THE
LOCAL CHURCH —
A LIVING BODY

THE
LOCAL CHURCH —
A LIVING BODY

JOHN KEITH DAVIES

First published 2001

ISBN: 0 85234 495 3

Printed and bound in Great Britain by CPD Wales.

Contents

Foreward

When Keith Davies suddenly died not only a friend and co-labourer had been removed from our circles, but a presence. There was that beautiful distinctive voice with its London-Welsh tones. Keith manifested a sense of authority and kindliness. I'm missing him at this moment as he comes back into focus, a big person, in heart and life, with a smile and one pertinent observation or another. His dry humour came out of observing the human condition in as diverse a range of churches as the Rhondda valley, Cornwall, London and Cardiff. He was a man of gifts. There were his musical capabilities – a tune that he wrote for a hymn was sung at his funeral. It was quite haunting, part of a living hymn-writing tradition at least three hundred years old in Wales. I knew from where he was coming and what he was doing, using his gifts to build the kingdom of God. I could take that for granted, and knew he was at peace about my work too. I never had to worry about Keith Davies. He continued in the vocation that he believed God had called him to as a young man, decades earlier and from which goals he was never deflected. He was a minister, and an elder, and a pastor, and an evangelist, and a theologian.

There was not a proud bone in his body. In the last years of his life he was not the secure pastor of a large congregation but he returned to what he did so well, church planting from scratch in a vast housing estate. It is the sort of thing my heroes do. I could rely on Keith Davies, and now he is not here and I feel it. How much more must his family and close friends lament his absence. He was a son, and a husband, and a father, and a grandfather. I sat with Keith and Pauline at a lunch table in a recent conference. We chatted in a peremptory manner as one does after some sessions of full addresses. It was another missed opportunity to hear from him, and talk more seriously and in some depth. So a life can drift away.

Whether he was full-time working in congregations or also supporting himself in other employment in order to start a new work in Cornwall or in Cardiff Keith loved the church of God that He purchased with His blood. Keith has gone, but he has left us something, a legacy which I or any minister would yearn to leave behind, some developed considerations, the mature convictions of a life-time's enterprise in building Christ's church. This book says, "Please think seriously about the church."

It is the work of an exegete and a scholar who wears his learning lightly, someone acquainted with church history and the theology of the Scriptures. Keith writes as a radical conservative. He accepts Scripture as the Word of God and the 1689 Confession of Faith as a faithful summary of Bible. He argues (rightly I believe) that even in accepting the plurality of elders the pastoral office is essential and most helpful for a congregation. He rejoices in independency in church government, but he sets out the need for one church to recognise, support and encourage other congregations.

Then there are fun things to discuss: pews, he thinks, are not as conducive to Christian fellowship as chairs. Children's talks are an unnecessary intrusion into a service. He also wonders whether one can administer church discipline to a stubborn member of a congregation if unbelievers are present. I cannot see why not. He is not committed to smallness in congregations but thinks ten congregations of a hundred members will do far more work than one congregation of a thousand. That makes sense.

Keith Davies presents that old position for a closed table and a closed membership to those who have been baptized on profession of faith, and he argues that as kindly and clearly as he can. Not all will be persuaded, nor are we sure that a head covering for women is essential. But for 1900 years, from 33 AD to 1933 not a woman entered a service with her head uncovered. Was that all 'cultural'? When fashions again change so that people will be wearing head-gear everywhere will they point then to their obedience to a passage from Scripture for the practice? But I have written more about that theme than Keith has. It was refreshing to find an unfashionable observation well set out. He wrote to make you think and his observations live on. In his fascinating chapter on the relationship of church and state he asks such questions as whether Religious Knowledge and religious assemblies should be part of state schools, and whether a poor evangelist of Jesus should accept income support and financial benefits from Caesar, and whether a church should comply with a local government's banning of open air preaching. Sparkling questions.

Keith writes well. Hear this: "The broken lives of this generation need something more than is offered to them. The well meaning 'Cheer up, remember God loves you,' will seem like mockery to those in terrible pain, conflict or despair. The real needs of people are too deep to be treated in such a way." That is a preacher writing. You can hear Keith's voice. Again, "Each church should examine carefully what it is doing locally and further afield, to ensure that it is being true to its calling as a church of God. Although we are moved first and foremost by the Lord himself (by his command and call) we should be aware of the glaring need of our generation: our cities have thousands of streets with thousands of homes, in which live thousands and thousands of souls. Yet how few churches are there to reach them." That is the not only the voice of an orator but of a pastor and evangelist. Hundreds of quotations like that characterize the book.

This is a splendid biblical study of the church. You notice at once its fourfold comprehensive structure – the life, membership, leadership and mission of the local church. You are confronted with a thinking man to whom lucidity mattered. He was also a humble servant of Christ. To splutter about 'not agreeing with everything here' is never the point. Keith would be amazed if anyone should think that he expected that. He had too much respect for the individuality of God's people personally and collectively. What this book does expect is that its readers take very seriously the church – not other religious modalities – but the local congregation of God's people to which every single Christian must belong. If this book does that in some of its many readers then Dr Keith Davies would have considered his mission accomplished.

Geoff Thomas, Aberystwyth. October 2000

Editor's Notes

Knowing Dad as we did made the task of editing his book both easier and more difficult to do. Easier because we always knew where he stood on any issue (and there was therefore little doubt what he meant in a phrase or paragraph) and harder because every word, so obviously his by phrase and content, reminded us of him and the fact that he died two years ago.

Editing his book was something we had to do, to get it into print and into peoples' hands, hearts and minds. Something we had to do because it was what he wanted and because we share his belief that such a book is a vital addition to every Christian's bookshelf. Dad was devoted to the biblical principles of the local church – not the least because the church is the bride of his beloved Saviour – whom he put before all else – but also because the church is God's chosen mechanism for spreading the Gospel to the world. For more just read the Author's Preface.

He would want every one of you to read this book – not because you will think more of John Keith Davies (he would never want that) but so that you *think* more about the church Jesus bought personally with his blood. He would want you to prayerfully read the book, look at the arguments set out, form your own opinion based on what the bible says and then <u>act on them</u>.

We must thank Geoff Thomas for an excellent foreword to this book and to Dr Nick Fiddian, Wilfred Kurt, Stanley Griffin, Pamela Bugden and Doris Foster for their diligence in proofreading. That said the responsibility for any mistakes is ours. We must also thank John Rubens and other members of the Evangelical Press for their helpful advice, comments and encouragement. Thanks also to those responsible for the cover design.

It is entirely proper to thank Mum – Mrs Pauline Davies, for the encouragement and help she has provided both when Dad was writing the book – she typed the original manuscript from his handwritten notes – and since his death when we took on the editorial responsibilities.

Dad was not a perfect man and he would never hear praise for himself. We however, were privileged and are proud to have known and loved him. We thank God for Dad's life and example to us, his family. In addition to the churches he planted in the service of his Lord and those his own life touched we trust that this, Dad's last book will teach and enrich the lives of many more.

This book is dedicated to *both* Dick Eccles' and Dad's memory – our world is a poorer place without them.

To God be the glory, great things He has done.

Andrew and Kathryn Gray

Author's Preface

The views expressed in this book are those of the author alone, although he believes they are the teaching of the Scriptures. It is his belief that the doctrine of the church, and that means particularly the local church, is one of the most important, indeed crucial, doctrines of the Bible.

The Apostle Paul wrote of the church, 'Christ also loved the church and gave Himself for her' (Ephesians 5:25). The church is the object of Christ's love and of his sacrifice at Calvary. Nothing is more important then, as the subject of study and interest, than that which is so highly regarded by the Saviour.

Teaching about the local church has long been neglected, but has in recent years been taken up again. As the doctrines of grace have been rediscovered and emphasised so attention has been directed to the church. Papers have been given and conferences held to discuss reforming the church to the teaching of the New Testament. A great deal of valuable material has been produced, but no comprehensive statement of the New Testament doctrine of the local church has been produced. This book, for all its weaknesses, is an attempt to address that need and is written with a general readership in mind, rather than a theological one.

It had long been the hope of the author and the late Pastor R.B.S. Eccles of Hebden Bridge to produce a book of some significance on this important doctrine. Although some initial work had been done on the book, Dick Eccles' death in May 1987 meant that it could not be produced as had been hoped. This book is not that hoped-for book. Dick Eccles is sadly missed, not least because of the vital contribution he made in this area of study. This book is dedicated to his memory.

This book is offered to the Christian public with the prayer that our Sovereign Lord God will use it for the benefit of the churches of Jesus Christ and as an encouragement to those engaged in the work of bringing New Testament churches into being. It is the firm belief of the author that the work of bringing into being New Testament churches is one of the greatest activities that anyone can engage in.

Within the purposes of God the great need of our times is for authentic Christianity to be seen. The best place for that to be seen is within local churches made up of godly people faithfully serving the Lord. To understand what a local church should be and to put that understanding into practice can do nothing but good and will bring great honour to the Lord our God and to his dear Son our Lord Jesus Christ. May God the Holy Spirit use this book to that end.

John Keith Davies, Cardiff.

Editor's Note: Dad's final paragraph of thanks to those who helped in producing the original manuscript has been amended and moved to the Editor's Notes so as to include others who have assisted us in getting this book to print.

PART ONE

THE LOCAL CHURCH
AND ITS LIFE

Chapter 1
The local church and its nature

The word 'church'

When people use the word 'church' today they can mean a number of different things and confusion reigns in many minds. The English word 'church' comes from the Greek word κυριακos – 'kuriakos' 'belonging to the Lord' or 'Lord's'. It is found in 1 Corinthians 11:20 – 'Lord's supper', and Revelation 1:10 – 'Lord's day'. When Christianity became acceptable and even popular from the time of the emperor Constantine in the fourth century onwards, even buildings set aside for worship were identified as 'belonging to the Lord' – 'kuriakos'. Thus buildings became know as 'churches'. The development of the word can be seen in the present day Scottish word 'kirk'.

The usual New Testament word for church is εκκλησια – 'ekklesia' – 'assembly'. The development of this word can be seen in the present day English word 'ecclesiastical', the French word for church – 'eglise', and the Welsh word for church – 'eglwys'.

The use of the word 'church' does express one important truth however. Those who are the church do belong to the Lord. They are his and his alone.

The word 'assembly'

The usual word for a 'church' in the New Testament, the Greek word 'ekklesia' – 'assembly', derives from 'ek' (out of) and 'kaleo' (call). It has the technical or grammatical meaning of 'a company of people called out in order to assemble together'. It was in common use in the Greek world where it meant 'an assembly of citizens', such as in a city-state, called together for a public meeting.

The Septuagint (the Greek version of the Old Testament, usually denoted by the letters LXX) consistently uses 'ekklesia' as a translation for the Hebrew word 'kahal'. 'Kahal' has the meaning of 'gathering together' usually with a set purpose. It is often translated into English by the words 'assembly' or 'congregation'. The word 'ekklesia' is found 114 times in the LXX, in each case as a translation of 'kahal'. The following examples will demonstrate how the word is consistently used of a gathering, assembly or congregation of people – Numbers 35:24; Deuteronomy 4:10; 9:10; 10:4; 18:16; Joshua 20:6; 1 Kings 8:14; Ezra 10:1; Nehemiah 8:1.

Turning to the New Testament we find 'ekklesia' 115 times (the critical text omits it in Acts 2:47). On three occasions the word means a meeting of citizens in a town as in normal Greek usage – Acts 19:32,39,41. The word translated 'robbers of churches' in the Authorised Version (King James 1611 Version) of Acts 19:37 actually means 'robbers of temples' ('hierosulous'). This shows how the false idea of identifying church and building had become dominant in the 16th and 17th centuries.

In one place (Acts 7:38) 'ekklesia' refers to the Israelite congregation in the wilderness. Undoubtedly this is an echo of the LXX usage. In all 111 other places 'ekklesia' refers to the Christian assembly or 'church'. Having established that, we are now faced with determining what exactly the word means when it refers to the Christian church. False ideas abound as to what 'the church' is, so we need to know what the New Testament means by the word. Clearly it must mean an assembly of people in one way or another.

New Testament use of 'ekklesia'

When we examine the New Testament usage of 'ekklesia' we are faced with a problem. It doesn't always mean exactly the same thing every time it is used of the church. In 1 Corinthians 1:2, for example, it explicitly states that it refers to the local church at Corinth. In Hebrews 12:23 the word is linked with another word meaning a 'festive gathering' and refers to all God's people, called the 'firstborn', whose names are registered in heaven, and means the general assembly gathered in heaven for all eternity. Here it has a prospective or eschatological meaning because it does not yet exist as a functional entity. It will be seen in glory made up of all God's elect from all ages gathered for all eternity. These two meanings of the word dominate the New Testament usage of 'ekklesia', and they are related to one another. The qualities and characteristics of the one are the qualities and characteristics of the other.

The local assembly, visible in time and space, is a 'microcosm' of the general assembly visible in eternity. The church is always a gathered company of regenerated people, whether local or 'total'. The church, as an assembly, is a visible company of believers. An assembly assembles, either locally in time or totally in eternity. It is therefore quite incorrect to use the singular word 'church' or 'assembly' to cover a number of companies of believers in different localities, because they assemble locally and cannot assemble collectively. So, to speak of the 'church in (or of) England' is to use 'church' in a way foreign to both the usage and the spirit of the New Testament.

In the New Testament the two senses of the word, referred to above, sometimes overlap. Consider for example Ephesians 5:23 and 25. Christ is head of the church, locally and totally, and he loved the church, locally and totally, and gave himself for it. This overlapping of meaning presents 'ekklesia' as a concept and uses it in a 'generic' sense. We use other words in a similar way, for example in the phrase 'trial by jury' where we are not referring to a particular trial in a particular court of law but to a legal concept. However, when we use 'ekklesia' in a generic sense it is only because the two uses (local and total) overlap in the New Testament.

Correctly speaking the church is not a building, a denomination, or a universal and invisible institution. For this day and age or 'dispensation' it is to be correctly understood as the local, visible, gathered company of believers united by a common life in Christ, under the authority of God's word and guided by the Holy Spirit.

The body of Christ

The New Testament uses some interesting titles and descriptions of the church, and they all express important truths concerning it. The church is God's church (Acts 20:28; 1 Peter 2:9-10), the bride of Christ (Ephesians 5:23-32; Revelation 21:2), the temple of the Holy Spirit (1 Corinthians 3:16-17; Ephesians 2:19-22); the pillar and ground of the truth (1 Timothy 3:15).

The highest designation the church receives in the New Testament is probably the 'body of Christ'. Christ loved the church and gave himself for it (Ephesians 5:25) because he is the Saviour of the body (Ephesians 5:23) of which he is the head.

Some uses of the phrase 'body of Christ' in the New Testament refer to the physical body of the Saviour. When using the phrase in reference to the church we must not regard the church as a kind of extension of Christ's incarnation. Christ is the Saviour of the body, and he is its head. The distinction between Christ and the church is made clear in that way. However the title 'body of Christ ' does identify the church with the Lord Jesus Christ in a very close way. The church's life is derived from Christ (Ephesians 1:23), he is its head (Colossians 1:18) and its members share his life and express that life in the gifts he gives for the benefit of the church (Ephesians 4:12). The body is a unity made up of many members (Romans 12:4-5) whose relationship to Christ includes their relationship to one another. Each member of the body is important, with a vital function to perform for the benefit of all (1 Corinthians 12:12-27).

Relationship to Christ

The church belongs to Christ. It is made up of sinners saved by the grace of God through the finished work of Jesus Christ. What the

Lord Jesus Christ has accomplished in his ministry on earth is central to the whole Bible. It is also central to the doctrine of the church. His saving work has brought the church into being by bringing regenerated sinners for whom he died into union with himself. Individual Christians are described as 'in Christ'. The local church is described in the same way (Galatians 1:22; Romans 12:5).

The Lord Jesus Christ identifies himself with his people very closely indeed. In Acts 9, Saul travelled to Damascus to persecute the church there as he had done elsewhere. When the risen Lord confronted him, he was challenged, not with his persecution of the church, but with his persecution of Christ (verse 4). The Saviour identified himself with the persecution suffered by his people. What happens to the church relates directly to him, for he is in the church and the church is in him – 'in Christ'.

A holy people

The close identification of the Lord Jesus Christ with his people is also apparent in the 'bride' description applied to the church. In Ephesians 5:22-33 the relationship between Christ and the church is used by the Apostle Paul to teach husbands and wives what their relationship with one another should be. The emphasis is upon a marriage of love, submission and union. Concerning the church, however, the apostle indicates that Christ's purpose is to sanctify and cleanse it so that he can ultimately present the church to himself as a glorious, holy and unblemished bride (Ephesians 5:25-27). That prospect is also anticipated in Revelation 19:7-9; 21:1-3 where the people of God, the church, are pictured as a bride adorned for her husband.

The church as a bride is a holy people (1 Peter 2:9). As a bride she must remain true and loyal to her husband. Purity of life and separation from all else to Christ is emphasised by this picture of the church. Doctrinal purity is included in this picture along with separation from sin and worldliness (see 2 Corinthians 11:1-4).

A spiritual life

This holy separation is not a physical isolation into some monastic community. The Lord Jesus Christ was 'separate from sinners' (Hebrews 7:26) and yet his life was lived in the world. He identified himself with people and entered into their lives. He was sent into the world by his Father (John 6:39-40,44,57; 7:16,28-29; 8:16,18,26,29) and in a similar way he sent his people into the world (John 13:20; 17:18). Jesus came from above into this world. He was not of the world (John 8:23) so the world hated him (John 15:18). His people would also be hated by the world because they would be identified with him (John 15:19-21; 17:14). They would not be removed from the world, but would be kept from its evil as they testified of Christ (John 17:15; 15:27).

The church is made up of human beings but it is no mere human organisation. The human beings who make up the church are a new creation in Jesus Christ (2 Corinthians 5:17). They are a distinct people who have the Holy Spirit living in them (Romans 8:9-11). The church is a living thing in which Christ's life is displayed by the Holy Spirit's guidance and activity. The Holy Spirit dwells in each church as he dwells in each member (1 Corinthians 3:16; 6:19). The church has a spiritual life that is more than that contributed by the individual members.

Both Apostles Paul and Peter describe the church as a temple to emphasise that it is essentially a spiritual structure or organism (see 1 Corinthians 3:16-17; 2 Corinthians 6:16-17; Ephesians 2:20-22; 1 Peter 2:5). Its life is spiritual and holy. It is separated from sin and sinful associations and is separated to God and his service. Its' activity is directed towards God in worship and service. It is these things that particularly distinguish the church from every other human organisation. Its life is spiritual and its activity is service to God.

A regenerate membership

The church is not a national or international institution or organisation. Nor is it a building in which people meet. It is a gathering or assembly of people who belong to Jesus Christ and have been regenerated (born again) by the Holy Spirit (John 3:3; Titus 3:4-7). As such the church is unique.

Jesus Christ loves the church and has saved it. He has died on the cross for each and every member of it. He has obtained their forgiveness and the renewal of their nature. Each member is redeemed by his grace and mercy. Each member responds to Christ by repentance and faith in him as Saviour, which leads on to devotion and obedience to his commands. Only those who have a faith to confess and demonstrate a new life are proper candidates for church membership. For only those who are united to Christ are united to his people. Church membership is for the regenerate only.

Regeneration is God's work alone. He gives new life to those who are dead in trespasses and sins (Ephesians 2:1-10). The Holy Spirit applies Christ's saving work to the heart and life of the sinner and transforms that sinner into a 'saint'. Evidence of that transformation is seen in repentance, faith and good works to the glory of God.

The church is made up of believers in Jesus Christ. It is necessary to maintain this New Testament principle because it affects the character of a church's life (e.g. Acts 2:41-42). Worship is a corporate act of the church, but only regenerate people can worship God in 'spirit and in truth' (John 4:24). The church is commanded to engage in evangelistic and missionary activity and this demands that the distinction between the world and the church be kept clearly defined. A proper exercise of discipline is required of the church by the patterns of life established by the New Testament, but where the church is a 'mixed multitude' with regenerate and unregenerate in membership true spiritual discipline is impossible. 'Wheat' and 'tares' might very well grow together in this age (Matthew 13:24-30), but they do so in the world (Matthew 13:38) and should not grow together in the church.

Disciples and discipleship

The church as a 'called-out' people ('ekklesia') is different from the
world around. As a company of identifiable people the church has
an 'inside' and an 'outside'. In 1 Corinthians 5 is an example of a
local church removing from membership an offending member who
is guilty of gross sin. He is then to be considered as one 'outside' the
church (1 Corinthians 5:2,5,11-13). The church is a holy and disciplined company. No one is forced against his will to join, no one
belongs whether he likes it or not. It is a voluntary matter and yet as
a holy and disciplined company the church has high standards of
life to maintain. All who join the church take to themselves responsibilities as well as privileges. These include living a consistent
Christian life that the church has every right to expect from its members. The church also has the right to act when the necessary standards of Christian behaviour are violated.

The church as a disciplined body is therefore marked off from
the rest of human society. It is made up of Christian disciples,
followers of the Lord Jesus Christ, committed to him and to one
another. They have a relationship to Christ and to one another which
is altogether different from other human relationships (see Luke
14:26-27; John 14:23; 15:12,17; 1 John 3:16,23). It is a relationship of love. This is the essence of Christian discipleship – love for
Christ and for his people. 'By this all will know that you are My
disciples, if you have love for one another' (John 13:35).

Any exercise of corrective discipline by a church must be motivated by that same love. All discipline is to be exercised to the glory
of God and for the benefit of his people. It is the corporate outworking
of collective discipleship.

Christian discipleship doesn't happen by magic. God's word, the
Bible, provides the proper basis for it, personally and collectively.
The word of God is to be taught to the church so that members,
individually and collectively, may live lives conformed to the
patterns and principles of discipleship found in it. The headship of
Christ over his church is exercised through the authoritative written
word that is interpreted by the Holy Spirit present in the church.

The glory of the church

The presence of the Holy Spirit in the church is the glory of the church. He is in the church in Christ's name (John 14:16-18,26; 15:26; 16:7,13-15), for it is his 'temple' and Christ's 'body'. The church depends on Almighty God (Father, Son and Holy Spirit) for its life, and displays that life to the surrounding world. The glory of the church is a visible glory, for the church as an 'ekklesia' is a visible assembly. Yet the glory is a spiritual glory. The church brings a foretaste of the glory of heaven to the activities of earth. In the pattern of life developed by the church, spiritual qualities will have greater consequence than material ones. Men will be appointed to office by recognising the gifts which Christ has given to the church in those men (Ephesians 4:8-16). Riches (or lack of them), rank and intellectual qualifications will not be the factors uppermost in the church's consideration. In addition, by determining the pattern of worship, the teaching of Christ in his word will weigh more heavily with a church than will cultural or aesthetic factors. In these ways, and others, the church displays its glory.

Everything a church does can display its glory. Worship services, sermons, prayers, evangelism, administration and expressions of fellowship and love all express the glory of the church. Even the most mundane of activities can express the holy living and growth in grace of the people of God. Christ's life through his Spirit is lived out in the lives of believers. What he gives to the church in those believers reveals his glory and life.

Unity in diversity

As the church closely conforms to the patterns of life expounded in God's word it reveals the mind and glory of Christ. The descriptive titles given to the church in the New Testament point to the kind of life the church is to display as it works out in practical terms Christ's life within. For example, the title 'body of Christ' expresses a number of important truths about the church, as we have already seen. It also points to the church's life as a unity in diversity, because each member of the church as a member of the one body has a vital part to play in the church's life. The contribution each member makes to the church's life has first been given to that member by the Lord of the church who gives gifts as best suit his purposes and glory (1 Corinthians 12:4-11). One effect of this is to prevent any member of the church from despising any other member's place or function in the body (1 Corinthians 121:14-27). Each member has a value and dignity which Christ himself gives.

The emphasis of Romans 12:4-5 is on the unity of the body. It is one, although it has many members. 1 Corinthians 10:17 similarly stresses the unity of the body, which is expressed in eating one loaf together. 1 Corinthians 11:29 indicates that it is the body of Christ (i.e. the local church) present at the table which can be abused and insulted by unseemly conduct. 1 Corinthians 12:12-25 is a passage set in a context which deals with gifts and manifestations of the Spirit in the church, and yet in the midst of such diversity the stress in these verses is on the unity within that body where such gifts are seen. Similarly Ephesians 4:4 insists 'there is one body' with the succeeding verses stressing unity within the body. That unity is a unity in diversity with each member making a vital contribution and having a high value.

The value of each member

As we maintain the unity of the church we must also emphasise the value of each member. There are no unimportant ones. All are important to the Lord and to the church. The Lord Jesus Christ had to lay down his life for every member of his body, and each is of great value to him. It is quite consistent with this truth to find Paul declaring in 1 Corinthians 12:14 that 'the body is not one member but many'. He also says that each member, even the apparently insignificant one, has a proper part to play in the life of the church. The Lord, in fact, gives honour where we overlook it (1 Corinthians 12:23). As the body is one, the life of each member affects the whole, and the life of the whole affects the individual member (1 Corinthians 12:26). In Romans 12:5, Paul takes the matter a little further and speaks of 'members of one another', so closely are members bound to one another.

Each member has a part to play, each has a work to do, for God gives gifts to all – to each one (1 Corinthians 12:7; Ephesians 4:7). If a church ignores this principle it impoverishes itself and rejects God's gifts. The individual Christian suffers too, having no legitimate outlet for his gifts and abilities. That has often led to unscriptural outlets being sought to the detriment of the true work of God. We greatly impoverish the life of the churches by maintaining a pattern of life that rules out the great variety of what God gives to a church in its members. This is not to advocate some chaotic free-for-all, for the command to do things decently and in order comes in the context of the church's worship, and participation by members was anticipated (1 Corinthians 14:40). Each member has something to contribute to the life of the church that God has first given him. There are gifts today that are appropriate for a church in the late 20th and early 21st centuries that would have been inappropriate for the first century. There are gifts appropriate for a first century church (such as the foundational 'signs of the apostles' – see 2 Corinthians 2:4) which are quite inappropriate today.

What does a church do to implement these principles? How do the members use their gifts in contributing to the church as a whole? The New Testament provides the answer to these questions, for it provides a consistent pattern for local church life that caters for the unity of the church and the individuality of the member. We shall consider this matter in more detail in the following chapters.

Chapter 2
The local church and its activity

Activity is important

The life of any body is shown by what it does. So a church's life is shown by what it does, and that life is developed by what it does. The Lord writes to the churches in the book of Revelation that he knows their *works*, for those works reveal their life (see Revelation 2:2,9,13,19; 3:1,8,15). It is often said that activism is no substitute for life. That is true as far as it goes. If, however, a believer does not have things to do to put his faith into practice, his spiritual life will stagnate. James says that 'faith without works is dead' (James 2:20,26). The same holds true of the church.

We must emphasise at this point the fact that the church as the body of Christ must live as a body with each part functioning fully. The local church as the body of Christ, functioning as he directs, is vital in every generation. A church which does nothing, does not work, does not function as the Spirit of God directs, is not a body – it is a corpse, it is dead. What we expect to see in a church as the body of Christ is life and work.

An integrated fellowship

A church is not a bunch of individuals who please themselves what they do. A church is the body of Christ that lives to please God. So, it is a disciplined fellowship, eager to obey the Lord's direction of its life. No one can justify an individualistic approach to Christian living and service from the New Testament. A local church is an integrated fellowship, and no sectional interest within the church should be allowed to endanger this essential unity. The individualism that enables a man or woman to please him or herself without consulting brothers and sisters in Christ should be viewed with disfavour – it is contrary to being part of the body. The disciplined life of a local church does, in fact, stimulate individual enterprise and endeavour, rather than stifle it. To be engaged in the Lord's work with the approval and support of the Lord's people is a great encouragement.

Organisation in a church

The church is no disorganised rabble. It is an organised body and the New Testament lays out how the local church is to be organised. The closer a church adheres to the teaching of the New Testament in this regard the better it will be equipped to take account of the needs of the present age. New Testament directions for the life of the church are eminently practical. We have no warrant to go beyond Scripture in this matter any more than in any other matter.

Organisation is essentially a spiritual matter for it is to do with the system the church adopts to ensure that its life, which is essentially spiritual, functions properly. Church life doesn't depend on one person. It is not a 'one-man-show'. Each member is involved. Organisation is necessary to ensure the involvement of each member.

The local church is an 'ekklesia', an assembly. In order to be an assembly in fact as well as in theory its members will assemble. They will meet regularly and often. The meeting together of all the members of the church is the centre from which all aspects of organisation spring. It is also an expression of other important things in the life of the church that we shall consider later.

The church meeting together

Why did the church meet together in the New Testament? In Acts 4:23-31 the members met for prayer. In Acts 6:1-6 they met to deal with the necessary business of the church and appointed the first deacons. In Acts 13:1-3 the church in Antioch met to send out missionaries called by God, and in Acts 14:27 they met to hear the report of the missionary work. Acts 15 contains accounts of two churches meeting because of problems that needed solutions. In verse three, the church in Antioch sends Paul and Barnabas with others to Jerusalem. Verses four to twenty-nine give the account of the church in Jerusalem meeting to handle a contentious matter. Acts 20:7-12 records the Troas church meeting for the 'breaking of bread' and the preaching of God's word. 1 Corinthians 10:14-40 is a lengthy passage dealing with various issues arising from the meeting of the church for worship. I Corinthians 5:4-5 refers to the church meeting to exercise proper discipline of a church member actively involved in gross sin.

All these matters are to do with the work of the Lord. They are all spiritual matters. When the church meets, it is a spiritual meeting, for the church is the body of Christ. The whole church should meet, with every member, as far as possible, present. Each member of the church is important, although the church is not a mere democracy subject to the rule of the majority. Christ is the head of the church and when decisions have to be made the church is concerned first and foremost, with knowing what his mind is (1 Corinthians 2:16). Christ governs the church by his word of truth. It is not accidental therefore that the man who leads the church, the pastor, is a preacher and a teacher. He pastors the flock, as a shepherd under Christ, with Christ's word. Similarly the church itself functions and regulates its own life by the word.

Leadership and responsibility

Although leadership of the church, as biblical leadership generally, is a singular thing, and the Scriptures give a large place to it, they also teach that churches are to be led by a body of elders (more than one). This may well be an ideal to be aimed at rather than a practical reality in many situations, and is a subject we shall have to return to, but shared aspects of leadership in this way mean that the church is beginning to use God-given abilities and gifts. Elders are not to do everything, nor do they operate a benevolent dictatorship over the church. Acts 6 speaks of assistance given to the elders by the appointment of deacons. Deacons are not the board of management of the church. They are appointed to serve the church in relieving the elders of practical matters relating to the church's common life and property. 1 Timothy 3:11 and 5:9-10 speaks of particular responsibilities falling on older women in the church as they too assist the elders. However that is not the limit of the work to be organised in the life of the church. There is a tremendous variety of activity that needs organising, for the whole church depends on the whole membership – all have a part to play. The church is wise, however, to delegate functions and tasks within its life according to the gifts given by God to the church in the members. When the church meets together it exercises an over-sight of those functions and tasks.

Church meetings

As we have noted already a local church meets for various activ-ities – worship, prayer, transacting necessary business, preaching etc. What we are dealing with here is the meeting of the church for the purpose of discussion and decision. In the New Testament no other authority for the government of a local church is to be found apart from what comes from the local church itself. Under the head-ship of Christ and the guidance of the Holy Spirit the local church is competent to govern its own affairs. The direction given to New Testament churches by the advice and encouragement of the apostles is given to churches today – by the New Testament itself, which we have in a complete form.

Although the word 'local' in 'local church' does not simply refer to matters of geography, it does emphasise that a church meets in a locality, in a particular location, and is a 'gathered' church. Evidently, New Testament churches gathered their members from a large area or were responsible in some way for Christians from a large area (see 2 Corinthians 1:1). Even so the 'church meeting' was a gathering of the whole membership. In Acts 6 the 'whole multitude' of the disciples chose the seven (verse 5) to be appointed to diaconate office. In Acts 15:22 it was the 'whole church' that chose men to accompany Paul and Barnabas.

Although officers or leaders of a church have a very important part to play in the life of a church and have an authority pertaining to their office that is recognised by the church, the final human authority in a local church is the church meeting. Clearly it would be difficult for a church to discipline a member (1 Corinthians 5:1-5) with unbelievers present (1 Corinthians 14:23). Equally the 'church meeting' excludes those who are not members of the particular local church.

Church 'meetings', if we understand the New Testament correctly, are not only occasions for transacting business. Church meetings should be times of fellowship for the members of the church when they have opportunity to grapple with matters of mutual concern – doctrinal issues, the spiritual health of the church, relationships with others and particularly with evangelistic and missionary enterprise. The church should also be involved in the activities of the individual members and that involvement can find expression in the church meeting when advice and support can be given.

In 1 Corinthians 10:14-40 the meeting together of the church provides the background to the various points Paul makes in writing to the Corinthian church about its many problems. He sought to correct abuses in the church but did not prohibit what was evidently a common pattern among the churches. 1 Corinthians 11:18 and the following verses suggest that church meetings included the Lord's supper.

Where to meet

1 Corinthians 5:3-4; 11:17; 14:26 seem to imply that the local church should meet regularly, certainly on the Lord's day, the first day of the week (Acts 20:7; 1 Corinthians 16:2). In order to meet, the church will need premises large enough to house the congregation (not only the members) regularly. The New Testament phrase 'the church in your house' (Romans 16:23; Colossians 4:15; Philemon 2) does not mean small 'house-churches' or one family churches. It refers to houses that were big enough to accommodate the whole church. Accommodating the church today in a private house is usually impossible and is often unwise. Hired premises may be suitable (Acts 19:9) but in these days if it is at all possible, the church would be wise to buy its own premises. This will be found to be more convenient and will avoid conflict with others who may use or own the property.

Any building, however, whether hired or owned, should not be too large for easy maintenance. Its size should reflect the needs of the church and its life. The church itself, similarly, should not be too large for fellowship to be real and meaningful. When a church gets too large for meaningful fellowship it is time to plant another church. The building should be adaptable so that it can be used to the full, and so that it can become a useful tool in the church's life and work. Together the members of the church will spend a lot of time in that building and will be involved in a great many activities there.

The reality of fellowship

A church is a fellowship, but fellowship is not only a state to be in, it is an activity to be done. The Greek word used in the New Testament is 'koinonia' and means 'partnership' or 'participation'. It is associated with the word 'koinos', which means 'common' or 'belonging to many'. The idea underlying fellowship is 'sharing', and in the New Testament fellowship is first of all to do with sharing what God has given. It is particularly fellowship with God

himself (1 John 1:3) because it is sharing a common life in the Lord
Jesus Christ. It is also fellowship in the truth, for the life Christians
have in common is capable of definition. It is centred in a person
(Jesus Christ) who can be described. It has to do with facts, historical
and theological, which can be stated. To deny the truth makes
fellowship impossible.

Fellowship can be broken, bruised, strained and undermined; yet
it is of the essence of the Christian life – a life meant to be lived in
fellowship with God and fellow believers. To read Romans 12 and
1 Corinthians 12 is to see how close the bond is between believers.
Believers are part of, sharers in, and contributors to the body of
Christ. In the local church the members are one body. Fellowship is a
'state of being', but it is only seen and experienced in a life of doing.

The activity of fellowship

True biblical fellowship has to be worked at and catered for in the
programme of the church. It is many sided but is essentially a
practical sharing in the things of the Lord. It isn't just sitting
together in the same place at the same time. It is much more than
that. Much of what Paul says in Romans 12 has a relevance to the
practical outworkings of fellowship between believers. The supreme
expression of fellowship within the church in Paul's day was the
Lord's Supper and the common meal that went with it. (1 Corinthians
10:16; 11:18-34, especially verse 22). Paul's condemnation of the
Corinthians' conduct was because of the lack of love for the church
revealed at such a meal (1 Corinthians 11:18,22,29). He did not
condemn the meal as such. Churches would gain much from sharing
such a meal together with the Lord's Supper from time to time. It
could also include a time of sharing in the things of God in worship
and testimony, and the ministry of the word of God. Love is the
keynote of Christian fellowship and may be expressed in any number
of ways to enhance the life of the church. It is significant that the
common meal linked to the Lord's Supper came to be known as a
'love feast', or using the Greek word for love – agapè (pronounced

'agapay'), an 'agapè meal' (see Jude 12 and the parallel in 2 Peter 2:13).

Everything that is expressive of the life of the church involves fellowship, but it is particularly expressed and enjoyed in activity – doing things together. Sharing with the people of God in life is fundamental to the practical reality of Christian living. See Hebrews 10:33; 2 Corinthians 9:13; Philippians 1:7, for examples of this shared experience. Fellowship is experienced as prayer is offered for other believers (Philemon 22; Ephesians 6:18-19), and support and encouragement is given to them. Worship in the church is a shared experience (e.g. 1 Corinthians 10:16-17). Believers who are in fellowship with one another will care for one another (2 Corinthians 8:1-5; Romans 12:4-13), because they need one another (1 Corinthians 12:14-26). They will bear one another's burdens (Galatians 6:2), and will do good to one another (Galatians 6:10; John 13:35). All aspects of fellowship have a practical dimension, but being together (Hebrews 10:25), living near to one another and the church's meeting place, talking, sharing information (not gossip), all contribute to fellowship. Absence from the meetings of the church by a member is hurtful to the church because the church is deprived of the fellowship and unique contribution of that member. Fellowship in the church is too precious to miss.

The unity of fellowship

Unity in a church is vital if it is truly to live as the body of Christ. Our Lord prayed for it in John 17 and the Apostle Paul wrote to encourage it in Ephesians 4:11-16 and Philippians 4:2-3. It is an essential factor underlying the life of the church as the body of Christ as taught in Romans 12 and 1 Corinthians 12. The local church as a real 'body' will discover that the spiritual health of the members of the church will affect the other members profoundly. Where both joys and sorrows are shared the practical realities of fellowship will be evident. The unity of the church is very precious but many things can harm it and the church's fellowship as a result.

Unity in fellowship demands loyalty to one another. A church is a family – the family of God – and such loyalty is family loyalty. Members should trust one another – but trust has to be earned. It is earned by keeping confidences and by the ability to keep quiet when it is needed. It is also earned when members keep their word and honour their promises. Unity in a church is so important that special vigilance is necessary lest cliques, parties or exclusive friendships spring up in a church and destroy that unity (Romans 16:17; 2 Thessalonians 3:6,11,14).

Preserving unity

A church is wise if it takes active measures to encourage and preserve its unity. No sectional interest in the church should be allowed to endanger this unity. For instance, if the church operates a Sunday school, it should never be allowed to operate as if it were separate from the church. The same applies to other activities sponsored by the church. The leadership of the church should involve itself in all the church does. The members of the church need to be encouraged to think of their activities in a church context and every effort should be made to ensure that activities are seen as church activities.

Such a spirit of unity stimulates individual enterprise and endeavour. It is what makes Christian fellowship real and invigorating. True Christian fellowship does not stifle the individual enthusiasm of the believer. When the Lord's work is done with the approval and support of the Lord's people greater things are achieved. For one thing, there is greater prayer support. It is important to know what other members are doing in order to pray for them effectively. Sometimes helpful advice can be given to a young and enthusiastic Christian by older Christians if they know what he is intending to do. The loving and uniting power of Christian fellowship can be an effective check on unwise individualism where that individualism involves compromising scriptural doctrine.

Provision for fellowship

For fellowship to be real and actual in caring and sharing, it needs to be catered for in the church's life. Members need to know one another and what are one another's needs. Information should be circulated regularly at prayer meetings and every member should know what is going on in the church. Members should be encouraged to talk to one another about what is happening in their lives so that others can join them in prayer and praise. Both problems and blessings may be shared. Every member needs to be a good listener. However care needs to be taken to avoid gossip and a morbid concentration on calamity. In order to receive confidences it needs to be demonstrated that they can be kept.

To some extent fellowship comes automatically due to the unity of life in Christ enjoyed in the church and joint activity in his service. Yet it can be encouraged and catered for in the life of the church in order to give opportunities for members to be together. Of course by definition spontaneous fellowship cannot be organised but it may develop during other more organised events. Maintenance work on church premises, evangelistic activity and conversations after meetings of the church are examples of occasions when spontaneous fellowship occurs. A church might feel that organising certain social activities will provide opportunities for fellowship – walks, outings to places of interest, weekend conferences, holidays, are examples. Even the arrangements of chairs in meetings can help or hinder fellowship. Pews do not seem to have been designed to encourage fellowship, but even their physical limitations can be overcome.

Fellowship meetings

Although Christians enjoy fellowship with one another in times of worship and prayer, a church can arrange meetings specifically for fellowship. Such fellowship meetings can deepen the sharing aspect of the church's life. The blessings of the Lord to the church are many and various and so it may be appropriate from time to time for the church to gather together to enjoy the gifts and talents given to it by the Lord in the members of the church. But where did New Testament churches particularly express their fellowship? It was as they gathered around the Lord's Table. As we have already noted, the local church in New Testament times gathered for fellowship in sharing a meal as it remembered the Lord Jesus Christ in his death and rejoiced in the blessings of salvation received through his sacrifice. Fellowship with one another in the church is deepest at those times when fellowship with God is uppermost. Times of worship, when the word of God is proclaimed and the people of God praise him for his majesty and his grace, can be times of warmest fellowship for the church as hearts are united in giving honour to the God and Father of our Lord Jesus Christ.

Fellowship in worship

If nothing else a church is a worshipping community with a spiritual dimension to its life. As it meets, for whatever purpose, it has its eyes directed heavenward; it always comes together in the presence of God. There is a completeness about the worship of the church that must not be lost sight of. If every member of the church is to participate fully in the life of the church, the worship of the church must have a pattern that takes account of every member. Corporate worship is by definition what the body does together. Church worship is worship of the whole church.

Services of worship

At the centre of the church's worship are the regular services of worship on the Lord's Day, Sunday. The weekly services of worship are the focus of the worshipping activity of God's people. Every aspect of the church's life is gathered up together and presented or offered to God. The attitude of devotion to God that must underpin the whole life of the church (2 Corinthians 8:5) is expressed in a service of worship where the whole church gathers together at a specific time in a specific place for an act of worship which has a particular form, pattern or structure.

The service of worship should be the highlight of the church's weekly activity. If the worship of God is the highest activity of which a redeemed creature is capable then the service of worship expresses something of the fulfilment of the purpose for which God created us. The 'quality' of the worship offered to God in that service is not primarily dependent on the form or pattern of the service. The state of heart and mind of the worshippers has a lot to do with it. When worshippers come expectantly, looking for the presence of the Lord and lifting up their hearts to him, a service of worship, however structured, may be a time rich with the honour and blessing of God. If hymns of praise are sung with enthusiasm and meaning and a humble and attentive attitude is displayed towards the preaching of God's word the service of worship can be an experience of the glory of God.

Attempts to make services of worship more meaningful

It is important that services of worship should not be meaningless religious occasions. Where there is true worship from believing hearts and God is praised and honoured there is meaning enough. However attempts to make services more meaningful to people of today have been attempted, but in many cases they have had the reverse effect and appear as an intrusion into the corporate worship of the church. All attempts to make worship meaningful to unbelievers will fail, because it is only those who have been redeemed who can truly worship God in spirit and in truth (John 4:24). This is not to say we can carry on in a meaningless way and call it worship just because believers do it.

A running commentary on every part of the service in order to explain what is going on can often end up as a talk for the sake of a talk. A children's address designed no doubt, to 'give the children something' can be an interruption in the service that distracts the worshippers and encourages the children not to listen to the sermon. Choruses, introduced to 'liven things up' can have the same kind of effect – generating the attitude that hymns are boring although probably necessary.

Having said all that, we do need to think carefully about what actually happens in a church's worship service. What we really need to know is what the timeless New Testament teaches us to do. Form or pattern in worship is important, as important as the heart and mind attitude of each worshipper. To understand that worship is not disorder (1 Corinthians 14:40) is basic to any consideration of the teaching of the New Testament on this subject. It is not a disorganised free-for-all any more than it is a straight-jacketed pattern full of 'vain repetition'. It has a proper form and structure, and that we can discover from the New Testament. That form or structure is there to encourage worship and facilitate the regular expression of the church's responsibility toward God.

The church at worship

The worship we are concerned with here is corporate worship, the worship of the body of Christ – the church at worship in its regular week by week activity as it meets on the Lord's day for services of worship. The worship of the church is a corporate activity of the whole church. Whether a service is led by an individual or not the worship is that of the whole church. The congregation or assembly of believers attending the service is not a collection of spectators watching someone else do something for them. It is a worshipping body, and every part of that body has a share in worship. The feelings, concerns and needs of the whole body of the church should be reflected in the church's worship, and not simply those of the man leading. If the priesthood of all believers (1 Peter 2:5,9) is to have any practical reality in a church's worship a church needs to ensure that the life of the whole body finds expression in worship. Worship for the church is a shared activity.

The Lord Jesus Christ in John 4:23-24 spoke of worship in spirit and in truth. The beginning of the fulfilment of his words is to be found in the worship of New Testament churches. While we must never imagine for one moment that these churches were perfect (reading 1 Corinthians will quickly dispel such an idea), certain features of New Testament worship emphasised its living quality and need a similar emphasis today. If that emphasis is given, the quality of a church's worship will be affected for the better.

Features of New Testament worship

There are three particular features of New Testament worship that both reflect the origins of distinctively Christian worship and emphasise its character in both form and content: the Jewish synagogue, the upper room, and the day of Pentecost. Each makes a distinctive contribution and brings a vital emphasis into Christian worship. Yet every aspect of Christian worship should direct the attention of the worshippers in heart and mind to Christ. Without that emphasis on Christ it is not Christian worship at all.

The contribution of the Jewish Synagogue

The Jewish synagogue was noted for its emphasis on the Scriptures – readings, expositions, and prayers. The first New Testament churches were entirely Jewish, so it was inevitable that they should carry over this vital emphasis into Christian worship. That being true, it is all the more understandable that the Apostle Paul went first of all to the synagogues of the towns he visited on his missionary journeys and there expounded the word of God. This was his practice in Christian communities too (1 Corinthians 15:3). Other evidence of the importance of the word of God in the worship of New Testament churches can be found in Colossians 3:16 and 1 Timothy 4:13.

The word of God declares who God is, what he has done and what he has said. Worship is a response to all God is, has done and has said. God's word must therefore initiate, feed and direct true worship. All we know of God is found in his word. He speaks to us in it and we respond to that by believing and in humble worship. Whatever else Christian worship is, it must have at its foundation the word of God and nothing less. Christian worship should never be thought of apart from the preaching of the word of God. Preaching has a primacy. The sermon – the public proclamation of an exposition and application of the word of God – should always have a substantial place in a service of worship. It should always be the word of God, the Bible that is preached. It should be based on it, should explain it, expound it (explaining it in detail) and apply it to the people of today (2 Timothy 4:2). It should be proclaimed with conviction; it should be direct, relevant, and understandable and should call for a verdict in the hearers.

The contribution of the upper room

At the heart of worship is the fact of the sacrifice of the Lord Jesus Christ. Grace, redemption, forgiveness of sins are some of the themes at the heart of worship and they all derive from Christ's sacrifice for sinners. The ordinance of Christ to remember him in his death 'until he comes' (1 Corinthians 11:26) originates in the intimate fellowship of the Saviour with his disciples in the 'last supper'. When the church meets around the Lord's Table it is obeying that command. This is the distinctively Christian contribution to the worship of the church, for it makes the church concentrate its mind on its origin in Christ and its continuing fellowship in him. The fellowship of the church at its deepest level is seen at the Lord's Table. Present day believers may experience something as profound as those two on the road to Emmaus in Luke chapter 24; they reported how, 'he was known of them in breaking of bread' (Luke 24:35).

The Apostle Paul draws on this truth in 1 Corinthians 10:14-22. Because the believer eats of the loaf and drinks of the cup that speaks of participation in Christ and fellowship with his people, it is unthinkable that he will eat and drink things involved in pagan worship. Having come to know Christ he will have nothing to do with demons. That one cup and one loaf which believers share at the Lord's table with the church proclaim fellowship with Christ and with fellow believers in Christ.

The Lord's Table is a constant reminder of Christ's sacrifice and of the fellowship of the church, which that sacrifice has brought into being and taken believers into. It is a time of remembrance (1 Corinthians 11:23-29) and of thanksgiving – for Christ and for one another. It is also an act of commitment to one another in sharing the same loaf and the same cup within the fellowship of the local church (the one body which is expressed by that one loaf). There-fore, any attempt to detach the Lord's Table from the local church will impoverish this sense of commitment and fellowship. The Lord's Table is no private matter – its place is within the corporate worship of the local church.

The contribution of the day of Pentecost

The Holy Spirit is essential for the life of the church for he makes the church a living body. He is the life-giving Spirit (1 Corinthians 15:45). The Holy Spirit regenerates, empowers and sanctifies believers. He gives gifts for the benefit of the church and for the glory of the Lord Jesus Christ (1 Corinthians 12:11). His coming upon the disciples on the day of Pentecost transformed timid followers of Christ into bold ambassadors of Christ. He brought liberty from fear and gave power to testify to Christ.

So today as then, he brings direction to the church so that its activity in the world is not done by guesswork. He also equips the church to fulfil Christ's commission. He invigorates the church's life and its worship that without him is but an empty form. He excites the hearts of worshippers as they contemplate the glory and grace of the Lord Jesus Christ, especially in the preached word. He unites their hearts in prayer as he guides and inspires their praying.

He humbles believers by convicting them of sin and comforts believers by applying the blood of Christ in cleansing and forgiveness. He puts to death trust in self, and elevates the Lord Jesus Christ to become the believer's supreme delight.

He gives gifts to the members of the church for the mutual edification of the church and for the glory of God. Following his coming upon the church on the day of Pentecost the worship of God offered by believers was marked by the liberty they enjoyed in Jesus Christ. When the local church met together for worship in New Testament days, believers could edify one another by participating in the service as the Holy Spirit moved them (1 Corinthians 14:26). Yet the Holy Spirit does not promote disorder; his interests are centred in promoting the honour of the Lord Jesus Christ. The gifts he gives to members and the participation he encourages are all for the honour of Jesus Christ. He gives gifts to the church for all sorts of purposes and only some of them would be suitable for corporate worship. The lists of gifts we find in such places as Romans 12, 1 Corinthians 12 and 14 and Ephesians 4 do not give the appearance of being comprehensive. Rather, they appear to be examples given by the Apostle Paul of the variety of gifts bestowed upon the church by the Spirit. Some are offices serving all the churches, some are itinerant ministries, some are local church ministries, some are foundational and are no longer appropriate for today, some are mundane, and some would be expected in all believers. We might therefore expect to find gifts given to churches today which would vary from church to church, and some which would have been inappropriate for New Testament times.

What then would be appropriate for a service of worship today? Each local church must determine this for itself, but such things as leading in prayer, choosing hymns, reading the Scriptures, testifying to God's goodness might be considered appropriate. Worship is essentially directed towards God, and this must never be overlooked. The worship service of the local church is the worship of the whole church and so the varied spiritual experiences of all the members should find a place. The Holy Spirit gives gifts and blesses every member of the church in one way and another. Each member has a vital contribution to make to the life of the church as a body. That contribution might well have its place in the corporate worship of the church, but corporate worship does not require every single member to contribute individually. Fellowship in worship may be experienced in various ways, for example in listening attentively to the sermon, in sharing in the prayer led by another, in singing hymns congregationally.

Worship through Jesus Christ

The three features discussed above should find a regular place in the worshipping activity of the church. The word of God is fundamental and is the controlling factor. Congregational participation should always be in response to God's word. Its direction should be towards God. It is Spirit inspired worship. We do not now need those direct Spirit inspired utterances that were given to certain foundational prophets in the New Testament because the Spirit now uses the word of God in his ministry to the church. Nevertheless the congregation will sing (Colossians 3:16; Ephesians 5:18-19) and will vocally express its love for God.

When the church meets for worship it meets to worship a holy God. The approach to God will be in humility and godly fear with an awareness of the need for sins to be forgiven. Yet the church may approach God with boldness because of Jesus Christ by whose grace it has come into being. It may now approach the throne of grace (Hebrews 4:14-16). Christ must be central in the life of the church if ever its worship is to be truly Christian. The Holy Spirit always bears testimony to him. Without the presence and ministry of the Holy Spirit the church's worship will be a mere form without life; when he is at work in the church its worship can be a joy and a delight.

The worship of Almighty God lasts for all eternity, but our worship here on earth lasts only until Christ comes again. For that glorious event we look and long and pray. When we meet in worship we meet in anticipation of that great and glorious day when

Christ our Saviour shall appear. We meet here and worship him on earth only 'until he comes'.

Children in worship services

In the life of the local church the meetings of the Lord's Day will usually be meetings at which non-members and unbelievers will be welcome. The preaching of the word of God on such occasions will, of course, make application to them as well as to the members of the church present.

Although unbelievers cannot worship God in the fullest sense they should not be turned away or barred from such services on the Lord's Day. The testimony of the church at worship, the hymns and the word of God read and preached will all make an important impact upon their hearts and minds. Faith comes through the hearing of the gospel (Romans 10:17), and the gospel will be preached in the services of the Lord's day. The Apostle Paul expected the presence of unbelievers in the services of the church in Corinth (1 Corinthians 14:23; see also James 2:2).

Similarly, it was expected that children would be present when churches in New Testament times met. In some of his letters (e.g. Ephesians 6:1-3; Colossians 3:20) the Apostle Paul directly addresses them. Plainly they were expected to be present when Paul's letters were read to the church. Although unregenerate children cannot worship God in the fullest sense they can certainly observe, learn and hear the word of God. They can learn to reverence and respect God; they can see the church at worship and can hear the word of God expounded and the gospel proclaimed. (cf. Exodus 12:26). Regenerate children can and do worship God in the fullest sense along with regenerate adults. A children's address is usually an unnecessary intrusion into a service of worship if the church's teaching is organised properly. If children are present in a congregation the preacher should not ignore them. A church might consider the provision of 'worksheets' on the sermon as a suitable aid to concentration and learning. Children should be encouraged to attend the church's services on the Lord's day when they are old enough to sit quietly without the aid of comic books, colouring books and sweets.

Prayer and prayer meetings

Prayer is an essential part of any believer's individual Christian life and relationship to God. It is not our purpose here to discuss private prayer as such, but corporate prayer – the praying activity of the church. Corporate prayer can often supply what is lacking in private prayer but neither should be a substitute for the other. As an individual's prayer life will reveal the state of his spiritual health so a church's prayer life will reveal the state of its spiritual health. The prayer meeting has sometimes been described as the powerhouse of the church. That description only indicates something of the importance of the prayer meeting.

Churches in New Testament times met to pray (e.g. Acts 1:14; 2:42; 4:24-30; 12:12). The church in Philippi was born out of a meeting for prayer (Acts 16:13), and prayer provided the foundation to the many expressions of fellowship found in Paul's letters. So it is not to be wondered at that today the prayer meeting is vital in the life of a church. At the root of every church knowing the blessing of God is the prayer meeting. A church at prayer is a church being blessed. The church prayer meeting is the whole church at prayer. The effective praying of the church is undermined if but a few members are present. Leaders in the church must be present if their leadership is to have spiritual reality.

The church prayer meeting is the ideal occasion for sharing needs and joys; for to pray for one another realistically requires a knowledge of one another. Specific prayer can be made for specific needs, and news of answered prayer can provoke praise from the whole church. Regular prayer can be made for the church's continuing responsibilities in outreach and missionary work. The church prayer meeting reflects accurately the church's attitudes and its priorities.

The prayer meeting is where the whole church comes to God in a state of dependence and gratitude. As it is a meeting of the whole church, those who lead in prayer should be more than a few. In order to facilitate the vocal praying of as many as possible in good order, prayers should not be too long, topics for prayer should be known before prayer begins, and in order to involve the whole congregation the language of prayer should be simple, direct and to the point. The congregation will join in the 'amen' at the close if it is truly involved in the praying.

The teaching activity of the church

Christian churches are made up of disciples of Jesus Christ – they are followers and learners. A very large area of church activity comes within the category of 'teaching' in order to provide for the needs of members to learn from God and to grow in grace. However the teaching responsibility of the church does not end with members – the church must also teach unbelieving adults and children.

Instruction in God's word of truth giving due weight to the whole counsel of God will occupy a great deal of a church's time and attention. Indeed the whole church, in one way or another, is involved in the teaching ministry. New Testament churches lived in this way. The letters of the Apostle Paul and others, for example, provided doctrinal and practical teaching as those called and equipped by the Lord expounded the word of God for the members (Acts 20:29; Ephesians 4:11; 1 Peter 5:2). The word of God was to have the supreme place in the local church (Colossians 3:16) for it was the very truth of God (John 17:17).

The whole Bible should be taught

Teaching needs to have content and form to it – see Romans 6:17; 1 Corinthians 15:3-4; 2 Timothy 1:13. The whole Bible should be taught – the whole counsel of God (Acts 20:27) – for all Scripture is profitable (2 Timothy 3:16). The teaching should therefore be expository: explaining, opening up and applying the word of God. The balance of Scripture should be maintained and the particular emphasis of God's own mind revealed in his word. In fact the whole spectrum of God's revelation is to be taught. Themes and subjects need the weight of the whole Bible when they are explained. The teaching should ensure that it is plain where the various books of the Bible fit in with one another, where the characters of the Bible fit in and how the history of God's dealings with mankind has developed.

No one should be left out

No one should be left out of the church's teaching. Adults and children of all ages should be taught (Deuteronomy 31:11-13; Nehemiah 8:2-3). The prime responsibility for the training of children in the things of God belongs to the parents (Deuteronomy 6:7; Proverbs 4:1-4; 2 Timothy 3:15), but the church has a responsibility to give instruction suited to the age and understanding of children as well as adults. We do not neglect to teach wives in the church simply because they should be in subjection to their husbands! In addition the church has a responsibility to teach the truth to children from non-Christian homes as much as it has a responsibility to teach adults from such homes. There is a very important evangelistic dimension to teaching God's word that should not be overlooked.

Teaching given in small groups appears to have biblical support, (e.g. the Lord Jesus Christ and the twelve) and the careful preparation of gifted teachers has biblical encouragement (2 Timothy 2:2,15). This is a ministry that the men in the church should undertake particularly, although women are often especially gifted in teaching small children. Each local church needs to work out carefully with its knowledge of local circumstances when such teaching should best take place. Sunday may or may not be the best day.

Catechetical instruction

Those enquiring after the Christian Faith and those young in it need special consideration. A church might helpfully arrange a series of special classes where foundational and basic matters in the faith can be handled simply. The pastor or one of the elders of the church would be the one to teach such a class. However it is not only enquirers and those young in the faith who would profit from a system of instruction; it is a most helpful thing for everyone. A catechism is such a systematic presentation of the teaching of God's word that can bring great benefit. A catechism is a series of questions and answers and can be learnt by heart. It usually contains Scripture references relating to the questions answered.

'Catechism' comes from two Greek words meaning 'to sound in the ears' and therefore means 'oral instruction' (see Luke 1:4; Acts 18:25). If a catechism is used in the church it might be helpful for a young Christian to be instructed (catechised) by a mature Christian as his 'catechist' appointed by the elders of the church for an appropriate length of time. It is possible in this way for the young Christian to be firmly established in the teaching of God's word.

Building up

Apart from the evangelistic dimension mentioned above, the fundamental purpose of teaching in the life of a church is to build up the church and its members (Colossians 1:28; 2 Timothy 3:17). The body of Christ is to grow in knowledge, holiness and spiritual activity (Ephesians 4:11-16).

In order to grow we need to know. Information is vital. Christian books can provide information or knowledge of the Christian Faith. Reading good books should be a major part of a Christian's personal life. Knowing what the Christian Faith is and involves is necessary to growth. It is wise, therefore, for a church to provide a bookstall stocked with good Christian books to encourage such reading.

Minds are important and Christian minds need feeding with what opens up and submits to God's word (Proverbs 23:7; Romans 12:1-2; 1 Peter 1:13; Deuteronomy 17:18-20).

Inspiration needed too

Information is not enough – inspiration is needed too. A church will need times for special teaching – special meetings or weeks of meetings. These would be meetings where a preacher would be invited to expound the Scriptures to the church to stimulate and enthuse believers with God's truth and to generate an excitement when God's word is expounded. There is great 'uplift' in hearing God's word in the company of others (Deuteronomy 27:26, 'and all the people shall say, Amen'. See also Nehemiah 8:6, 8-12).

Outreach activity

The whole subject of 'outreach' involves the very mission of the church in the world. It is a large subject that will occupy Part IV of this book. As it is such a large part of a local church's activity we will also deal with it here but much less thoroughly.

The church is responsible to its Lord to proclaim the gospel and to live as Christ's body in the world. The reasons behind the outreach activity of a church are the glory of God and concern to obey his commands, and a concern for the plight of the lost (2 Corinthians 5:11,14). The outreach activity of a church is that activity where it endeavours to reach outside its membership with the gospel of God's saving grace. God has decreed that he will save his people through the proclamation of the gospel (1 Corinthians 1:21,23-25; Romans 10:14). This gospel is for people everywhere (Acts 1:8), all nations – every creature (Mark 16:15). The local church needs an expansionist view of the gospel for we still have a responsibility to preach Christ where he is not known (Romans 15:20; 2 Corinthians 10:16) both in the church's locality and further afield.

The gospel to be preached

The gospel is 'good news'. That is what the word 'gospel' means.
As good news it contains important information that we are
commissioned to pass on to men and women in the darkness of
sinful ignorance. The gospel first of all contains information about
God and his law. It also includes information about man and his sin.
But what makes the 'news' particularly 'good' is the information it contains about Jesus Christ the Saviour of sinners. The good
news is about forgiveness of sins, adoption into God's family, the
Holy Spirit's work, love, joy, peace and the church. The gospel
message includes a call for men and women to repent of their
sins and believe in Jesus Christ. It is announcement and application
of truth.

The motive force behind the outreach activity of the church is
the love of God for men and women, and our love for them too.
Associated with this is the desire that Christ's kingdom shall be
extended and increased by sinners being saved and joining the
church.

Conversion is God's work alone, so no unworthy pressures should
be applied to seeking souls to provoke some kind of response. The
gospel is proclamation, not getting 'results'. Evangelism must never
be thought of merely in terms of its results. A great deal of true
evangelism is not apparently successful and yet is genuine evangelism. On the other hand we must not assume that a lack of success
automatically means that evangelism is 'faithful'. It could be that
the lack of success is well deserved.

Reaching out

We are commanded to 'go' (e.g. Matthew 28:19) to those who are
'outside' the church and its fellowship (John 20:21; 15:27). We are
commanded to witness to the truth as it is in Christ, by life and by
word of mouth. The impact of the lives of Christians on those around
can be most significant (Acts 4:13; 5:13; see also Galatians 6:10;

1 Peter 2:12). The church is to present Christ's life by holy living and 'social concern'. That is true of individual Christians as well as of the church as a body. Christians are also to be always ready to speak for Christ (1 Peter 3:15). Words are important, but they must be understandable, truthful and loving (Ephesians 4:15). The 'Great Commission' includes words – teaching (Matthew 28:19) and preaching (Mark 16:15; Luke 24:47). Later in this book we shall return to these matters for a longer consideration. However at this point a few brief remarks are in order on where and how outreach is to be conducted.

Where?

The simple answer to the question as to where outreach is to be conducted is, 'everywhere'. An obvious first consideration is where people live – their homes. The outreach may be by door-to-door visitation, visitation of those with some existing contact with the church or by distribution of leaflets, invitations or tracts. The local church basis for this work is vital, for the local church is the corporate proof of the reality of the gospel.

Other activities may be held in the homes of members of the church to which 'outsiders' are invited, or on premises belonging to the church. Other outreach activities can take place where people normally gather. So open air preaching may be possible or the setting up of a bookstall in a street market.

How?

All methods of outreach must be subordinate to God's word and must be consistent with God's honour, the truths of the gospel and the dignity of the church. Entertainment-centred evangelism must be repudiated, for it centres on gimmicks, personalities and emotionalism.

In many of the church's evangelistic activities it is wise to use teams of people; for example door-to-door evangelism is often done best by members going in pairs ('two by two'). Also, a church is wise if it endeavours to concentrate its evangelistic energy on reaching men. It is easy enough to gather children, and it is not too hard to gather women, but to win men opens up a much greater potential for establishing Christian homes.

'Regions beyond'

When we come to consider outreach beyond the immediate area around the church's regular meeting place we are concerned to establish in a new area a similar base for evangelistic work. That is the work of church planting and we shall consider it in great detail later. The local church is God's ordained means of reaching the lost in a particular area and is the most effective. Each area or identifiable community needs a local church to bring the gospel to it. Where a church recognises areas around where no such testimony exists it should prayerfully consider how best a church may be planted there. The vision should always be that of expanding the work of Christ's kingdom.

Chapter 3
The local church and its relationships

New Testament churches and their independence

The plain teaching of the New Testament is that local churches are independent of one another. A local church does not depend on anyone or anything outside of itself in order to be a proper church. It has within its own life and being everything it needs to be a complete church. No outside organisation of any kind can tell the church what it can and cannot do. No one outside the church may speak on behalf of the church without the church's permission. The local church does not gain anything as a church by being linked in some way to other churches – it does not become more of a church than it would have been had it not been so linked.

Let us consider the New Testament evidence. There are various references in the Acts of the Apostles, which indicate that in their relationships with one another, local churches acted as independent entities. How such churches came into being, by what authority and with what recognition, we shall leave for a later chapter.

Acts 13:1-3

A new church having been established in Antioch under the leadership of Barnabas with teaching help from Saul of Tarsus, the Holy Spirit led the church to send out a missionary team. Without any doubt, other churches already in existence had an interest in what was happening, not least because Paul and Barnabas went to largely

Gentile areas. However, the church at Antioch acted alone. It did not consult with, and it certainly did not ask permission from those other churches. It was under no external jurisdiction at all, because it had everything needful within its own life and authority. It is also interesting to note that the other churches raised no objections to Antioch's action.

Acts 15:1-35

The events of this chapter are sometimes called the 'Council of Jerusalem'. Nothing, however, could be further from the facts. When the chapter is examined we do not find any evidence of the presence of representatives of various churches meeting to decide a difficult issue and reach a verdict binding on all the churches. What took place in Jerusalem in Acts 15 is no Synod or Council of the churches acting with authority over them.

What provoked the meeting was a problem that had arisen between two churches – Antioch and Jerusalem. Men had gone from Jerusalem and were teaching in Antioch things contrary to what was already being taught there. The situation could not be resolved locally (verse 2), so the Antioch church sent men to Jerusalem to sort out the matter with the church from which the teachers causing the problem originated. They were obviously the responsibility of the church in Jerusalem although they were neither sent out by the church nor authorised by it (verse 24).

The brethren from Antioch were received by the church in Jerusalem (verse 4) and reported the matter. What then took place was nothing less and nothing more than a meeting of the Jerusalem church with various brethren taking part and evidence being called from Barnabas and Paul of the church in Antioch (verse 12). The whole church then came to certain conclusions and wrote to the church in Antioch (verse 22), sending trusted and authorised representatives with the letter. The Antioch church received the letter with joy (verses 30-31). In due course the conclusions reached by the Jerusalem church were shared with other churches (16:4).

What the letter does is distance the Jerusalem church from the disruptive teachers who caused the problem in Antioch. It also expresses the considered response of the church to the issue raised by the Antioch church and recommends Gentiles to leave utterly their former pagan ways.

At no time does the meeting that took place in Jerusalem (as recorded in Acts chapter 15) exercise authority over any other church than the church in Jerusalem. The working out of the relationship between two churches gives full recognition to the independence of those churches.

Acts 20:17-38

Paul's 'farewell' to the elders of the church in Ephesus dealt exclusively with matters relating to Ephesus. At no time did he suggest that Ephesus had 'metropolitan' status over other churches and he evidently did not feel it necessary to call together the elders of other churches close by (e.g. Laodicea and Colosse) in some kind of synod. What he said to these men was in no sense a directive from an apostle. He offered advice to brethren who would undoubtedly heed it because it was wise and came from one with a unique position as an apostle. Yet Paul did not seek to interfere with the independence of the church.. Those with responsibility for the church were within the church – its elders.

Paul's letters

Paul's letters in the New Testament are addressed both to churches and to individuals. His letters to churches are each addressed to an individual church in a particular place. The one exception is the Galatian letter. This is not written to a single church in one place but to several local churches throughout a large Roman province. Nevertheless Paul addresses them as 'the churches of Galatia' in the plural, maintaining the individuality and independence of each church. He does not write, significantly, of 'the church (singular) of Galatia' as if each local assembly was only a part of a larger whole. Each local church/assembly is 'the church'. Throughout his letters Paul maintains this position.

The Corinthian church

Throughout the two letters to the church in Corinth Paul treats it as a full, complete and independent church. In the first letter he assumes that the church as one body will share in one loaf to express unity as members of one local body at the Lord's table (10:17). In the Lord's supper the members were to 'come together as a church' (11:18). They, the individual members of the church at Corinth, were together the body of Christ (12:27), and were able, as a whole, to gather in one place (14:23).

The local church in Corinth was a complete church, a whole church. It needed nothing from outside itself to make it a church. It did not need to associate with any other body of believers to make it a church. It was a church of Jesus Christ. The local church of today is similarly the church of Jesus Christ.

The Ephesian church

The letter written by the Apostle Paul to the church in Ephesus is another letter written to a specific church. Christ's headship over the church is referred to in chapter 4 verse 15 (see also 1:22 and Colossians 1:18; 2:19). The context of chapter 4 is the life of the local church. Although verse 11 also refers to apostles, prophets and evangelists whose ministry was wider than one particular local church, their ministry of equipping the saints (verse 12) could only take place in one local church at a time. Paul's purpose in this chapter is to encourage unity and service within the church in Ephesus.

Christ is head of the local church and he is also the foundation upon which the church is built (2:20-22). He is the Saviour of the church (5:23, 25) and so it bears a holy responsibility to him for its life and work. The local church must be free to follow Christ who is its head. It must be free to discover the will of Christ and to obey it. No one outside the church has authority to determine Christ's will for the church.

The churches of Revelation – Chapters 1, 2 and 3

These seven churches in Revelation 1-3 are addressed individually and independently. Close to one another geographically they are never considered as a unit. They do not collectively make up the church in Asia. They are individual churches and each received a letter from the risen Christ. Chapter one pictures them as seven separate candlesticks (or lampstands). This is a significant contrast with the seven-branched candlestick of the Old Testament tabernacle and temple. Collectively they are referred to as 'the seven churches' and individually they are referred to as 'the church in ...'. Each is fully and properly a church which depends on no authority or structure outside itself.

Acts 9:31

In some recent English versions of the New Testament the following phrase is found: 'the church throughout all Judaea, Galilee and Samaria had peace ...'. It is based on a few very old Greek manuscripts which differ from the majority of early Greek manuscripts which have: 'the churches throughout ...'. I do not believe the textual evidence warrants the singular 'church' covering such a wide geographical area. I am happy that the textual evidence emphasises the individuality of the various local churches in Judaea, Galilee and Samaria. Those who hold to a collective view of the church in one of its forms, if this verse is cited as support, must find themselves on very shaky and inadequate ground.

Even given that the singular is correct (a view to which I do not subscribe), there is no hint in the context of this verse of any inter-church organisation or union that had authority over the local assembly.

The meaning of independence

From what we have seen in the various New Testament references above we can state what the independence of the local church means in its day-to-day life. In the first place we can state that each local church is a proper church. It is fully a church and does not need something outside itself to make it a church. The local church is not merely a part of the church that is made up of other parts – other local churches – to make a whole church. The local church itself is a whole church. It has within itself everything it needs to be a church.

In the second place the local church has authority to determine and act upon the will of Christ. It is under no external human authority in matters of faith and practice. This applies to governmental bodies, national and local, and to religious bodies and individuals. The teaching given within the local church is the responsibility of the local church alone. It is responsible to Christ as its head and is under the authority of his word alone.

Thirdly, the independence of the local church means that no one outside the local church may speak for it, act for it, or make decisions for it. When inter-church bodies make decisions affecting the local churches that ostensibly make up those bodies and then apply to the churches for approval, that is a violation of the independence of those churches. Sometimes, of course, a local church will find it necessary to use someone outside its membership to speak for it, as in times when it needs to be legally represented in a court of law, but on such occasions specific permission and authority is granted by the church beforehand.

Fourthly, the independence of the local church carries heavy responsibilities for the church. For the church, independence does not mean liberty to please itself. The local church is the body of Christ. Christ is its head, its Saviour and its Lord. It must, therefore, be concerned to please him above all else. It is not under external authority, but it is under Christ's authority. Its' liberty is not to do what it likes; it is to do the will of Christ.

Similarly the local church has a responsibility to Christ in the way it comes to conclusions and makes decisions. A local church is ruled by Christ through his word and may be described as a 'Christocracy'. Decisions are therefore arrived at in more than a merely democratic way. It is not the people who govern the church but Christ. In seeking to reach conclusions and make decisions members will prayerfully seek Christ's mind on the matter in hand. Personal opinion, majority rule, party point of view, and other normally legitimate attitudes of the democratic process are inappropriate in the local church's affairs. Each member is responsible to know the mind of Christ and so is able to speak, express an opinion and take part in the decision making process. But each member must also submit to the word of God in that decision making process.

There is also another important area of responsibility falling upon independent churches. Independence does not mean isolation. Some isolate themselves from other churches out of principle and some do so out of fear of losing their independence. However independence does not mean having nothing whatsoever to do with other churches; the New Testament indicates that local independent churches had a great deal to do with one another and even engaged in joint endeavours without for one moment compromising their own independence.

New Testament churches and their fellowship with one another

Although fellowship between independent churches is not necessary in order to make them proper churches, it is very helpful nevertheless, as an encouragement and support to their life and witness.

That New Testament churches enjoyed real fellowship with one another is not hard to discover. Letters from the apostles demonstrate something of the reality of fellowship in New Testament times. Letters from Paul, Peter and John as well as those from James and Jude, together with the anonymous letter to the Hebrews, are all full of communication from one to another – between individuals, between individuals and churches and between churches. A good example of such varied communication may be found in Colossians 4:7-18.

There was genuine interest in the well being of others and the condition of the various churches. They shared a common life and faith in Jesus Christ and relationships were brotherly relationships. They shared the 'faith once for all delivered to the saints' (Jude 3) and the truth of the gospel was high on their scale of priorities. Error when it appeared was warned against, corrected where possible and withdrawn from where necessary (e.g. Romans 16:17; 2 Corinthians 11:13; Philippians 3:2; Colossians 2:8). Concern for one another was also expressed in various other ways, especially in prayer and practical help. We shall return to consider these and other matters again, but of this fact we can be sure: genuine fellowship existed between New Testament churches, for which we have considerable evidence. Without any doubt, the various churches of New Testament times, although independent of one another, benefited enormously from this fellowship.

Fellowship and its basis

When we considered fellowship as part of the active life of a local church in chapter 2 we noted that fellowship is essentially sharing a common life in the Lord Jesus Christ. That life in common is capable of definition because at its centre is a person (Jesus Christ) who can be described. Fellowship in Christ has to do with facts, historical and theological that can be stated. Fellowship is in the truth. To deny the truth is to make fellowship impossible. There is then nothing in common and we must conclude that there is no life there. Such is true also of fellowship between churches. Fellowship is essentially to do with spiritual life and biblical truth. It requires trust and confidence otherwise it does not exist.

How, then, do independent churches deal with fellowship with other churches today? Do they remain pretty much isolated from one another except for occasional contacts with friends, visitors on holiday and visiting preachers? The 1689 London Baptist Confession of Faith says the following: 'the churches, when planted by the providence of God, so as they may enjoy opportunity and advantage for it, ought to hold *communion among themselves*, for their peace, increase of love and mutual edification' (Chapter 26 paragraph 14). New Testament churches did not allow their independence to be isolation. They had genuine fellowship with one another – they had 'communion among themselves' on the basis of what they had in common – life and faith in Jesus Christ. There is no suggestion anywhere in the New Testament of any church wishing to remain isolated from other churches.

Fellowship based on truth

Fellowship between churches in New Testament times was not a vague thing. It had a basis in truth. The question of whether a work was a true work of God and the matter of the correct teaching of the gospel were sufficiently important for the apostles in Jerusalem to send Peter and John to Samaria when they heard that the Samaritans had received the word of God (Acts 8:14). No doubt they investigated what was happening, as well as exercising a ministry among them (verse 25). Later Peter himself had to give an account to the Jerusalem church of another new thing in Acts chapter 11, and the church rejoiced when it recognised an authentic gospel work with God's gracious hand upon it (verses 17 and 18).

When a new work began in Antioch, Barnabas was sent there when news reached the church in Jerusalem (Acts 11:22). He continued in the Antioch church for some time, teaching and leading them. The very nature of the gospel as the underlying basis for fellowship between churches and in Christian work came under urgent and lengthy consideration in Acts chapter 15. Paul and Barnabas were in Jerusalem on behalf of the church in Antioch to consult with the Jerusalem church. The Jerusalem church decided to send a letter to Antioch about the matter (Acts 15:22-31) accompanied

by trusted brethren. Concern for the truth was clearly a very important part of fellowship between churches in New Testament days.

Verses such as 1 Corinthians 7:17; 11:16; 1 Thessalonians 2:14
suggest that the New Testament churches tended to adopt a common
practice as they applied the truth to their lives. In order for this to be
effective it was necessary for each church to be equally committed
to the truth and for widespread communication to exist between the
churches.

In today's world we must state that fellowship between churches
should still be based on truth. How do we define that? Is it enough to
hold that the word of God is our authority as today's equivalent of
apostolic authority? In New Testament times the faith could be
defined – ('the pattern of sound words', 2 Timothy 1:13; 'the faith
once for all delivered to the saints', Jude 3). It is therefore important
that a local church today states clearly what it holds to be true.
Often this will mean adopting a convenient but comprehensive
confession of faith already in existence as a suitable expression of
its position.

Fellowship expressive of love

New Testament churches recognised the existence of other true
churches and were in close contact with them, but their fellowship
went far beyond that. The churches were very interested in what
was happening in other places. They were keen to know of the
progress of the gospel (see Acts 14:27; 15:3, 4) and expressions of
love and fellowship in prayer and practical things arose naturally.
As scriptural doctrines found their outworking in changed lives the
churches found many ways to express love and fellowship.

Prayer for one another was vital. Paul appeals for it in Ephesians
6:18-20 and Colossians 4:2-4 and implies it in the many greetings
from one church to another contained in his letters. 2 Corinthians
9:13-14 contains a most interesting indication of the bond between
churches – the praise and prayer of one church express their longing
for the other. This was due in no small part to the acts of love on
behalf of needy churches by those in better circumstances.

Financial support for the poor in Judaea features prominently in Paul's letters to the Romans and Corinthians (Romans 15:26; 1 Corinthians 16:1; 2 Corinthians 8 and 9). Another example of fellowship is the way the Philippians seem to have especially supported Paul in his ministry (Philippians 4:14-16).

In Romans 16:1-2, Paul commends Phoebe, who is from the church at Cenchrea, to the church in Rome and encourages the members to receive her 'in the Lord' and assist her in whatever way they can. Verses 3 and 4 also speak of the warm regard in which the churches generally hold Priscilla and Aquila. Paul's own care and concern for all the churches is mentioned in 2 Corinthians 11:28 and is indicative of the interest in and relationship with one another which existed in New Testament days. Such care and concern was not limited to individuals, whether apostles or not, it was the general attitude of the churches towards one another too.

These New Testament examples place upon us today some responsibility to exhibit the same attitude and do the same things. But certain questions have to be asked:For whom and for what do we pray? To whom do we display loving concern in practical ways? Whom do we support in gospel work? In one sense we wish to pray for everyone but the prayer we are talking about here is that fellowship in prayer which was experienced between the churches of the New Testament. Fellowship between independent churches can only really exist where those churches truly belong to the Lord.

Fellowship in gospel service

The close involvement of the Jerusalem church in early gospel endeavour can be noted in Acts 8 and 11 where work in Samaria and Caesarea received the close attention of the church. The new work in Antioch also received help and authentication from Jerusalem.

Paul's developing missionary work involved a number of churches. He was sent out by the church in Antioch and took Silas from Jerusalem with him on his second missionary journey

(Acts 15:22, 34, 40). He was subsequently joined by Timothy from
the new church at Lystra (Acts 16:1-3) who was also commended
by the church at Iconium. The presence of Luke (from the church at
Troas) the author of the Acts of the Apostles, can be detected from
time to time in the narrative of Acts when he changes from the third
person (he, they) to the first person (we). He evidently joined Paul at
Troas but remained at Philippi to care for the new church there
(Acts 16:8,10,12,16,40; 20:6). A large team of men is referred to in
Acts 20:4. They evidently came from a number of different churches.
Also 2 Corinthians 8:16,18,22 mention Titus and two other breth-
ren who had the confidence of the churches, who accompanied Paul
on his way to Jerusalem.

There does appear to have been considerable amounts of
co-operation between the churches in gospel work in New Testament times. Although churches were independent they did not need
to act entirely on their own. Paul, a member of the church at Antioch,
was supported financially by the church at Philippi and prayerfully
by a number of other churches. Independent churches can co-operate
with other churches in many ways without losing their independence. Joint action is not inconsistent with independence.

Implications of fellowship between churches

Fellowship is more than simply contributing to the needs of another.
You can do that out of a compassionate interest in the needy, and it
is not necessarily fellowship. Fellowship involves partnership,
association with and identification with your fellow. That is what
lies beneath the various examples of New Testament fellowship given
above. The churches identified with one another, they shared in the
activities of the other, and they even had a sense of belonging to one
another in Christ. Fellowship has not lost this meaning today, but
that does present us with problems.

When two individuals enter into a partnership one shares in the
life, actions and words of the other. The actions or words of one
become the actions or words of the other. Such a partnership

involves a joint or corporate liability or responsibility. Clearly there are limits to this and they are determined by the extent or level of the commitment in the relationship. What that means is that relations entered into, for example, for business purposes only involve matters consistent with those purposes.

When we transfer these things to the relationship between independent churches and their fellowship in joint action it follows that there is a joint or collective responsibility in matters relating to the Christian Faith, its doctrines and its practice, for that is the area of co-operation between them.

If a relationship is entered into with a 'church' that holds a different position theologically, acceptance of the validity of that position is implied, even if it does not involve acceptance of the position itself. Further, it also implies approval of that position and what goes with it. Non-acceptance and disapproval would mean repudiating the relationship.

These implications of fellowship between churches – joint responsibility, acceptance of the validity of another position, approval of another position - can be examined more closely as we consider what the Scriptures teach on these issues. We will then be in a better position to determine our present day activity. Problems invariably arise when the plain teaching of the Scriptures is abandoned or ignored and some other basis for life and conduct is adopted.

Joint responsibility

Joint (or corporate) responsibility can involve us in things both good and bad and is a clear biblical principle going back to Adam. The whole human race is involved in what he did in the Garden of Eden, as Paul argues in Romans 5:12. Cain could not abandon his responsibility for his brother Abel simply by claiming ignorance of his whereabouts (Genesis 4:9). The sin of Achan in Joshua 7 involved his family in its consequences (7:24). The whole Corinthian church was involved in the sin of the man in 1 Corinthians 5 if it was left undisciplined. The stern words of the Lord to certain churches in

Revelation 2 and 3 speak of the responsibility of the church as a whole (and not just its leadership) for the presence of sin and error within its life.

Acceptance and approval

Acceptance and approval of those who engage in gross sin is involved when one associates with them (cf. Romans 1:32); acceptance of error or at least its validity is involved in Peter's compromise in Galatians 2:11-14 for which he was reproved by Paul.

The devastating effects of contamination by sin and error are suggested by a number of New Testament passages. Matthew 16:6,11-12 warn against the leaven of the Sadducees and Pharisees; Romans 16:17 urges avoidance of those who cause division in a church; 2 Corinthians 6:14-16 warn against being unequally yoked with unbelievers; 2 John 10 requires refusing a welcome to your home for a person who holds to error. Some of these passages will be considered again because their application is wider than merely contamination by sin and error.

We are concerned here however, with the local church and its fellowship with other churches. The Scriptures briefly considered above have important things to say to us in that regard. The church is 'the pillar and ground of the truth' (1 Timothy 3:15). Truth as a basis for fellowship must never therefore be relegated to the level of the unimportant. Doctrine is always essential; it must never be overlooked because it might be awkward or embarrassing. The church has a responsibility to maintain the truth, to be true to its calling as Christ's body. It must uphold it and abide by it. Fellowship must be in the truth otherwise it cannot be Christian fellowship at all. Acts 2:42 indicates that from the very beginning the truth – the Apostles' doctrine – formed the basis for fellowship between the Lord's people. Christian fellowship is sharing in the truth, so there can be no fellowship with those who deny the truth.

When withdrawal of fellowship is necessary

The strong words used in the New Testament about the importance of truth and the dangers involved in the entrance of error also suggest that there are occasions when disassociation or withdrawal of fellowship is appropriate, and even essential. For instance see the strong words of 2 Peter 2:1-2 and Galatians 1:8. If withdrawal is necessary from an unruly man (2 Thessalonians 3:6) it is obviously more necessary from one who is a heretic (Titus 3:10). Those who reject the truth concerning Christ are to be rejected and are to be given no encouragement in their evil work (2 John 10). Those who are guilty of gross sin are to be avoided (1 Corinthians 5:9-11). Even partnership with unbelievers is to be avoided (2 Corinthians 6:14-16).

Although these matters have a reference to the individual Christian they are also relevant for the local church itself. In many cases these passages were actually written to churches not individuals. We live in an undisciplined age, and such actions will inevitably be misunderstood, especially as some people believe that 'love' renders discipline unnecessary. However love on its own is not a proper basis for fellowship, if that fellowship is to be biblical and Christian. A love that ignores the truth is mere sentimentality. Although we are indeed urged by the Apostle to speak the truth in love (Ephesians 4:15) it is still the truth we are to speak.

In the case of the individual Christian within the local church, conduct and belief are to be under the authority of God's word. Where error or gross sin appears, appropriate discipline has to be exercised. In the case of churches and their relationship with other churches, similar standards apply. Fellowship has to do with commitment and trust. Where a local church exercises discipline faithfully and another church ignores, rejects or contradicts that discipline, truth has broken down, and fellowship is strained to breaking point. The same is true of a church's doctrinal position. Little fellowship if any can be enjoyed with a church that ignores, rejects or contradicts that doctrinal position.

Where truth is denied

Where truth is denied there can be no fellowship at all. Any organisation or so-called church that denies the truth is to be avoided or
withdrawn from. Doctrines necessary for salvation and for local
church life are fundamental to fellowship between churches. Any
relationship with another church has to be approached carefully and
the basis for that relationship must be clear at the outset. It makes
no sense at all for churches that believe the Scriptures to be their
final authority in all matters of faith and practice to belong to an
organisation that does not. Similarly it makes no sense for such a
church to belong to an organisation where error is accepted as valid
and is thereby approved. It is impossible for an independent church
to have organic links with churches belonging to a connexional body
that denies the truth, even if we dignify those churches with the title
'church'. Their relationship with the other body creates critical
tensions affecting commitment and trust, both of which are essential
for meaningful fellowship.

It is not enough for churches to hide behind their independence.
The New Testament churches were independent and yet had meaningful fellowship with one another. Where an independent church
has fellowship with other churches, in whatever form that takes, the
principle of joint responsibility applies. This is particularly true if
the fellowship involves actual membership of some body or other,
for the local church becomes part of that body for the purposes of
that fellowship, and becomes directly involved in what that body
does and says.

Where difficulties affecting fellowship arise, where strains
undermine commitment and trust, what cannot be put right should
be withdrawn from. Fellowship is a positive thing and is entered
into on the basis of something real and tangible. It is not fellowship
where there are areas of embarrassment that cannot be spoken of;
nor is it true fellowship when the only thing holding it together is a
common reaction against something else. Truth unites, error divides.
When error appears, fellowship is ruined. True biblical fellowship
between churches is based on truth and truth alone.

Relationships inconsistent with the independence of the local church

Relationships between local churches are organised in a variety of different ways in the modern world. Some have arisen because of historical developments, some have arisen because of conviction that they conform in some way or another to the biblical pattern, and others have just arisen by a process of development. We shall concentrate here on a few broad categories as examples of relationships that fly in the face of the New Testament's teaching on the independence of the local church. Particular situations in different parts of the world vary yet nevertheless fit into these broad categories. It should be noted that as the relationship between churches becomes more organised or institutional the tendency is for a progressive departure from the independence of the local church and therefore from the teaching of the New Testament.

Episcopal systems

The Greek word 'episkopos' means 'overseer' and is so translated in Acts 20:28 in the King James Version of 1611. In 1 Timothy 3:2 it is translated 'bishop'. An 'episcopal' system is that in which authority or rule is exercised over local churches by an individual usually known as a bishop. In fact it is an hierarchical system with government over local congregations exercised by individuals in a kind of graded system up to an 'archbishop' or 'patriarch' or 'pope'.

Roman Catholicism, Eastern Orthodox Churches, Lutheran and Anglican Churches all follow some form of Episcopal or hierarchical government. They do so because they rely upon tradition and history. The appearance of the 'monarchical bishop' who exercised authority over a number of churches in the early Christian centuries is reckoned to be sufficient reason for such a position today. The antiquity of a practice is considered a convincing reason for the position. Some Lutherans and Anglicans try to find the system in the New Testament that uses terms such as 'presbyters' (elders) and 'bishops'. Presbyters are now called 'priests' and are the ministers of local congregations whereas bishops have authority over a number of congregations. Similarity of title is insufficient evidence for identity of function. The New Testament uses 'presbyter' and 'bishop' of the same office in the local church, and there were often a number in each church.

Connexional systems

Other hierarchical systems place graded authority not in individuals as such but in meetings of individuals – courts, synods, and assemblies. Local congregations are connected to one another within this system to form one 'church' within a wide geographical area. The 'Connexion' of those congregations is the 'church'. Presbyterian, Methodist, Reformed and Elim Churches all follow some form of connexional government of local churches, and the higher courts of the connexion exercise authority over lower courts and over the local congregations. Local congregations or 'societies' are merely the local expression of the larger church.

This form of church government appeared on the scene at the time of the European Protestant Reformation and appeals to the New Testament for support. It does so on two counts: the scriptural office of elder, claiming a wider authority for him than the local church; and the so-called 'Council of Jerusalem' of Acts 15, which it is claimed was a gathering of church representatives from more than one church and which exercised authority over the churches generally. We have already seen that such ideas do not in fact have the support of the evidence of Acts 15.

Committee power

This is not a thought-out system as such to compare with episcopal and connexional systems. It nevertheless undermines local church independence in practice. Independent churches in seeking to do things together often yield to the temptation to hand over executive power to a committee made up of a small group of elected 'representatives'. One or more of a church's officers or members may represent them, but it is not necessarily the case that all churches are represented. The committee still acts on behalf of all the churches.

When any body or committee acts on behalf of churches, makes decisions or speaks for them, it is violating the independence of those churches. It is not enough to say that the committee is answerable to the churches. The churches should be taking the action and making the decisions, not the committee.

The system can in no way be supported from the New Testament nor can it be supported by some necessary principle; in fact it undermines the necessary principle of the independence of the local church. Committee power is the result of expediency – the desire to get something done as efficiently as possible. Sacrificing a little independence for the sake of the project means sacrificing a vital New Testament principle.

Although committee power grows out of the independence of the churches it does so only where adherence to the principle of independence has grown weak. Although the power exercised by the committee is not as strong as in the episcopal or connexional systems it is still a violation of the New Testament teaching on the independence of the local church.

There are certain danger areas that need to be noted. Sometimes a committee or panel continues in being long after its original and temporary function has ceased and takes decisions and claims for itself functions quite apart from the will of the local churches. Sometimes an individual ministry, say of one church, finds wide acceptance among other churches and those churches are tempted to accord some kind of unofficial primacy of respect or authority to that individual or church. Sometimes the committee distributing funds to churches can exercise authority over those churches requiring the fulfilling of special and even unscriptural conditions to qualify for receiving such funds. Such things are all a violation of the scriptural principle governing the independence of local churches.

Inter-church organisations – principles and dangers

Independent churches today do co-operate and consult with one another. They do so in various ways and try to make sure that the relationships they enter into are consistent with their independence. They are not always successful. Sometimes the description 'inter-dependency' is used of these relationships. The problem with such a description is that it suggests the local church is somehow 'dependent' on other churches. It is not. It has within itself all it needs for its life as a church. It may be weak and it has the right to seek help from other churches, but it is under no necessity or compulsion (humanly speaking) to do so. Where a local church is weak in some area of its life it is wise to seek help from other churches. That help should be given without the needy church losing its independence. Inter-dependency suggests some loss of independence, for a church cannot be both dependent and independent at the same time.

The basic principle governing inter-church organisations is the independence of the local church. Any relationship between local churches, any fellowship between them that violates that principle must be regarded as contrary to the mind of Christ as revealed in his word. Even the loss of a 'little' independence must be rejected. The independence of the local church is too important a matter to be undermined for whatever motive, however apparently worthy.

Limits to be placed on inter-church organisations

Local churches can, and should, have fellowship with one another in co-operative action. Where some form of organisation is set up to express that fellowship its actions must be scrutinised carefully lest it steps over the line of the independence of the churches co-operating together. No organisation can make rules governing the churches. Any rules it makes can only govern its own administrative procedures. Equally gatherings of local church representatives must not make rules governing the churches. No organisation can speak on behalf of the churches. Gatherings of representatives must not make declarations on behalf of the churches. They can speak for themselves as individuals from a number of churches meeting on a particular occasion. What they say will be given due weight by local churches seeking the mind of Christ – but it is local churches which must seek that mind for themselves as individual churches.

No organisation can act on its own authority on behalf of the churches. It is the independent local church that has the right to act in a way it believes to be in accordance to the will of Christ. No official of the organisation must act on his own initiative on behalf of the churches. Such action is a violation of the independence of those churches. No organisation has power to impose its will on the churches. It has no authority over the churches and cannot require the churches to act in a particular way. It has no power of discipline. Only local churches can exercise discipline and that is by withdrawal of fellowship from a church where fellowship is broken for one reason or another.

Where there is some form of general meeting, made up of representatives of the local churches co-operating together, those representatives must not be reckoned to stand in place of their churches. They cannot make decisions on behalf of those churches, which should properly belong to the meeting of members of those churches (the church meeting). Great care needs to be exercised in this area. Decisions that commit churches to action of one kind or another are properly made by the churches themselves. The decisions taken in a general meeting or assembly must be limited to the conduct of affairs in that general meeting and administrative matters relating to the inter-church organisation.

Organisationism and the independence of the churches

The word 'Organisationism' is used here to describe the situation where an inter-church organisation has a life of its own apart from the local churches that co-operate together in it. It is a situation of profound danger for the independence of the local church.

The local church alone has authority to decide whether it wishes to have fellowship with other churches and how that fellowship is to be expressed. It is also free to withdraw from that fellowship at any time and for whatever reason. No external pressure should ever be applied to a church to be involved in or to remain in fellowship with other churches. Pressure of financial assistance or threats of loss of premises are examples of what have been used to entice churches into and keep them in some organisation of inter-church fellowship. Such things are total violations of a church's independence and are glaring examples of the excesses of 'organisationism'. Independent churches have expressed their inter-church fellowship in various ways: Associations, Unions, Councils, Fellowships, Conventions, Assemblies. They all have the potential to become institutionalised and thus become the vehicle of 'organisationism' which steadily erodes the independence of the local church. The tendency to centralisation of decision-making, often because of a desire for 'efficiency', is to be observed in all such organisations. Committee power grows slowly but surely and the independence of the local church is compromised more and more.

The spiritual vitality and perception of the local church tends to be obscured where the centralised body sets the agenda of concern and action. What is of real and necessary importance for the local church in its own local setting is relegated to the lower levels of priority in favour of what the inter-church organisation regards as important. Inertia often follows from this and the local church finds itself leaving decisions and actions to the central organisation because its own burdens and concerns are not 'important' enough. The local church even begins to think that the central body is the only one that can make decisions. It is a short step from that attitude to the one that sees the central institutional organisation as the main representation of the church on earth and the local church as but a part of it with no particular importance in and of itself.

Compromise of independence

Where the inter-church organisation is set up for one particular purpose it is easy for local churches to decide if they wish to fellowship with other churches for the fulfilment of that purpose. If they no longer wish to continue that fellowship it is a simple matter to withdraw. Where that inter-church organisation is active in a number of areas, even going so far as to do everything a local church may want to do in fellowship with other churches, compromise of that church's independence is inevitable.

If for instance, a church wishes to co-operate in publishing but not in overseas mission support, it is difficult to withdraw from the one without withdrawing from the other. If the church does not agree with what is going on in one sphere but is happy about others, unless it withdraws from all it will be involved in what it is unhappy about. That is a compromise of its independence.

It is much wiser for inter-church fellowship to be organised according to each separate activity. In that way only those things that the local church wants to co-operate in will actually receive its support and fellowship.

A pattern for inter-church fellowship

Inter-church fellowship in New Testament times was evidently a practical thing. Churches had fellowship in joint action. The problems arise for us today at precisely that point – joint action, or rather how that joint action is organised. We have considered above some of the dangers and pit-falls to be avoided in the organising of that joint action. Fellowship in joint action is good for a church but how that fellowship in joint action is organised can undermine the necessary independence of that church to its lasting detriment. We need to give very careful consideration to the matter of establishing what is the right pattern for inter-church fellowship. New Testament examples can help us in that consideration.

Fellowship between churches in New Testament times started on the somewhat basic level of recognising each other's existence. Jerusalem and Antioch recognised each other. In fact the commencement of the Antioch church was 'authorised' by the Jerusalem church.

Antioch recognised the churches formed during the missionary labours of Paul and Barnabas (Acts 14:27) and the churches in Galatia recognised each other (Acts 16:1-5). Such examples abound in the New Testament. Yet recognition was not enough, personal contact was normal and expected. There are many instances of contact between churches and not only in the ministry of the apostles. Antioch and Jerusalem had considerable contact, not all of it helpful. Phoebe of the church 'at Cenchrea' had contact with the church in Rome (Romans 16:1). Priscilla and Aquila appear in different places at different times (Acts 18:2,18,26; Romans 16:3; 1 Corinthians 16:19; 2 Timothy 4:19).

Communications between churches were quite normal and were not limited to letters of commendation of visiting individuals. The communication between Antioch and Jerusalem is but an example. Paul's letters, although personal also contained church communications (e.g. Romans 16:19). Paul's letters circulated among the churches from the earliest days (Colossians 4:15-16) and of course Galatians was written to several churches at one time (Galatians 1:2). So it should be no surprise to discover that the churches had much in common even to the extent of doing things in the same way (1 Corinthians 7:17; 11:16; 14:33,34).

Fellowship between the churches was mutually edifying and encouraging. Help was sought and was given. Advice was shared and support for gospel endeavour was received from a wide constituency. Fellowship between the churches was real but at no time impinged on the proper independence of those churches.

Practical Fellowship

There are two obvious areas of practical fellowship between the churches in New Testament times that are the most plainly documented. They are support of missionary labour and the collection for the poor in Judaea. There is much that we can learn from the New Testament record concerning a pattern of inter-church fellowship in the practical realm that does not violate the independence of the local church.

We have established already the importance of decision making being in the hands of the local church, but when joint action is undertaken by a number of churches together, sometimes urgent decisions have to be taken by some body without waiting for the churches to hold their church meetings and discuss the issue thoroughly. It is not too extreme to say that sometimes decisions are to do with life and death situations. This is especially true in some aspects of missionary labour in dangerous and remote places. Is it enough to place such decisions in the hands of one local church? Sometimes that is a satisfactory answer so long as the other supporting churches have sufficient confidence in the church making the decisions. But that is not always the case.

In some situations one local church trying to make proper decisions finds itself 'out of its depth', when dealing with a foreign government, for example, on behalf of the missionary it supports. In today's complicated world such situations can arise all too often. Does this mean that the independent local church is forced to submit to some form of external executive power in order to get its work done in such situations? What may we learn from the New Testament?

Decisions made apart from the local church

The decisions made in New Testament times, in both practical areas of missionary labour and support for the poor, were not always made by the churches! Paul's home church was Antioch in Syria. It was from there he was sent out into missionary labour (Acts 13:1-3) and to that church he reported on his return (Acts 14:26-27). He was also supported by other churches, notably Philippi (Philippians 4:10,15-16) and reported on his labours to many churches in the course of his travels (Acts 15:3-4; 16:4; 18:22-23; 21:7,17-19). What is plain, however, is that Paul did not refer practical decisions back to the church in Antioch or to the other supporting churches. The churches evidently trusted him to make decisions affecting the practical details of his ministry.

Paul's method of going first to the synagogue in the town he was visiting and then turning to the Gentiles when rejected by the Jews does not seem to have occasioned any comment from his supporting churches. Decisions about where to labour were made in response to other factors than the considered opinion of the Antioch church meeting (Acts 16:6-10). Paul does not seem to have consulted his home church about his desire to go to Rome (Acts 19:21) or Spain (Romans 15:24, 28). Although the Scriptures are silent on a good deal which took place between Paul and his supporting churches, and he indeed could very well have consulted them more than the record shows, we are nevertheless left with a very strong impression that Paul took many important decisions on his own responsibility in consultation only with his companions in the work. What is plain is that the churches trusted the missionary team to do the right thing in each situation, guided by the Spirit of God.

Turning to the collection for the poor in Judaea made by the churches in Macedonia and Achaia, we discover that the suggestion for a collection seems to have been Paul's. Perhaps his experience in Antioch provided him with a useful precedent (Acts 11:27-30). Paul made decisions concerning this project and encouraged the churches to participate. The only compulsion involved was what they themselves had promised to do. (1 Corinthians 16:1-4; 2 Corinthians 8:1-4; 9:1-5). Involved in this project was a brother who was trusted by the churches to administer their gifts faithfully (2 Corinthians 8:18-21). Paul was very conscious of the need to uphold the rights of the churches and his accountability to them.

Two levels of inter-church organisation

Two observations may be made on the evidence of the New Testament material. Firstly, independent local churches holding to the truth and sharing a common life in Christ can have meaningful fellowship with one another; in consultation, sharing of information and recognition of one another which involves some sense of commitment. This can be done without jeopardising their independence.

Secondly, independent local churches can work together on specific projects as the need arises without jeopardising their fellowship with churches that are not involved in those projects. This would mean that two levels of inter-church organisation would be necessary. For the purposes of this study we shall use the terms 'constituency' and 'co-operative' to describe these two levels.

'Constituency'

The 'constituency' is made up of churches that hold the common faith and are identified with one another by a broad common life and practice. There is a sense of commitment to one another because of that common faith and life. Mutual recognition, contact and consultation takes place in the ordinary course of events between the churches without the need for an elaborate machinery to facilitate the outworkings of fellowship. There is no reason to erect an executive power structure and the likelihood of damage being done to the independence of the churches is thereby reduced to a minimum. If the 'constituency' of churches is to have some place or platform for discussion and consultation it will probably be helpful to organise assemblies of messengers from the constituent churches. These assemblies will have no legislative, declarative or executive authority, and will have no continuing existence. An assembly exists only as long as it is meeting. The agenda for such assemblies should be set by the needs and concerns of the churches with a large part of the proceedings given over to questions, sharing information and discussion. The only organisation necessary within the 'constituency' is that which arranges the convening of the assembly. Each church attending the assembly should make a formal commitment to the other churches concerning adherence to the common faith expressed in the doctrinal standards of the assembly. The constituency has no formal membership as such but attendance at the assembly requires a formal commitment by a church before it can send messengers. This will mean that where there is doctrinal deviation the church involved will be forced to stay away as it will not adhere to the doctrinal standards of fellowship.

'Co-operative '

The 'co-operative' is a formal organisation in which individual local churches co-operate in joint action, e.g. missionary work, publishing, training, social concern. Some projects are long term, while others are of short duration. For long term projects the 'co-operative' will have a continuing existence and that will be reflected in its organisational set up, but for short term projects the 'co-operative' will simply be terminated once the project has been completed.

Churches are only involved in the various 'co-operatives' if they wish to be. They are not automatically involved simply by belonging to the 'constituency'. If a church withdraws from a 'co-operative' because it no longer wishes to be involved in the particular project it does not thereby necessarily withdraw from the 'constituency'. Its fellowship with the other churches in the 'constituency' is unaffected.

The 'co-operative' must nevertheless take careful note of the opinions of the co-operating or member churches. It must never be assumed that support or approval is automatic. Those appointed by the churches to further the work for which the 'co-operative' was set up must always be accountable to the churches. They are 'trustees' acting with the confidence of the churches because sometimes they will have to make administrative decisions in urgent situations without the opportunity of consultation with the co-operating churches. The appointment of such 'trustees' in the 'co-operative' requires great care and wisdom. Vigilance and conformity to God's word are always necessary if this area of a church's life is to be honouring to its head – the Lord Jesus Christ.

Chapter 4
The local church and the state

The persistent testimony of true churches

Down the centuries from New Testament times onwards the relationship of the churches of Jesus Christ to the state has often exercised the minds of Christian people and has usually affected their lives profoundly. The state has seldom been sympathetic to the existence of Christian churches and the churches themselves have often suffered as a result. Attempts to make true churches of Jesus Christ conform to the will of the state in religious matters whether pagan, atheistic or 'Christian' (so-called), have been met with strong and faithful resistance.

Throughout the centuries there have been faithful churches maintaining a testimony to God's truth, sometimes in the face of great opposition and danger. The Lord has maintained that faithful testimony to his truth even when error has flourished. He does not leave himself without witness (Acts 14:17). Hellish powers have never and will never finally triumph (Matthew 16:18). These faithful churches form a noble chain of testimony down the centuries as they have borne witness to such truths as salvation by God's grace alone, and that true local churches are made up of regenerate believers only.

We thankfully live in quieter days, although some true believers in Jesus Christ still face considerable hardship in some parts of the world. Even though state pressure is not as once it was we need to be vigilant still, and in our study of the relationship of the churches to the state we need care and wisdom to see clearly the issues involved. Different views of the relationship of the churches to the state have appeared at different times. Today many who believe they each have the teaching of Scripture to support them hold divergent views. In addition there are a number of serious practical problems that we shall touch on at the end of our study on this subject; but at this stage it will be helpful to grasp the meaning of certain terms.

What is distinctive about the church?

The distinctive nature of the church has already been discussed at some length in chapter one. For the purpose of our consideration here the mention of certain features of the unique nature of the church will be sufficient.

The church and by that we refer to the local church, is related to Almighty God in a unique way; it belongs to God. No other group or organisation of human beings has that unique relationship. For instance although both instituted by God, neither the family nor the state belongs to God. The members of the church have been redeemed, saved and delivered from sin and its consequences by Jesus Christ. They have been 'bought' by his blood – the cost of their redemption was his death on the cross. They have been regenerated by the Holy Spirit and have been justified by grace through faith in Jesus Christ. Numerous New Testament references could be cited here to support the above statements. The following will be sufficient: 1 Peter 2:9-10; Ephesians 1:22-23; 5:25-27; Acts 20:28; 1 Corinthians 3:16-17; 6:11. The head of the church is Jesus Christ and he exercises his authority over it by his word. It is led by the Holy Spirit and is yet responsible to exercise an obedient response to Christ's word and the Holy Spirit's leading.

The church is God's church, the body of Christ and the temple of the Holy Spirit. It owes everything to God concerning its being and its life. It is unique and the above factors affect its relationship in every area of its life with all other bodies and organisations including the state.

What exactly is the state?

The state does not enjoy that unique relationship with God that belongs to the church, the people of God. Nevertheless the state has an important place in the affairs of human beings and has been instituted by God for their benefit. However, in order to understand what we mean by the term 'state' we need to distinguish it from a number of other terms which are closely and commonly associated with it.

The following are such terms: nation, country, race, civil power, and society. We also need to understand what 'sacralism' is and what the term 'world' means. If we are clear about these terms we will find it easier to see at what point the state impinges on the life of the churches.

A *nation* is what we call the people who live in a *land* or *country*, and those who are identified with them but live elsewhere. A land or country is a distinct territory or geographical location with some independent identity for historical or political reasons. A *race* of people is a group, irrespective of numerical size, connected by common descent or of common stock. A nation might contain people from different races, and one race may be part of any number of different nations.

The *civil power* in a nation is the government of the people. The *state* is the form or expression of that governmental power as it exercises its authority over the inhabitants of the land. The state is part of *society* which is the environment of people and institutions in which we live and work. The state is the formal expression of governmental rule and authority. So we can refer to a 'totalitarian state' or a 'monarchical state' or a 'democratic state', for each is the exercise of governmental power in a particular way. Each will impinge on the life of the churches according to the way it exercises its power. Churches can, and do, exist within any state system. When we talk of the state in such a phrase as 'the churches and the state' we are referring to authority and power of the governmental system as it affects the people of God.

The sacral system

Sacralism is that system in which the state is identified with a particular religion so that all citizens are automatically involved in that religion. Officers of state are also leaders in religious matters, and religious officials are state appointees. The Roman Empire before Constantine was already a sacralistic society (Emperor worship). He didn't make it one by making 'Christianity' the official religion. All he did was change the sacralistic form of the state. If a sacral system is in existence and Christianity is involved, the 'church' becomes essentially a visible structure where outward conformity to religious practice becomes the important thing. Heresy even becomes a state crime. Nonconformity to the outward form of religion approved by the state also becomes a criminal offence. The conditions for membership in the state-approved 'church' are no longer regeneration and faith, but natural birth and citizenship.

When the Lord Jesus Christ commanded us to 'render therefore unto Caesar the things which are Caesar's; and unto God the things that are God's' (Matthew 22:21), he was making a very important point. The responsibility we have to the state is not identical with the responsibility we have to God. Acts 4:19 and 5:29 make it plain that Christians have a higher obedience than their obedience to the state system. The two are <u>not</u> identical. The church and the state, similarly, are not identical and because they are so different we must maintain their distinctiveness and separation.

The world and the church

The identity of Christianity and the state in the sacral system introduced by the Emperor Constantine, was developed by the Emperor Theodosius and was further developed by the North African theologian Augustine. Its effect was to leave no room for any distinction between the world and the church. Such distinctions as there might have been were seriously blurred; the blurring making a marked and detrimental effect on Christian behaviour. Holiness became reserved for special religious people such as 'priests' and 'monks'. Holiness became viewed as an outward conformity to negative standards rather than a positive expression of a person's relationship with God. In a similar way evangelism was affected. If all citizens were now Christians there was no need to evangelise them. The call to repentance and personal faith in Jesus Christ virtually disappeared, (except in those independent churches which retained biblical faithfulness and would not conform to the state system).

In the New Testament, however, the world is distinct from the church, as in the words of the Lord in John 15:19, 'If you were of the world, the world would love its own ... but I chose you out of the world, therefore, the world hates you'. Although the New Testament uses the word 'world' in various ways, the meaning can usually be determined by the context in which it is used. However, for our purposes here, the meaning of 'world' as distinct from the church, is that sphere of life and activity of natural man alienated from God, sin-laden, exposed to God's judgment, in open hostility to God, Christ and his church, and in need of salvation.

The uniqueness of the church distinguishes it both from the state and the world. The local church stands apart from its surrounding environment by virtue of its special relationship to Jesus Christ; a relationship that requires the involvement of the church in its environment to proclaim and live the gospel message in the name of Jesus Christ. Although involved, the church never becomes the same as the surrounding environment. The 'parish' never becomes the church.

This view is not universally held and over the years various other views have appeared and have dominated at different times. Views on the relationship of the church (or churches) to the state have broadly fallen into four categories with variations held at different times by different groups of people in different places. The four main views may be listed as follows: the Papal view, the Erastian view, the Establishment view and the Independent or Voluntary view.

The Papal view

This view holds that the state is subject to the church; including civil matters as well as spiritual. It presupposes a view of the church quite different from that put forward as the scriptural view in this book. Historically the Roman Catholic pope has claimed the right to appoint Kings and Emperors; he claims temporal power still. In countries today where Roman Catholics are in a majority the hierarchy of the Roman Catholic Church still attempts to control the legislative processes of government.

The Erastian view

This view holds that the church is subject to the state and takes its name from Erastus (1524-1583) who wrote at length on matters maintaining the inability of the church to discipline on moral grounds any who should wish to partake of the church's sacraments. (He was answered, also at length, by the reformer Beza). Those who share Erastus's view (Erastians) regard the church as a society that owes it existence to the will of the state. The church is subject to the state in spiritual matters as well as civil. Officers of the church have a delegated authority from the state for the purpose of upholding the religious system approved, endorsed and sponsored by the state. This system finds expression in the Anglican Church where the head of state, the Queen, appoints ecclesiastical dignitaries and is called the church's 'supreme governor'.

The Establishment view

This view holds that it is the duty of the state to recognise and main-tain true religion. The state may not interfere with the church in spiritual matters, and the church may not interfere with the state in civil ones. According to this view church and state are recognised as being quite distinct and independent from each other in matters that are the proper responsibility of each. They have, however, mutual duties and obligations. This is seen in a national recognition of religion and the church's duty to support the state's attempts to advance the spiritual interests of the people. This is the view of many Presbyterians.

All the above three views involve an adherence to some form of sacral system. They also share a common intolerance of nonconformity to the church/state system. Historically this has meant the persecution of those unwilling to submit to such a system.

The Independent or Voluntary view

This view holds that the church as a church has no formal relationship with the state as a state. The church is separate from the state. The people of God are a called-out people and the church is a called-out company (an 'ekklesia'), a gathered community of believers. It is a regenerated body made up of believers and believers only.

It is to this last view – that of holding the church and state separate – that we shall now address ourselves. We shall consider, therefore, the teaching of Scripture on this subject. In so doing it will become clear that the alternative views are unacceptable. It will also become clear why that is the case.

Old Testament anticipations

Even a casual observer will notice that in the Old Testament the covenant people, Israel, was a 'sacral society'. All the citizens of Israel, the descendants of Abraham, were in the covenant and were therefore involved in the religion of Israel. One entered both the nation and the covenant people by birth, and left it only by death. Abraham, for instance, acted both as a civil leader and as a religious leader of the people (his family). The two things were considered to be one. However, by the time of Moses things were not quite as simple. Aaron was appointed with a purely religious function, and the seventy elders were appointed to help Moses in civil matters.

During the monarchy the separation of function was marked. Saul was even rejected from the throne for usurping the priestly function of sacrifice. Even so, this 'separation' of function was still within the sacralistic framework. What we do discover, however, is the growing place of the 'godly remnant' within Israel – those who had not bowed the knee to Baal, the circumcised in heart. The basis of membership in this community was not birth but new birth. The godly remnant was a foreshadowing of the people of the new covenant who would have the law of God written in their hearts.

New Testament development

When we turn to the New Testament these ideas are further and fully developed. In the life and teaching of the Lord Jesus Christ emphasis is given to the particular place occupied by the civil power as distinct from the people of God. Mention has already been made of Christ's statement distinguishing the realms of God and Caesar in his directive to render to each what is due. It is clear from what the Lord says in that passage (Matthew 22:21) that the believer has responsibilities to the state (represented by 'Caesar') as much as he has responsibilities to God. But the two sets of responsibilities are not identical. While 'Caesar' represents civil government involved with pagan religion this is easy to see and accept, but it is equally true when 'Caesar' represents civil government involved with some outward form of Christian religion.

Christ's clear rejection of kingship because his kingdom is not of this world (John 6:15; 18:36) makes it plain that the spiritual realm does not run along the same boundaries as the civil and national. Over all authority, whether civil or religious, stands the sovereign lordship of God, as the Lord Jesus made clear to Pilate in John 19:11. Yet this does not mean that religious authority on earth has power over civil authority. Christ's statement simply means that all power and authority has its ultimate origin in God. God had delegated Pilate's boasted authority to him and as such he was responsible and answerable to God. It is God who removes kings and sets them up (Daniel 2:21). He is still in control of our world, whatever appearances may suggest.

At no time, however, did the Lord Jesus encourage a rebellious spirit with regard to human authority, even when betrayed and arrested in the garden of Gethsemane. But obedience to human authority, such as we see in the conduct of our Lord, must not be assumed to be approval of that authority. Nor does obedience to human authority mean that authority has power in religious matters. While Jesus acknowledged the teaching role of the scribes as sitting in Moses' seat (Matthew 23:2), he steadfastly rejected the traditions of men when they conflicted with the word of God. Clearly the higher authority in terms of personal conduct and religious life was the inspired word of God. That is still the case.

Apostolic application

The conduct of the Apostles continued in this general direction. Both Acts 4:19 and 5:29 teach that early Christians knew that civil and human authority had limits. Obedience to God was more important than obedience to an earthly authority. The church's commission to preach Christ must be carried out, whatever men might decree. The persecuting power at that time was Judaism, but the time would come when the Roman state would persecute the church. The same principle applied:'We ought to obey God rather than men'. The book of Revelation was written against a background of that Roman persecution.

Before that time, however, the Apostle Paul had a very different relationship with the Roman state. He was a Roman citizen and was not afraid to use that to advantage in his work of spreading the gospel. He was able to do so without in any way compromising the principles of maintaining a distinction between the church and the state. In Philippi (Acts 16:37) he had been flogged, which was unlawful for a Roman citizen to undergo. He demanded and succeeded in this demand that the town magistrates should come and get him out of prison themselves after unlawfully flogging him.

It is interesting to note also that Roman officials at that time sometimes acknowledged their lack of competence to deal with religious
issues affecting the churches, e.g. Gallio in Acts 18:12-17, and the
town clerk of Ephesus in Acts 19:35-41.

Turning to Paul's appeal to Caesar (Acts 25:10-12) we note that
Paul was more concerned with justice from the Emperor than with
purely religious matters. He was not seeking the validation of
Christianity by the Emperor. He was seeking a judgment on the
accusations of the Jews. Already it had been made clear that the
charge of insurrection was groundless, but Paul was still in captivity.
No doubt his desire to go to Rome encouraged his appeal, but Paul
knew the place of the state in God's order of things as the authority
among men for ensuring justice and peace. It was to that aspect of
the state's function that he now appealed.

The apostolic application of these principles is more fully
expounded in their epistles. Underlying all the comments about the
state seems to be the basic notion that justice is of paramount
importance. Such was the case with Paul's appeal to Caesar. This is
the primary task of government. Justice is not partial; it favours no
class or group. It originates in the very character of God. In the
sacrifice of his Son at Calvary, God upheld his justice and righteousness (Romans 3:21-31). The state is accountable to God whether
it acknowledges him or not. It is not accountable to any class or
interest group. God instituted it, he rules over it, and in the end he
judges it.

Peter's teaching concerning the state is found in 1 Peter 2:13-17.
Paul's teaching is found in two main passages, Romans 13:1-7 and
1 Timothy 2:1-2. Basic attitudes to the state and its officers are
determined by the description given to those officers. They are
'ministers of God' (Romans 13:4, 6), and are appointed by him
(Daniel 2:21; John 19:11; Romans 13:1-2). Obedience to them is
approved by God (1 Peter 2:13, 15; Romans 13:2).

The responsibilities of the state

We observe from the above passages that early Christians recognised that the state had certain God-given responsibilities. These responsibilities remain. The state is responsible for promoting and maintaining good order in society - the 'good' as Romans 13:4 puts it. This good order must not be at the expense of the individual citizen's liberty of conscience to worship God and to obey him. That liberty enjoyed by each citizen is, however, itself a matter of responsibility. It must be a liberty that does not infringe on the liberty of others. When it does, the state's responsibility for good order becomes involved to ensure that the liberty of one citizen does not become the means of denying liberty to another and so provoking disturbance of the peace and good order of society.

The state is also responsible for punishing evil-doers and for praising (and rewarding) those who do well (1 Peter 2:14; Romans 13:4). Care is needed of course in defining what exactly an evildoer is, for what might be considered an evil in one society might be approved of in another. It seems from what we read in God's word that the evil-doing which the state is to take notice of is that which does damage, distress or harm to our fellow human beings. No legislation can deal with the hearts of men, so the state will find it difficult to deal with matters of motive or desire.

In the further exercise of its responsibilities the state is also to ensure that its citizens are able to live a quiet and peaceable life (1 Timothy 2:2). In a sense this is part of the good order of society which the state is to maintain. In order to do this 'peace-officers' (police) of some kind will be required and some form of organisation for purposes of defence against external aggression (military forces). The state will need to levy taxes to pay for the services it provides (Romans 13:7), and these services can easily and properly be quite widespread. The state is to concern itself with the proper means of life for its citizens – justice, peace, safety, stability, ease of movement, communications, and adequate supplies of necessities. It is to promote those conditions that contribute to the well being of the life of its citizens.

It is good for a people when those who rule in a state acknowledge their dependence on the Lord and recognise that he rules over all. When he is honoured and righteousness reigns the nation is exalted (Proverbs 13:34). It is good for a nation when the mature and wise reign (Ecclesiastes 10:16-17). The blessings of godly leadership should not be minimised, even in a state.

Christian responsibilities

The same passages of scripture from the pens of Peter and Paul also teach us that Christians and churches have responsibilities to the state and the nation. A prime responsibility reflects the very reason for the church's existence, and that is the preaching of the gospel. It is only Christ who can do helpless sinners good, and so, helpless sinners are to be told the good news. Giving a reason for the hope that is in us (1 Peter 3:15) is to be constantly accompanied by a quality of life which faithfully represents the life of Christ within – we are to be salt and light to the world around us (Matthew 5:13-16). The concern that Christians have for the conditions of men and women in the world around will lead to prayer for them. Paul urges that prayer be made for all men, and not least for those in authority in the state (1 Timothy 2:2). Our Sovereign God is in control of all things so we go to him in prayer with our requests for those whom he has set over us. Because he has set them in those positions of authority, we are to give them the honour and respect due to them (1 Peter 2:17; Romans 13:7).

We are similarly to obey and to submit to the state as it acts within its God-given responsibilities. We are therefore to obey the law in so far as that does not involve breaking God's law. We should pay our taxes and live as directed by those over us (1 Peter 2:13; Romans 13:1,7; Matthew 22:21). All in all, Christians are to be good citizens, setting a good example to others and thereby silencing the criticism of foolish men (1 Peter 2:15). The laws of men are to be set aside only when higher obedience to God's laws makes it necessary.

Throughout the teaching of the apostles on this important matter, at no point do they allow any interference by the state in the life of the church as to its God-given role and nature. Similarly, at no point do they allow any interference by the church in the life of the state as to its God-given role and nature. Yet the individual Christian is at liberty to play his full part as a citizen of the state, and as a Christian he will strive to be a good citizen in every department of his life. He is also at liberty to engage in lawful political activity, as is any other citizen. If he holds office, attains some rank or dignity, or exercises authority in the state, it is because he is a good citizen, not because he holds a particular position in the church. A Christian is not forbidden by God's word from holding office in the State, but he will undoubtedly find it extremely difficult.

The relationship of the local church and the state

We learn from the New Testament that the local church is fundamentally different from the state and so the two must be kept separate. This separation has a number of practical effects. Officers in the one, for example, do not automatically become officers in the other. It also means that one does not control the affairs of the other. The state is not responsible for religious matters, and the church is not responsible for civil matters. It is not the place of the church, for instance, to fix the speed limit for traffic, but it is at liberty to express its mind on social and moral issues as it sees the need. The state has responsibility, for instance, for safe building regulations that will affect places of worship, but it is outside of its power to dictate what is taught within those buildings.

While recognising that the state and the church are distinct and independent from each other in matters that are peculiar to the proper sphere of each, some who hold to the 'establishment' view of the relationship between church and state claim that the civil ruler has a duty to recognise, protect and promote true religion. This is advanced as a national recognition of religion. It finds expression for instance, in the Westminster Confession of 1644 chapter XXIII paragraph III; 'The civil magistrate ... hath authority and it is his duty, to take order, that unity and peace be preserved in the church, that the truth of God be kept pure and entire, that all blasphemies and heresies be suppressed, all corruptions and abuses in worship and discipline prevented or reformed, and all the ordinances of God truly settled, administered and observed. For the better effecting whereof he hath power to call synods, to be present at them, and to provide that whatsoever is transacted in them be according to the mind of God.'

This is going far beyond what we can discover as the role of the civil power in the New Testament teaching of Christ and his apostles. It is surely significant that in the Westminster Confession the only verses from the New Testament used to support that position are Matthew 2:4-5 (Herod the king asking the chief priests and scribes where the Christ should be born!). What the Westminster Confession is proposing is considerable interference by an officer of the state in matters that are no business of the state, namely, doctrine, worship, discipline and the gathering together of church leaders. The London Baptist Confession of 1689 contains no such paragraph, and when the Westminster Confession was transplanted to North America the above statement was considerably modified.

Old Testament and New Testament reasoning

The reasoning behind the above statement about the civil power and its involvement in the life of the church is based on the Old Testament. In this connection, matters relating to the church, the Old Testament order was preparatory and temporary and came to an end. For teaching about the church and its relationship we must turn to the New Testament. There we find that Christ instituted the church separate from the state and gave it separate regulations and officers. In the New Testament we find the qualifications for those officers, and the church, not the state, is to judge whether a man has those qualifications or not. It is in the New Testament, and especially in the words of Christ himself, that we find the rules for admission to and exclusion from the church. The church itself and its officers are to apply those rules. The state has no part in that responsibility.

Where the state has sought to exercise the role expressed above in the quotation from the Westminster Confession it has inevitably employed some form of compulsion to enforce its will. This is quite inconsistent with Christ's example and his teaching as to the fulfilment of God's will. It is also inconsistent with the rights of individual Christians to serve God according to their consciences taught in God's word. Compulsion does not work, because true Christianity is not an outward conformity to a set form. It is a voluntary obedience of the heart to the truth and a living relationship with the Saviour. Compulsion can only, and does produce great harm to the cause of Christ's truth.

What is reckoned to be the duty of the 'civil magistrate' is in fact the duty of the church. It alone is responsible for unity and peace within its life. It alone is responsible for maintaining and promoting the truth. It alone is to deal with error and abuse of truth by careful and prayerful discipline. It alone is to appoint suitable men to office to serve and lead the church. Experience has taught over the years that in many cases the civil magistrate is the most unsuitable person to exercise authority over the church. Civil authority in whatever form it takes need not be Christian at all. It is certainly not assumed that it is in Romans 13 and 1 Peter 2. An unbeliever can be as effective a ruler as a believer, simply in terms of ensuring an ordered life for the citizens and similar responsibilities. Christians are to submit to him as much as to a Christian ruler. He is ordained of God, whether he be believer or unbeliever. Our submission is to God, and therefore to those he appoints, and they may not be Christians.

However, to give the civil power any authority in areas which are the special preserve of the church is to identify the kingdom of the world with the kingdom of Christ. The relationship taught in the New Testament is that the church and the state are separate. We have no need and certainly no right to alter that position.

Some present day problems confronting the churches

We live in confused days with the values accepted by previous
generations being questioned by this generation. The institutions of
the past are being questioned and to some extent attacked. Much of
the background to our present society is provided by history, and
history has its place in contributing to our present confusion. In
England and Scotland established churches and 'national religion'
permeate a great deal of the life of those nations and their institutions. In Wales this is not so much the case as Nonconformity has
had a much larger historic influence on national life. As Christians
and as churches we have many privileges that have been accumu-
lated over the years, and we have almost come to accept them as our
right. Another factor in the confusion is the existence of the Welfare
state and what is known as 'Social Security'; what formerly the
churches needed to do for people is now done by the state.

When we try to apply the principles of separate church and state
we come up against problems that need clear, biblical answers. The
state plays such a large part in the lives of ordinary people these
days that it is sometimes difficult to see where its power and influence ends. The established church in England has also traditionally
had great power and influence. Many within it still assume that it
has that power today. Even among independent churches there are
those who have an unhealthy 'respect' for the Anglican Church. To
have an established church of any kind is quite contrary to New
Testament teaching, but such unreasonable and unbiblical attitudes
do exist and contribute to the background of confusion we face when
trying to apply biblical principles to practical problems.

The state and the churches are separate with different functions
in different spheres. The state is not to be involved in the propaga-
tion of religion (of whatever sort) because it is not part of its proper
function. It is singularly inappropriate for the state, therefore, to
pay people as employees to teach religion to the people, be they
children or adults. It is similarly inappropriate for 'Religious Knowledge' to be part of the curriculum of a state School and to be taught
by teachers employed by the state. It is no doubt necessary for children

to know something of Christian beliefs in a general way when doing Social Studies or other related subjects such as History, but for them to be taught a particular religion is not the work of the state. In a similar way it is inappropriate for the state to employ men to preach and teach Christianity to military personnel and prison inmates. (Chaplains do not limit their role to social work if they are true Christians). If chaplains are appointed they should be paid for by the churches and not by the state. Their work then becomes primarily evangelistic within a particularly needy 'mission field'.

Because the churches and the state are to be kept separate it is wrong for the state to pay money to the churches to support their work. Often 'public money' is available to churches for their work among the young. State financial aid can lead to a loss of freedom of action and can eventually lead to state control. As the old saying has it, 'He who pays the piper calls the tune', and state financial aid can easily lead to a church losing control of its own work and having to abide by policies and regulations which undermine the distinctive testimony of the church.

Other financial matters

There are other financial matters confronting churches today where the issues are not as clear as we would like and have to be considered very carefully.

In Great Britain everyone who is employed (and unemployed) is obliged to pay money in taxes and National Insurance contributions. Pastors of churches benefit from the services provided by the state paid for out of the state's income (tax revenue etc.), just as every other citizen does. So there is no difficulty whatever about a pastor receiving sickness benefit when he is ill, nor is there any problem about him receiving a state pension on his retirement. Both of these things are part of National Insurance provisions and the pastor has been paying his share just like everyone else over the years.

But what of other Social Security benefits such as those paid to families on low incomes? Such benefits are paid to families with children where their income falls below a certain minimum. Many pastors of churches have an income below that minimum. Should they claim such a financial benefit from the state? In answer to that question, the first thing that should be said is that it is a scandal for a church to pay its pastor such a low stipend! It is sometimes argued that some churches cannot afford to pay more, but that only raises serious questions about the attitude and condition of those churches. Should a low paid pastor claim state benefit to supplement his low income when it seems it is the only way his family can manage? It can be justly argued that he has paid his National Insurance contributions over the years as everyone else and he can claim what is his right when in need. Such benefit is not paid to the church as such so is not a payment made by the state for the support of the church's ministry. It is paid to the family in need, any family in need, not only to the families of pastors of churches. Such benefits can be viewed in the same way as tax allowances for a wife, for dependants, for insurance premiums and mortgage payments. No church should ever take into account when determining a pastor's stipend any possible benefits he might be entitled to. A church should pay as high a stipend as possible, for pastors are worthy of 'double honour' (1 Timothy 5:17).

This leads us easily into a consideration of other concessions made by the state, but this time to the church as such. In Britain churches are 'registered charities' for purposes of taxation, and relief from the burden of taxation is granted to charities. Gifts made to charities by taxpayers can qualify for the repayment of tax paid (e.g. if gifts were made under a deed of covenant). It is not wrong for churches to benefit from these benevolent concessions made by the state. They are not rights, but privileges, and no conditions contrary to the biblically based purposes of the churches are made. They should never be regarded as a permanent feature of local church life. A change in legislation could easily bring about a withdrawal of these privileges.

The blurring of the edges of separation

As a result of the peculiarities of British history with the position of the Anglican church embedded in it and because Nonconformist churches have had to fight for their rights over the centuries, there are any number of areas of contact between the churches and the state where the clear principle of separation becomes blurred. Such a problem occurs where an office holder in a local church (e.g. pastor or youth worker) is invited to take part in state activities by virtue of being an office holder in the church. An example of such a thing would be an invitation to sit on a local government committee, because of being pastor of a particular church. It is often done with ministers in the established church presumably as some kind of recognition of their peculiar position in society. But where the invitation goes to the pastor of a church holding to the separation of the churches from the state the situation becomes much more difficult.

When the pastor of a church is invited to lead in prayer at local council meetings is he not becoming involved in some form of state religion? Does not the holding of so-called 'civic services' in places of worship imply the same thing? Any local government (or national government) official can attend the place of worship at any time, it is when the services are regarded as 'official' and held under the auspices of the local governmental body that the separation of the churches from the state becomes blurred.

Occasions of conflict with the state

When we face state directives, orders and restrictions which conflict with our God-given responsibilities we have problems of a much more serious order. For instances, how does a church react when laws (or by-laws) are passed which forbid open-air preaching? How does it react to restrictions placed on meetings in homes as there are in some areas? In the case of preaching in the open-air there are many other ways of reaching people with the gospel. A church may feel free to engage in this form of activity but only if it is prepared for those involved to be charged with a breach of the peace or some-thing similar, should law enforcement officers decide to act against them. In the case of meetings held in homes there are often alterna-tives available to a church, but where a church is unable to meet anywhere else and it must meet somewhere. It is obviously better to find a home where the restriction does not apply. Christians do not break laws just because they don't like them.

Christian involvement in public affairs

Sometimes issues arise in the life of a nation that are of concern to the churches and to Christian people generally. Is the principle of the separation of the churches from the state violated by the sending of protests and petitions to the government on such issues? Surely, Christians and churches are at liberty to make their views known as widely as they wish so long as they are not denying the principle of liberty of conscience and the separation of churches and state. Surely the churches have a clear responsibility to make known the mind of the Lord in his word on moral and social issues relating to the good of God's creation.

The individual Christian has even greater opportunities to express his concern about such matters because he is able actively to become involved in person in the social or political scene. Some believe it is quite wrong for Christians to be involved in 'public life', arguing that it is impossible for a Christian to be true to his Christian profession in such a position. It is certainly very difficult, but it is not impossible, for that would be a denial of God's keeping and enabling power. Obviously this is an area for the exercise of personal liberty among believers.

It is necessary, however, for Christians generally, and especially the churches to which they belong, to pray earnestly and regularly for those who are involved in public life, that they may be kept from danger, pride and compromise, and that they might set a good exam-ple to their fellow men and point many to the Saviour.

This whole subject – the local church and the state – has many pit-falls and problems, but even in a minefield of difficulties we can know the help of the Lord and the wisdom that comes from above. Each church needs to seek the Lord's help and guidance as it endeavours to obey his word and walk in his ways.

PART TWO

THE LOCAL CHURCH AND ITS MEMBERSHIP

Chapter 5
Membership, baptism and the Lord's Supper

Conversion and Baptism

A true Christian is one who has been 'converted' (Matthew 18:3; Acts 3:19), has been 'born again' of the Holy Spirit (John 3:3,5; Titus 3:5; James 1:18; 1 Peter 1:23), has repented of sin and has trusted in Jesus Christ for salvation (Acts 20:21).

When a person becomes a Christian an old life has come to an end and a completely new life has come into being. The new Christian is now a new creation in Jesus Christ (2 Corinthians 5:17). This is no secret event to be kept hidden. If someone has been made into a new person by God's grace that newness will show. If Jesus Christ has truly died to bear the punishment for sins that a sinner deserves, then the reality of that will be seen in a new life of gratitude and service to Jesus Christ.

The true Christian is united to Jesus Christ and that union will be seen in the Christian's new life. Baptism expresses that union with Christ. It depicts the cutting off of the old life and the commencement of the new life. It is a public act of identification with Jesus Christ for in it there is a visual representation of death, burial and resurrection as the believer is submerged in the baptising water and rises again from it. No other public act can express the truth of conversion in such a forceful way. The old life is dead and buried and the new life has been raised up, all because of Christ's death and resurrection. Baptism is meaningless where this kind of conversion is not present (see Romans 6:3-4; Colossians 2:12).

The command to baptise

Christian baptism has been practised from the very beginning of the existence of Christianity. John the Baptist received a divine command to baptise and prepare a people for Messiah (John 1:33; Mark 1:7-8), and in a very real sense Christianity, in its distinctive place apart from Judaism, began with John the Baptist. Mark's Gospel opens with these words: 'the beginning of the gospel of Jesus Christ, the Son of God' and he then proceeds to describe the ministry of John the Baptist. John's ministry of preparation for the Lord Jesus Christ meant gathering a company of believers who in due time would be the disciples of Jesus Christ. John's decreasing ministry meant that Christ's would increase (John 3:30). That community of disciples continued the baptising work in the name of Jesus (John 4:1-2) as an increasing company was gathered to him.

When the risen Saviour issued his worldwide evangelistic commission just prior to his ascension to heaven at the close of his earthly ministry, he commanded the church to baptise new disciples. The normal practice of his earthly ministry was now incorporated into the 'Great Commission' recorded in Matthew 28:19-20. Baptism is part of the evangelistic obligation that the Saviour placed on the church then and continues to require of the churches now.

Disciples and baptism

Making disciples is the work of gospel preaching, outreach and missionary endeavour. Disciples are those who have repented of their sins and are now trusting in Jesus Christ for salvation. Those who become disciples of Jesus Christ as a result of the evangelistic endeavour of the churches are to be baptised. Repentance and faith are the response demanded by the gospel in an inward and spiritual sense. Baptism is the physical response demanded. It marks out the beginning of the new life of faith in Jesus Christ. Baptism comes at the beginning of discipleship, even before Christ's other commands are taught (Matthew 28:20).

In Mark 16:15-16 the close connection between discipleship (believing) and baptism is emphasised. Those who believe are to be baptised. Both belief and baptism are necessary responses to the preaching of the gospel coming at the beginning of a new life of discipleship – one of the heart and life and the other of the body. For believers not to be baptised is disobedience to a clear and unmistakable command. These verses do not say that baptism is necessary for salvation – those who are condemned are those who do not believe, not those who have not been baptised – but they do teach that baptism is necessary for discipleship and is the proper physical response to the preaching of the gospel.

This being so, we expect baptism to feature as the required physical response to the preaching ministry of the apostles. That is exactly what we find. In Acts 2:38 the Apostle Peter, preaching on behalf of the church on the day of Pentecost, commanded his hearers to be baptised on their repentance and conversion to Jesus Christ. His hearers gladly received his word (verse 41) and trusted in Jesus Christ. They were then baptised. Their baptism demonstrated their response in repentance and faith and marked out the beginning of their new life of Christian discipleship.

When Saul of Tarsus (the Apostle Paul) was converted he was also told to be baptised (Acts 22:16). He was told to call on the name of the Lord Jesus Christ and to trust in him. In that way he would find that Jesus Christ would wash away his sins. In a separate act, baptism would symbolise that washing away of sins and would mark the beginning of his life as a Christian disciple.

Baptism is commanded by the Lord Jesus Christ and is subsequently treated in the rest of the New Testament as a command and obligation to be obeyed. It is not an optional matter – it is a command that all true Christian disciples should obey to mark the beginning of their life of discipleship and following Jesus Christ.

The meaning of baptism

The Apostle Paul writes about union with Christ using the

illustration of baptism in Romans 6:3-6. The submerging and emerging from the baptismal water is symbolic of being united with Christ in his death, burial and resurrection. Baptism is a symbol of being overwhelmed by Christ, by his death and resurrection. He referred to his coming death as a baptism in Matthew 20:22-23. He was to be given up to it, overwhelmed by it, as he died for sinful people on the cross.

Baptism, as an outward act marking off the end of the old life of sinful rebellion against God and the beginning of a new life of loving submission to God, expresses the believer's commitment to the rule of Christ in everything. As the new believer is totally immersed in water it is as if he has died and has been buried. Then as he is raised up from the water it is as if he has been raised up from the dead. No other form of 'baptism', either by sprinkling or pouring of water, can adequately reflect this spiritual truth.

In fact, in the Greek language, the language in which the New Testament was written, the word 'baptise' means 'dip', 'immerse', or 'submerge'. To baptise is to immerse – that is what it means. To use the word 'baptise' of sprinkling or pouring is to talk nonsense because you cannot immerse by sprinkling or pouring water on someone! The person being baptised goes into the water, the water is not applied to them. Baptism is immersion.

In Mark 7:8 the word βαπτιζω 'baptizo' has to do with washing utensils and that would mean immersing them. In John 13:26 the word βαπτω 'bapto' means 'dip', again involving an immersion of the object.

Baptism as immersion is confirmed by various New Testament accounts of baptisms taking place. In Matthew 3:16 when Jesus was baptised by John the Baptist he 'came up from the water' having been down under the water. John 3:23 tells us that John was baptising in Aenon and the reason given is 'because there was much water there'. There would need to be plenty of water there because John immersed those he baptised. The baptism of the Ethiopian eunuch is recorded in Acts chapter 8. In verse 38 Philip and the eunuch 'went down into the water' because Philip immersed the eunuch when he baptised him.

In the great commission of Matthew 28:19-20 baptism is said to be 'into' the name of the Trinity. The little Greek word used is εις 'eis' and means 'into'. When Christian disciples are baptised they express their union with Almighty God and they express God's ownership of them. Being saved by Jesus Christ means entering a new life and being submerged in the life of the living God. Baptism is immersion, and no other form will do!

Baptism and believers

The New Testament contains numerous references to baptism and those references treat baptism in various ways. There are examples of actual baptisms taking place, there is teaching about baptism and it is used to illustrate and teach other truths. Many of these references to baptism make particular mention of those for whom it was instituted. Baptism is for disciples or believers.

Discipleship refers to the whole of the new life Christians now live in Jesus Christ. They follow Christ (as his disciples) and learn from him (as disciplined followers – disciples). They have become disciples of Jesus Christ by repenting of their sins and believing in Jesus Christ as Saviour. Regeneration by the Holy Spirit has enabled them to repent of their sins and believe in Jesus Christ. Repentance and faith are two graces in the hearts of regenerate people, each implying the existence of the other. Both or either are mentioned in many New Testament references as the qualifications for baptism.

John 4:1 refers to disciples being baptised; Mark 6:15-16 links believing with baptism; Matthew 28:19 commands the baptising of disciples; Acts 2:38 and 41 bring together repentance and receiving the word of God and baptism; Acts 8:12 shows that those who believed were baptised; Acts 8:36-37 also links believing with baptism; Acts 10:47 associates the Holy Spirit with baptism; Acts 16:14-15 describes regeneration as the heart being opened by the Lord and baptism followed; Acts 16:33-34 speaks of baptism following belief; and Acts 18:8 similarly links belief and baptism.

The significance of this evidence should not escape us, and it is confirmed by the references to baptism in the Epistles. Repentance and faith in Jesus Christ are necessary qualifications for baptism. Only the regenerate are to be baptised. Baptism is reserved for professing believers in Jesus Christ.

An unbeliever who goes through what is supposed to be baptism of believers is mocking the Lord. Conversion must come first. Baptism does not save in and of itself, so there is no reason for an unconverted person to be baptised. Similarly there is no reason for infants to be 'baptised'. Conversion must precede baptism, for without faith in Jesus Christ baptism is a meaningless bath.

For all believers

Baptism is for believers only, and for all believers without exception. Peter commanded 'everyone' who repented of their sins on the day of Pentecost to be baptised (Acts 2:38). Peter evidently considered baptism to be necessary for all the new disciples who gladly received his word (verse 41).

New disciples are 'new born' (James 1:18; 1 Peter 1:13), and baptism has been likened to registering the birth of a new baby. It doesn't make the baby any more real or alive than before, and baptism doesn't make the believer any more real or alive than before, but the Lord Jesus Christ commands it in the Bible. A true disciple of Jesus Christ will want to obey everything the Lord commands. Baptism is the biblical act of public profession of faith in Christ and identification with his people (Acts 2:41). When a person is baptised he or she is joined to the people of God because he or she has been joined to Jesus Christ.

Baptism and the church

Because Christianity is a religion for all peoples the good news of the Christian gospel is to be proclaimed. No true Christian can be a secret disciple. The new life in Jesus Christ will be seen in one way or another. This will mean the believer being identified as one of the people of God. Baptism is a public act, carried out in the presence of witnesses (1 Timothy 6:12). Being identified with Jesus Christ necessarily involves being identified with his people. It is impossible for a believer to accept Christ and reject Christ's people.

The command to baptise was given to the church corporately (see Matthew 28:19-20, where Christ addresses his people in the plural) rather than to the individual Christian disciple. It is a public act carried out in the context of the church and by the church. It is an act of great significance that marks out a great change in a person's life. The new believer has been separated from his previous life by his conversion to Jesus Christ (Acts 2:40; 2 Corinthians 6:17). This separation requires a formal and significant public act that Christ has ordained for that very purpose. Going down into the water and being submerged as if buried by the water signifies the death of the old life. The new life now lived in Christ is signified by rising up from the baptismal water as if rising from death (Romans 6:4; Colossians 2:12). The old life and all that was associated with it has now been replaced by the new life which has new associations and it is necessary for a public act to take place which identifies the new Christian with that new life and its associations (Galatians 3:27-28).

Baptism into Christ, which expresses union with Christ in the new life, is also baptism into his body and expresses union with Christ's church (1 Corinthians 12:13). Both Galatians 3:27 and 1 Corinthians 12:13 emphasise that to be submerged into Christ is to be submerged into his body. In baptism the public renouncing of the world by the new believer is accompanied by a public identification with Christ and his people.

Union of the believer with Christ means union with the body as well as the head. One must not be separated from the other. The new Christian is to be taught following baptism, (Matthew 28:20), by the church, Christ's visible body. New Christians are to take their place in the life and work of the church where they will grow and will contribute to its life. All membership responsibilities and privileges are theirs and they enter into those by that act of commitment to Christ and his people that marked out their separation from the world, namely baptism.

The baptising church

The command to baptise was given by the risen Saviour in the 'great commission' of Matthew 28:18-20 to the church. The church at that time was a local company of disciples who met together in the upper room in Jerusalem (Acts 1:13-15). Following the events of the day of Pentecost and the widespread success of the gospel, other churches came into being and they also continued steadfastly in the apostles' doctrine (Acts 2:42), preaching the gospel and baptising the new disciples in obedience to that 'great commission' passed on to them.

Those who actually did the baptising did so with the authority of the church to which they belonged. So Peter, Philip and Paul all baptised on the authority of the churches to which they belonged – Jerusalem in the case of Peter and Philip, and Antioch in the case of Paul. Baptism is not to be done by just anyone – it is a church ordinance and is to be conducted under the authority of a true church.

False immersions of one kind and another evidently did take place (e.g. Acts 19:1-7). This was not baptism by John the Baptist as with Apollos in Acts 18:25, but baptism into John as if he were the Messiah. It had to be put right by the disciples undergoing proper baptism administered by a true church teaching the right things about Christ, about salvation and about the church.

False immersions can take place today administered by churches with erroneous views of Christ, salvation and the church. Such churches are not true churches and therefore have no authority to baptise. Where a Christian has undergone an irregular immersion in a non-scriptural setting that should be put right by a proper baptism conducted by a true church with which the believer will be united. A true church will reject all false immersions however they are carried out, as it will reject infant 'baptism' and so-called baptism carried out by sprinkling or pouring on the candidate.

The church and its membership

Baptism into Christ includes entering the church as a visible body.

Identification with him means identifying with his people; but where is the church visible? The usual word for church in the New Testament, as we have already considered in chapter one, is ekklesia or assembly. An assembly assembles somewhere. The church assembles locally – in a particular location. The church is *seen* in a locality gathered as the people of God, the body of Christ. When new disciples are 'baptised' they become members of the local church. They become part of the body of Christ, a visible company of God's people; and they enter that visible company by the visible act of commitment, namely baptism.

The Apostle Paul wrote to the church in Corinth and referred to it as the body of Christ (1 Corinthians 12:27). The individual members were involved in its life as closely as the various parts of the human body are involved in its life (see 1 Corinthians 12:14-27). As it is unthinkable for say, a finger to have a separate life apart from the human body, so it is unthinkable for a Christian to live a Christian life apart from the local church.

The local church is not an optional extra to personal Christian living. Membership of and faithful participation in the life of the local church is commended and commanded in the New Testament. In the New Testament, membership of a church was limited to those who professed faith in Jesus Christ and were baptised on that profession.

The membership concept

'Membership' as a concept is no recent innovation. Some believe that being joined to the so-called 'universal' church is all that is necessary for Christian discipleship. Such an idea completely misses the point that Christian discipleship is following Christ in fellowship with his people. Membership of a local church is not simply having your name on a church roll. It is commitment to brothers and sisters in Christ and identification with them in the various circumstances of life, in joy and sorrow. It is being part of a body to which you make a vital contribution and from which you receive support, help and fellowship in the things of Christ. No other organisation of human beings has the same character or quality of life. This is because the head of the church, Jesus Christ, is vitally involved in the church's life.

On the day of Pentecost the preaching of the Apostle Peter was blessed by God so that 'about three thousand souls were added to them' (Acts 2:41). The word 'added' means 'placed to' or 'beside'. The adding of the people was not the unseen response of their hearts to the gospel. The word is used of the visible act of joining the church in Jerusalem by baptism following faith in Jesus Christ.

After God's judgment had fallen on Ananias and Sapphira (Acts 5:1-11) we read that 'none of the rest dared join them' (verse 13). Insincere and hypocritical people did not try to attach themselves to the church after they saw what had happened to Ananias and Sapphira, but true converts did. The word 'join' used here means 'cement together' or 'unite'. No one has the right to assume that belonging to a church is automatic. There has to be a deliberate act of commitment both by the church and by the new Christian. That act of commitment is baptism by which a new Christian is accepted into the membership of the church.

After his conversion at Damascus, Paul went to Jerusalem and wanted to 'join (himself to) the disciples' (Acts 9:26 – the word 'join' is the same word as in Acts 5:13). The Jerusalem church, however, would not receive his application (Acts 9:27-28). Paul could have attended the meetings, but he wanted more than that. He wanted to belong. There was a clear difference between being a member of the 'congregation' and a member of the church. Belonging to the church was for those who belonged to the Lord and made that fact known in baptism. That baptism involved a church commitment to and acceptance of the Christian as well as a commitment to and acceptance of the church by the Christian.

When the Christian moves to a new area and joins another church the baptism is not repeated. It is part of the evidence of commitment with which the Christian is recommended to the new church. Baptism has to do with the beginning of the Christian life as it symbolises Christ's saving work. The Christian does not start a new Christian life when he moves to another church any more than he has to be saved again.

It is interesting to note also how 'membership' was even anticipated before Pentecost. Luke's mention of the fact that the number of names was about a hundred and twenty (Acts 1:15) suggests that a membership roll of some kind with the *names* listed was even then in existence.

Membership and discipline

The usual word for church in the New Testament, ekklesia (assembly), meaning those who are 'called out' (and called together to assemble in one place), is a Greek word that was used in the Greek world of assemblies called together for specific purposes. It doesn't merely mean a crowd of people. The church as an ekklesia called out and called together for a specific purpose is marked out as different from the world around. It has been called out of the world by the grace of God for a very definite purpose – to serve God.

As a special company of identifiable people who belong to God the church has an 'inside' and an 'outside'. There are those who belong (believers) and those who don't (unbelievers). In 1 Corinthians chapter 5 we see an example of a local church removing an offending member from the membership of the church. He had been guilty of gross sin and was evidently unrepentant. On his removal from membership he is then to be considered as one 'outside' the church (see 1 Corinthians 5:2, 5, 11-13). The church is a holy and a disciplined company. It is made up of disciples who are learners and followers of Christ. They are under his discipline and his rule. So the church is itself under Christ's discipline and there are very high standards of life that have to be maintained.

The act of commitment to the church is a voluntary act on the part of the believer. The requirements and standards of discipleship are willingly taken up; there is no compulsion. However, where there has been flagrant disregard of those standards of discipleship, in behaviour that is inconsistent with the Christian profession that has been made, the church must act to maintain the high standard of life expected from all members of the body of Christ.

Membership and life

The local church is the centre of the Christian's work for Christ. The contribution the Christian makes to the church's life is the active expression of his discipleship. He has been separated to Christ and his people. This also means being separated from the world. The world is no longer to be the Christian's centre of life. Christ and his church is now that centre and loving service to Christ is now to be the consuming interest of his life. That service is to be rendered particularly through and to the church. That is true even if the church sends the Christian into missionary service, for the church supports and advises even when distance makes physical fellowship difficult.

Christ is the church's head, and it is this headship that distinguishes the church from a merely human club or society. The local church is not simply to be understood as the sum total of its members. It is the body of Christ and derives its life from Christ as its head (Ephesians 4:15-16 – 'Christ: from whom ...'). It therefore has a life that is more than simply the collective life of its members. It is this life – Christ's life – that marks the church out from all around it. Now, while it is true that a couple of Christians meeting in fellowship do not properly constitute a New Testament church, it is also true that a church need not have hundreds of members and can be a true church with quite a small membership. Be it large or small, however, a true church – made up of a regenerate people – displays Christ's life in the locality in which it is set.

Not all so-called 'churches' are true churches, however. A true church has a regenerate membership, believes and teaches the Bible as the word of God and seeks to live according to Christ's rule in the New Testament. Where such a church does not exist in an area the Christian may have to travel some distance to join one, or it may be possible in fellowship with others to form such a church in the locality at present without one.

Local church life is expressed in many different ways and we have already looked at local church activity in chapter two. We had reason to touch on the subject of the Lord's Supper in that chapter because of its place in the regular activity of the church. Here we shall spend some time on the subject because of its connection with the membership of the church and its life.

Breaking bread and early church practice

Sharing a meal together was evidently significant for the Lord's people in Bible times. The Old Testament carries various references to worshippers sharing in a meal at times of national and family celebration at the place of worship. (e.g. 1 Samuel 1:1-7). The Passover was perhaps the most significant meal of all as the people looked back to the deliverance of the nation from Egypt by the sovereign work of the Lord.

The disciples shared meals with the Saviour during his public ministry and often they were significant occasions. See for example Luke 24:13-35 where two disciples enjoyed a meal with the risen Saviour and recognised him in the 'breaking of bread' (verse 35). The breaking of bread was evidently a special act. A fundamental activity of the church in Jerusalem from its earliest days was 'continuing steadfastly ... in the breaking of bread' (Acts 2:42).

As the gospel spread and other churches came into being the believers in the churches 'came together to break bread' on the first day of the week in the evening (Acts 20:7). So it would appear that what was known as 'breaking bread' was an important feature of New Testament church life. It was something more than merely eating a meal together. Its significance was in its origin; as the Saviour, the Lord Jesus Christ, established it. It would have no special significance apart from him.

Passover and supper

It was during a celebration of the Passover that the Lord Jesus commanded us to observe what came to be known as the 'Lord's Supper'. Although first observed within the Passover the Lord's Supper is not a reconstituted Passover meal. It is a Christian meal instituted by the Lord Jesus Christ. It is to be kept as Jesus said, 'In remembrance of me' (1 Corinthians 11:24-25) and in this meal bread and wine are used; each having significance in the remembrance of Christ. When Jesus said, 'This is my body which is given for you' (Luke 22:19), he was saying that the bread was a symbol of his body. In the Passover the bread was unleavened (no yeast used in baking) and is a symbol of his pure and sinless body. In a similar way he referred to the wine as ' ... the new covenant in my blood' (Luke 22:20). The Lord's Supper places great significance on the cup and again the wine should be 'unleavened' but there is debate as to whether this means alcoholic or non-alcoholic. Nevertheless it should be from the fruit of the vine – grapes (Matthew 26:29). (The personal view of the author is that the wine should be non-alcoholic as a more fitting symbol of the pure blood of Christ).

The bread and wine used in this meal do not at any time become something else. The bread does not become the actual body of Christ and the wine does not become the actual blood of Christ. They remain ordinary bread and wine and yet in the context of the meal have symbolic importance. The blood of Jesus completed or sealed the new covenant. The new covenant has to do with God working in the hearts of his people (Jeremiah 31:31-34), and their faith in Jesus Christ. Jews remember God's mighty act of deliverance of his Old Testament people from Egypt by sharing in the Passover meal; Christians remember Christ's mighty act of deliverance of his people from sin by his death on the cross, as they share in the Lord's Supper.

The Lord's Supper is not a sacrifice. It is a memorial, a remembrance service and a joyful reminder of Christ's sacrifice of himself to save his people. It concentrates the mind and heart of Christians on the Lord Jesus Christ as often as they participate in it (1 Corinthians 11:26).

A command of Christ

An ordinance is a practice ordained or ordered by the Lord Jesus Christ to be observed by his people, having a symbolic meaning and bringing blessing to believers. Both baptism and the Lord's Supper were commanded by Christ (Matthew 28:19; Luke 22:19-20). Both symbolically speak of the central historical events of the Christian faith - the death and resurrection of Christ. Baptism is the mark of entry into the church and belongs to the beginning of the Christian life. It happens only once in a believer's life. The Lord's Supper refers to a continuing life and fellowship with Jesus Christ and his people and takes place regularly in the life of the church. It is a particularly important expression of the fellowship of the church and its oneness in Christ.

The word 'ordinance' is preferred to 'sacrament', a word derived from Latin 'sacramentum' [a soldier's oath of allegiance]. 'Sacrament' tends to suggest that the rite so designated has some mystical meaning and conveys some blessing by virtue of its observance, whether by believers or not. 'Ordinance' – from Latin 'ordinare' (to put in order) merely indicates that baptism and the Lord's Supper have been put in order, ordered or ordained by Christ.

Both ordinances have particular reference to the local church. Both take place within the setting of the local church. Neither is the act of any individual alone. We have noticed already how this is true of baptism where the local church alone has authority actually to carry out baptisms, and as we proceed we shall see how this is also true of the Lord's supper which has no place outside the local church and its membership. In 1 Corinthians 10:16-17 Paul emphasises the corporate nature of the meal as those who belong to one body (the local church) share in the one loaf. 1 Corinthians 11:18-20 mentions both the local church coming together and the Lord's supper being shared. Although, in this case, the apostle is exposing bad behaviour in the church, the practice of coming together as a church for the supper is plain to see. When the believer enters the visible church by baptism, he enters a worshipping fellowship which expresses its unity as it remembers its Saviour by sharing the loaf and the cup at the Lord's table (1 Corinthians 10:16-21). The meal marks the church as a holy, Christ-centred fellowship. The Lord's Supper is the fellowship meal of the church.

The Lord's Table

The 'Lord's Supper' or 'breaking of bread' is referred to as the 'Lord's Table' in 1 Corinthians 10:21 in contrast to pagan meals of celebration associated with idolatry. When the church meets around the 'Lord's Table' it is engaged in an act that contains a number of important facets. It is engaging in an act of obedience to Christ's command. It is remembering Christ in his death. It is offering thanksgiving to God for the sacrifice of his Son. It is sharing in rededication as the members commit themselves to Christ and each other afresh. The meal is an act of worshipping the risen and ascended Lord and is an experience of fellowship with him in that worship. Importantly, the meal also expresses the fellowship in Christ that exists between the members of the church as they gather together around the table – the Lord's table.

The Lord's Table emphasises two things: fellowship and worship. Both are taught in 1 Corinthians 10:16-21 and 11:17-34. The one cup and one loaf shared in the meal and the 'love feast' shared by the church in Corinth are expressive of fellowship (at Corinth that fellowship was tarnished by unloving behaviour). By contrast with the idolatrous feasts enjoyed by pagans, the fellowship of the church at the Lord's Table is conducted in a framework of suitable and appropriate worship of God. This is especially true in its declaration of Christ's death and its triumphant anticipation of his return. Although the Lord's Table is not the only expression of fellowship in the New Testament, nor is it all that worship is, it does teach us a great deal about fellowship and worship.

The church meeting together

The Apostle Paul assumed that the church in Corinth would meet for various purposes, not only for worship. For example, in 1 Corinthians chapter 5 the church is urged to meet for the discipline of a member. Members of a church had a heavy responsibility for the affairs of the church when they met for discussion and decision (Acts 6:3, 5; 15:22). 1 Corinthians 5:3; 11:17; 14:26 suggests that meetings of the church were for more than fellowship and that acts of worship were involved.

However, it is difficult to see how discipline of the membership (1 Corinthians 5:4) could have taken place at meetings where outsiders and unbelievers were present (1 Corinthians 14:23). It is obvious, therefore, that the church would meet privately on some occasions and on other occasions more publicly.

Where does the Lord's Supper take place? Is it a private matter or a more public one? Asking the question is almost to answer it. The whole sense and purpose of the meal has to do with the members of a church rather than with the 'general public'. The 'general public' are to be evangelised, and that is by preaching the gospel. The Lord's Supper is for those who have responded to the gospel by faith in Jesus Christ confessed by baptism. The Lord's Supper is for the church, for church members and for the 'church meeting'. It is not an 'open' meeting for many to observe, it is a 'closed' meeting for members to participate in.

The love feast

An important expression of fellowship in the church in Corinth was the common meal to which each brought a contribution (1 Corinthians 11:18-19). This has come to be known as the 'love feast' (see also Jude 12 where the Greek word αγαπη 'agapè' – meaning 'love' – has this technical meaning of 'love feast'). This meal, together with sharing of bread and wine in remembrance of Christ, was all called the 'Lord's supper' (1 Corinthians 11:20). What should have been a joyful and blessed expression of fellowship was abused, however, in Corinth by unseemly behaviour. Where the church should have been most united, around the Lord's Table, it was most divided. Paul disapproved most strongly of the Corinthians' behaviour (1 Corinthians 11:22) and wrote to correct the abuses. By their behaviour the Corinthians were despising the church (verse 22). The sense of the church being the body of Christ was missing (verse 29). All the spiritual graces that should have been present – love, unity, fellowship – were absent.

Paul did not condemn eating together as such, but the behaviour of those who despised their brothers and sisters in the body of Christ by refusing to share food with them. They would do better to eat their fill at home where they would cause no offence to hungry members of the church (verses 22 and 34). There was a right way of sharing such a meal together and Paul points the Corinthians to it in verse 33. Such behaviour as Paul condemned in Corinth is a total contradiction of the Christian's fellowship with fellow believers in the body of Christ.

Christian fellowship can helpfully be expressed and enjoyed in a shared meal. Perhaps we today have lost something valuable by neglecting the shared meal merely because it was abused in Corinth. When such a meal includes remembering the Lord Jesus in his death by sharing bread and wine, a church can experience sweet fellowship in him in a way not provided by any other occasion. When the members of the church meet in such a way, any church business transacted becomes a further expression of fellowship in the work of Christ, not mere 'business'. Leaving aside matters of a mundane or routine nature for those whose responsibility they are, the church can usefully deal on such occasions with matters relating to its spiritual health, its obligations to those outside its fellowship, its relations with other churches and its outreach to unbelievers.

The loaf and the cup

The Lord's supper is eaten when the local church comes together

(1 Corinthians 11:20). The New Testament gives no support to ideas of the supper being a service provided for individual Christians or a suitable vehicle of inter-church fellowship. Nor does it give support for the supper being held at Conventions, Conferences, Assemblies and similar gatherings. The Lord's supper would be meaningless without the local church meeting as a body (1 Corinthians 11:18, 22, 29).

Exactly the same criticisms as Paul offered to the church in Corinth were offered by Peter and Jude concerning abuses at the Lord's table (2 Peter 2:13; Jude 12). The fellowship of the local church was being destroyed as well as the Lord himself being insulted. The matter was all the more serious because those participating would have eaten from the same loaf and drunk from the same cup. The emphasis on the one loaf and one cup in 1 Corinthians 10:16-22 is to do with participation, fellowship, sharing in the life of Christ together. The oneness of the church is effectively symbolised in this way. The simple act of eating one loaf together emphasises that the church is one body (1 Corinthians 10:17) and the simple act of drinking from one cup together emphasises the bond of fellowship the whole church has with God (verse 21). It is a 'communion' or fellowship meal (verse 16) that is profoundly expressive of the church's oneness in Jesus Christ. It is therefore reserved for the members of the church as a regular expression of their corporate love for Christ.

The word used for bread (loaf) in 1 Corinthians 10:16-17 is the Greek word αρτοσ 'artos'. It is the same word used in Matthew 26:26, (the Last Supper) and Mark 6:38; 8:5 (feeding the 5,000 and the 4,000). The word sometimes means 'bread' in a general sense but particularly means 'loaf of bread' – a particular object to be eaten. It has this specific meaning in 1 Corinthians 10:16-17 and emphasises Paul's meaning.

Those out of fellowship with the church are not to participate (1 Corinthians 5:11). The practice of allowing any and all to share at the Lord's Table whether members or not gains no support from the New Testament.

Attendance at the table

In the New Testament those who attended and shared in the Lord's Supper were members of the church. The supper was not and is not a public event. Sharing in the supper makes no one a member of the church as those who participate already belong.

Christians in New Testament times seem to have carried letters of commendation with them when they travelled from one church to another (Romans 16:1-2; 1 Corinthians 16:3, 10; 2 Corinthians 3:1). However there is no evidence that such a commendation would entitle the bearer to a place at the Lord's Supper with the receiving church.

Acts 20:7-12 records that Paul met with the church in Troas on the first day of the week 'when the disciples came together to break bread'. Paul spoke for a long time to the church – until midnight, (verse 7) and then until daybreak (verse 11). He broke bread and ate before talking with the brethren until daybreak (verse 11), which suggests that as an apostle he exercised some form of presidency at the Lord's Table of the Troas church. The brethren who accompanied him to Troas evidently went on ahead and met him at Assos (Acts 20:13-14). Again there is no evidence that the visiting brethren accompanying Paul shared in the Lord's Supper with the Troas church – Paul appears to have been there on his own.

Paul's attendance at the Lord's Table in Troas should give us no difficulties with the established principle that the Lord's Table is for members of the local church alone. He was an apostle, and as such in a sense belonged to all the churches. Plainly the circumstances of the visit to Troas were most unusual (e.g. the Eutychus incident), so it would be unwise for us to use these exceptional circumstances as a reason to question the well established New Testament principle regarding the Lord's supper and membership of the local church.

Another interpretation of this passage (Acts 20:7-12) suggests that the 'disciples' who met to 'break bread' were the various brethren who accompanied Paul, and the breaking bread was an ordinary meal. If this is so there is no suggestion of the Lord's Supper being shared by others than a local church. Who was Eutychus? He was present but is not listed with the brethren in verse 4. His presence presents some problem for this particular interpretation of the passage.

Problems faced by churches today in this area are largely because today's society is much more mobile than ever before, making the presence of visitors from other churches more common than before; and because many believers hold to erroneous views that membership of the so-called universal church entitles them to participate in the Lord's supper wherever it is held. The problem is compounded when a church makes the Lord's Supper a semi-public occasion.

The problem of 'open table' practises

Where a local church practises what is known as an 'open table', a minimal invitation is given for attendance (e.g. 'all who love Jesus Christ in sincerity and truth'). Such a practice, however, makes church discipline impossible to exercise. The emphasis of such an invitation is on 'let a man examine himself' (1 Corinthians 11:28). It takes responsibility away from the church and lays it on the individual. The phrase in 1 Corinthians 11:28 relates, however, to the manner of a person's participation in the supper (contrast verse 21) and does not refer to a person's spiritual 'worthiness' to attend.

Where a church limits membership of the church to baptised believers but practices an 'open table' there is a tendency to magnify one ordinance above another. It appears to be a grave and serious matter to enter into the fellowship of the church, but anyone in whatever condition can meet at the highest expression of the church's fellowship! The Lord's Table is thereby treated as of less importance than entrance into the church. On the other hand, those who attend the Lord's Table without first being baptised and joining the church, treat baptism as of less importance than the Lord's Supper.

It is vital that we assert firmly that the two ordinances (baptism and the Lord's supper) are of equal importance. Both are commands

of Christ with equal emphasis. We must not give one more prominence than the other. 'Open table' and 'open membership' churches
(allowing the non-baptised to participate and belong) emphasise the
Lord's Supper more than baptism. It will not satisfy the evidence of
the New Testament to insist that believers attend the Lord's Supper
while treating baptism as an optional extra. The Lord has made
provision for us in both ordinances - both strengthen our weak minds
and hearts. It is both inappropriate and disobedient to accept the
privileges of the table while evading the responsibility of baptism,
and it is unthinkably disobedient to confess Christ in baptism and
then ignore his command to remember him regularly at his table.

The table and the local church

The fundamental issue with regard to the Lord's Table, is not whether
un-baptised believers may attend or not, it is whether it is exclusively a local church matter or not. If it is, the local church under the
guidance of the Holy Spirit and seeking to be obedient to the Word
of God is free to organise the Lord's Supper within its own responsibility. What does the New Testament teach?

    The institution of the Lord's supper occurred in the setting of the
Passover as recorded in the Gospels (Matthew 26:20-29; Mark 14:17-25;
Luke 22:14-23; John 13-17). One or two references to 'breaking of
bread' occur in the Acts of the Apostles (Acts 2:42, 46; 20:7). Apart
from these references we rely almost entirely on what Paul wrote to
the Corinthian church and this is because he was specifically writing to correct abuses in the church. Nevertheless, although the
material at our disposal is limited, it is sufficient for us to see that
the Lord's Supper is indeed exclusively a local church matter.

    In 1 Corinthians 5:1-13 Paul is dealing with the local church and
its obligation to discipline a man guilty of gross immorality. When
the church gathered together, Paul required that the guilty man be
expelled. If 'keep the feast' (verse 8) refers to the Lord's Supper, it
shows that the local church has both an obligation and the right to
exclude such a man from the table. In verse 11 the church members

were required 'not even to eat with' those disciplined and guilty of equally evil things.

Turning to 1 Corinthians 10:16-22 we find Paul contrasting fellowship with Christ and fellowship with demons. It is impossible to have both. Fellowship with Christ is in some way a 'participation' (communion) in Christ and this is expressed in the Lord's Supper as the members of the church share in the one loaf and the one cup. All have participated in Christ's saving work, all have been baptised into his name and all share in the supper that symbolises his death, by which they are saved. Participating in the loaf and the cup, the one loaf and the one cup, speaks of the essential unity of the church, the body of Christ (verse 17). This 'body' must be the local church, the local body of believers who are physically able to share in that loaf and cup. It must be the local church gathered at the Lord's Table (verse 21) for the symbolism to have meaning.

In 1 Corinthians 11:17-34 we find the clearest evidence. The Lord's Supper is never an end in itself as if the act of eating bread and drinking wine conveyed some kind of merit; nor is it a purely individualistic thing left to the conscience of the individual believer with no reference to others present (otherwise it could not be ruined by division in the fellowship and abuses of the solemnity of the occasion). The words and phrases used by Paul to describe the meeting are significant. They emphasise the overriding importance of the local church as the setting for the Lord's Table. Verse 17 – 'you come together'; verse 18 – ' when you come together as a church'; verse 20 – 'when you come together in one place'; verse 22 – 'do you despise the church of God ...?'; verse 29 – 'not discerning the Lord's body' (the word 'body' refers to the church); verse 33 – 'my brethren, when you come together to eat'. All these references show that the proper setting for the Lord's Table is the local church, meeting together in one place to eat and drink in remembrance of Christ in his death. Remembrance of Christ, in a context of unity and fellowship, is what the table signifies. Only those who have joined themselves to Christ and to one another in the church are the proper participants in the Lord's Supper in the local church.

Visitors and the table

All questions of admission to or exclusion from the Lord's Table are totally within the discretion of the local church. No one has rights of admission to any church privileges merely on the grounds of belonging to Christ in some 'universal' sense. Church privileges, and the Lord's Table is one, are matters within the life of the local church alone. Submission to the discipline of the local church is a pre-requisite for all church privileges including the Lord's Table. The qualifications for admission to the Lord's Table are the same as for church membership.

Because the Lord's Table is within the responsibility of the local church, the local church has the right, if it wishes of course, to welcome visitors to the table. However, that is not a practice that can be supported from the New Testament.

Non-attending members

From time to time in the life of a church, situations arise which require the exercise of careful pastoral responsibility. Such a situation obtains when a member has been absent from the Lord's Table for some length of time. A variety of reasons will be found to account for this but they may be categorised under three broad headings: discipline, distance and disability.

A persistent non-attending member may be passing through a time of serious spiritual need and therefore will require sympathetic pastoral care. Another such member on the other hand may be expressing a spirit of rebellion against the word of God by stopping away and will require the faithful exercise of loving *discipline* by the church. Such absence from the Lord's Table is often an evidence of some deeper problem in the member's heart that therefore requires careful enquiry rather than hasty action. Standards of behaviour for church members are to be very high and the church is right to insist on that. It is also necessary to act when those standards are persistently and deliberately ignored or repudiated. A church is a disciplined body and indiscipline affects the honour of Christ's name.

In these mobile days, members of churches often move to other areas and so absent themselves from the Lord's Table where they are members. Long *distance* prevents them. The solution to this problem is for them to join a New Testament church where they are now living. Before moving to a new area it is always wise to ensure that such a church is close by. Where that is impossible because no such church exists in that area, the believers who have moved there should consider prayerfully whether they can play a part in bringing such a church into being. It is always unwise to attend regularly and become involved in a 'church' that does not hold to and practise the teachings of the New Testament.

Illness afflicts the people of God as much as other people. Sometimes long-term illness or *disability* prevents a member from attending the Lord's Table for some considerable time. Again, the sympathetic pastoral care of the church might find a solution. It is plainly inappropriate for the Lord's Supper to be observed by two individuals together (e.g. the pastor and the sick member) because it is a local church ordinance and a meeting of the church as a body. But the church as a body (or as many as possible) could meet in the home of a housebound member or at the bedside of a bed-ridden member. This would only be possible if the member was well enough to receive a large number of friends together at one time. If the sick member were in hospital or somewhere similar the co-operation of the medical staff would be necessary. If however, such arrangements are impossible to make, regular visits by the members should be encouraged so that the sick member may benefit from the fellowship of the church.

Christian duty and the ordinances

No Christian, to be faithful to the Lord, should fail to undergo baptism by total immersion in water. No Christian should ever live in isolation from a local church that is the local body of believers. He should join them and serve the Lord with them. Regular attendance at the Lord's Table is also of vital importance because the Lord's Table is one of the most important gatherings of the church. Anything that weakens the connection between members of the local church and attendance at the Lord's Table should be resisted. Attendance is not an optional extra additional to membership. Absence without good cause is a failure to exercise proper responsibility as a member.

There is no evidence in the New Testament of anyone being admitted to the Lord's Table who was not a church member and thus a baptised believer. It is our duty today to abide by the correct practice and pure doctrine of the apostles who learnt directly from the Saviour. This is not a matter of choice; it is simply carrying out and obeying the instructions and examples of Christ. Both ordinances are to be honoured by giving them the place and order Christ himself gave them. No person or institution has any right to cancel or add to what Christ ordained.

The life of the local church must be disciplined and directed by the word of God (as must the life of the believer). This should include teaching about the place and meaning of the ordinances. In Romans 6 and Colossians 2 the Apostle Paul refers back to the fact of baptism as a reminder and incentive to continuing and persevering in holy Christian living. He assumes that all his readers have been baptised. The memory of baptism becomes a means of discipline and is revived each time the ordinance is observed.

Similarly with the Lord's table. In 1 Corinthians 10 and 11 the Apostle Paul refers to the continuing remembrance of Christ in his death at the table as a challenge to holy living and loving fellowship. The continuing observance of the ordinance acts as a continuing spur to discipline and holy Christian living.

The Lord in his sovereign wisdom has given two ordinances to his people. Both are to be obeyed and observed. Both are set within the life of the local church and both are related to membership of the local church. No other setting does justice to the teaching of the New Testament. No other setting does justice to the significance of the two ordinances. Christ has put together the local church and the ordinances of baptism and the Lord's Supper. Let no man put them asunder!

Chapter 6
Membership and service

Christ's gifts to the church

In Ephesians 4:11-12 Paul writes that the ascended Christ gave gifts to the church so that the church would benefit. Apostles, prophets, evangelists and pastor-teachers were given so that believers (saints) should be equipped for service (Greek: διακονια 'diakonia'), in order that the body of Christ should be built up (Greek: οικοδομεω 'oikodomeo'). Each member has an important share in this (verse 16), for the growth of the body depends on the whole membership. The service rendered by each member is vital to the life of the church. The church's life is the life of the members; its activity is the activity of the members.

The specific gifts mentioned above, which were given by Christ so that the members of the churches should be properly equipped for service, were not the only gifts given to the church by the Lord. 1 Corinthians 12:4-6 speaks of different gifts (Greek: χαρισμα 'charisma'), service (διακονια 'diakonia') and activities (ενεργημα 'energema'), given by the Holy Spirit to each one for the benefit of all (verse 7). Always the emphasis is on the good the individual members can do for their fellow members. No gift was ever given for individual or personal benefit only. Always the good of the body determines the giving of the gift. There is no source of pride for the gifted member here. God gives gifts as he wills (verse 11) and always for the benefit of others.

However, in this matter of 'gifts', we are faced with controversy. Some are saying today that the gifts of the Spirit, all of them, including the miraculous gifts, are for the people of God in all ages, and so should be expected today. Because this matter impinges on the life of local churches we must address ourselves to it briefly. It affects the whole area of what the Holy Spirit gives to the churches for their blessing, what we should expect in the life of the churches, and how we are to interpret such Scriptures as 1 Corinthians 12 and 14.

At this point it is important to state that we reject what is known as 'second blessing' teaching. This teaching holds that a second work of grace occurs subsequent to conversion and is known as the Baptism of the Holy Spirit (or some similar description). Baptism in the Spirit (as distinct from baptism in water) always applies in the New Testament to the pouring out of the Spirit on the day of Pentecost (and the 'Gentile Pentecost' of Cornelius in Acts 10). In 1 Corinthians 12:13 believers are baptised (in water) into the body (the church) *in* one Spirit. The word usually translated 'by' has, in fact, a number of meanings the most prominent of which is the word 'in'. The Holy Spirit is the source of the local church's unity and the verse is set in a whole context that deals with the unity of the local church made up of different members. The one Spirit endows them with different gifts. These gifts are bestowed as the Holy Spirit determines, to every member of the church. As a result all the members possess one or more of the gifts given by the Spirit.

But what gifts are they? Do all the gifts given in Romans 12; 1 Corinthians 12 and 14; and Ephesians 4 continue today? The controversy today surrounds those deemed 'miraculous' – tongues, prophecy, healing, miracles, and interpretation of tongues – where direct divine intervention into human affairs is experienced in speech or activity. How are we to understand these gifts in their New Testament setting?

The purpose of the miraculous gifts

In 2 Corinthians 12:12, Paul refers to these gifts as they had been experienced and observed by the Corinthian church. He describes them as 'signs of an apostle ... signs and wonders and mighty deeds'. In Romans 15:19 he speaks of 'mighty signs and wonders by the power of the Spirit of God', associated with his position as apostle to the Gentiles. Hebrews 2:3-4 also records that the testimony of those who heard Christ (i.e. the apostles) was confirmed by 'signs and wonders ... miracles and gifts of the Holy Spirit'. It is evident that the miraculous gifts were closely associated with the limited period of the ministry of the apostles. They confirmed and supported that ministry which was laying the foundations of Christianity following the ministry of the Lord Jesus Christ (Ephesians 2:20).

1 Corinthians 13:8-10 indicates that prophecy and tongues are only of temporary duration. If the 'perfect' (verse 10), which was yet to come when Paul wrote 1 Corinthians, is the completed canon of Scripture with the complete New Testament added to the Old Testament, that would be reason enough for the miraculous gifts to cease, being closely associated with the foundational ministry of the apostles. We are, therefore, not to be on the lookout for such things today. They are part of the temporary authentication of certain of God's servants that happens from time to time in the working out of God's purposes, e.g. Moses, Elijah/Elisha, Daniel, and Christ and his apostles.

Diversity of gifts

The various lists of gifts in the passages mentioned above do not appear to be exhaustive. What Paul appears to be doing when including various things in a list is using them as examples of what he means in his arguments about diversity in one body. There are some twenty gifts listed and many are quite ordinary in appearance – 'ministry' (or 'service'), 'helps', 'governments', 'giving' and 'showing mercy'. Some refer to offices and responsibilities in the church – 'teachers', 'pastors' and 'evangelists'. Some refer to supernatural endowments whilst others seem to suggest a heightening or enhancing of a natural ability or talent which itself is God given.

The Lord distributes all these things through his Spirit. All are for the common good and for the building up of the body, the local church. It is evidently the Lord's desire that each church should benefit from the service rendered by each member, using to the full what he has graciously bestowed for the common good. Each member has something to contribute to the life of the church; something that the Spirit has first given him. To ignore that or to deny it is to despise or quench what the Holy Spirit is doing in the church.

If this principle were to be generally accepted the pattern of life of the churches might well alter considerably. It is possible we would not be doing some of the things we do now. It is more likely that we should be experiencing a greater variety of God-honouring activity. Even so, we must always keep in mind Paul's exhortation that everything should be done decently and in order (1 Corinthians 14:40). The Holy Spirit does not inspire chaos or disorder. Diversity within the one body is possible with humility and discernment, and local churches could well become quite different from each other in activity and life-style. Uniformity is no more God-honouring than variety is. Leaders of the local church will have to be more alert to see what the Lord is giving to the church in each member, while at the same time ensuring that nothing enters the church's life that would damage its testimony to the truth.

It is surely better for members to be at work doing wholeheartedly those things for which the Holy Spirit has suited them, than to be doing things deemed 'necessary' but for which they are unsuitable. Perhaps some of the things we consider 'necessary' may not have such a high priority for the Holy Spirit, particularly if he has not equipped anyone in the church to do them.

The churches are all the poorer because we are fearful of taking the risk involved in allowing the members of the churches actually to do what the Holy Spirit has equipped them to do. In fact, the churches could be quite exciting if we took seriously the gifts given to the members by the Spirit. The Holy Spirit has brought liberty – we tend to encourage a bondage to questionable virtues found in the traditions of the world rather than encouraging biblical sobriety, for which there is an important place in the Christian's life. Why do those who love the great Bible doctrines of salvation by God's grace alone not get more excited about the faith? We ought to!

Service in the church

The service rendered by the members of a church is first and foremost service rendered to Christ. It is significant that Romans 12:1-2 begins the chapter in Paul's letter that speaks of the church as the body of Christ and the members of the church having gifts to contribute to the common good. The presentation of our lives to Christ is our 'reasonable service'. We are to live our lives in every aspect as before God. It is him we serve in the things we do in the church and in our daily living. So as we come to consider how every member of the church is to serve in the life of the local church we affirm first of all that such service is not to be a parade of ability to gain the admiration of men. What the Holy Spirit gives to the church will always be for the glory of Christ. What God gives to his people will encourage the praise of his Son to whom has been given all authority in heaven and on earth.

The service rendered by the members of the church to the glory of God and for the common good is also to be motivated by love. We are to do good to all men, but especially to the household of faith (Galatians 6:10). Love is self-giving not self-glorifying and so brings a quality to our service which marks it apart from so much other human activity which could be considered good. The Christian is not to think of himself more highly than he ought to think (Romans 12:3). We need one another in the church because each has an essential part to play. It is not we who give honour to the members of a church, it is the Lord (1 Corinthians 12:24). We are to have 'the same care' for one another (1 Corinthians 12:25). Each part has a vital contribution to make. What every part contributes, as it takes its full share, causes the local body to grow and work properly and lovingly (Ephesians 4:16).

A further necessary requirement of the service rendered by the members is faithfulness. 1 Corinthians 4:2 declares that stewards (trustees, managers, servants) are required to be faithful. Success is in God's hands and faithfulness in ours. Wholehearted, committed and obedient service is required of all God's people. Our sovereign Lord requires nothing less of his redeemed people than the faithful service of those who love him. Although success is entirely in his hands, there is never any success without faithful service.

How does all this work out in practice? We have already considered the activity of the local church in a previous chapter. Here we shall consider similar things from the standpoint of the service of the members exercising those gifts bestowed by the Holy Spirit for the benefit of all.

Service in the church's organisation

The church is not a disorganised collection of people. Its organisation is mapped out for us in the New Testament. Each member is important and has an essential ministry (or service) to exercise. The New Testament teaches us concerning the important place to be given to the office of pastor of a church, and we shall consider that in greater depth in a later chapter. His office is not a solitary one; we learn in the New Testament that a church can be blessed by the Holy Spirit in having elders to assist and share with the pastor in his care and leadership of the church. This may well be an ideal to be aimed at in many churches rather than a practical reality. For each church is dependent on the sovereign bestowal of gifts by the Holy Spirit. It is a recipe for trouble if ungifted men are appointed to this holy office.

If the work of leadership is shared in this way it becomes apparent that God-given abilities and gifts are beginning to be used in the church. Shared pastoral care, teaching, wise leadership, discipline and rule are all involved, for no one man has every virtue or gift. The Lord blesses the church with a variety of talents and skills that are to be used – first of all here in the leadership of the church.

However elders are not to do everything. The Lord has made gracious provision in his word for assistance to be given to them.

Acts 6 indicates that deacons are appointed to assist and relieve the elders. They were appointed to do those practical things relating to the common life and property of the church which otherwise would have to be done by the elders. Deacons should be appointed by the church with the necessary authority to get on with their work. They don't need to hold meetings to do that. In fact, we have no record in the New Testament of the deacons meeting together in a 'deacons' meeting'. There are a number of instances of elders doing so, however, and for a variety of reasons (cf. Acts 11:30; 13:1-3; 20:17; James 5:14).

1 Timothy 3:11 (lit. 'women' not 'wives') and 5:9-10 indicate that there are particular responsibilities falling on older women in the church as they also assist the elders. But the great variety of jobs to be done in a church includes every member. Such passages as Romans 12:4-8 and Ephesians 4:16 point to that variety. There are many things that need doing simply to ensure that the church's life runs smoothly – stewarding, keeping records, writing letters, preparing prayer lists, catering, visiting one another, and so on. Each church will have different features in its life depending on who the members are and what they can do. The whole church depends on the whole membership. The whole church is to serve the Lord and one another. The appeals and instructions of Paul's letters were addressed to the whole church in a particular place, not just its leaders (e.g. Romans 1:7; 1 Corinthians 1:2). When the whole church meets together to discuss the work of the church in the 'church meeting', all the members should be there, for they all have a part to play and each has opportunity to contribute to the decision-making process (1 Corinthians 5:4; Acts 6:2; 14:27).

Service in worship

The service to be rendered by the members is first and foremost to be spiritual service. The gifts given by the Holy Spirit for service in the church, however 'ordinary' they may seem to our understanding are essentially spiritual gifts. The church is a worshipping community with a spiritual dimension to its life.

If Christian service is to be exercised in the church's worship the church member must be present to do it ... 'Not forsaking the assembling of ourselves together, as is the manner of some' (Hebrews 10:25). He must be eager to give as well as receive in the worship, for the 'service' of worship is expressive of the believer's service ('diakonia') to God as God's servant ('diakonos').

If worship is to be service, the members of the church must 'contribute' to the worship as gifted by God. As we have already considered in Chapter two the worship service of the church needs to take account of this. It is not the activity of one man. All are involved. We have no earthly priest performing some ritual for us. We all approach God's throne together and join our hearts in the worship.

So, on the other side of the coin, all the service rendered by the members is to be seen as 'unto the Lord'. It is worship too – it is the service of God done with a sense of his majesty and glory (Hebrews 12:28).

Service in prayer

Although prayer is delightful communion with Almighty God as our heavenly Father, it nevertheless requires effort and work. It is as natural for a Christian to pray as it is for him to breathe, but it is still an exercise to be worked at and improved. Within the life of the local church, prayer as a corporate activity is part of the Christian's service to God and similarly requires effort and work.

Prayer as service to God may be highlighted when we consider corporate prayer and especially the church prayer meeting as an exposure of the church's spiritual life. The audible praying of the members (leading others in prayer) exposes the spiritual health (or ill-health) of the church. The prayer meeting should be the power centre of the church, but it is often plagued by problems.

Sometimes church prayer meetings are afflicted with long embarrassing silences. Silence in itself is not necessarily a bad thing. It can sometimes be a great blessing aiding meditation and calm reflection on God's word and God's glory. But where very few people lead in prayer and silence becomes awkward so that audible prayer is offered because you can't stand the silence any longer, serious problems exist.

Although the silence might be due to shyness on the part of the members that is not the whole reason if it happens time after time. Church members should know one another well enough for shyness not to be a factor. Silence is not usually a problem in church business meetings! The persistent silence and lack of audible prayer is a serious matter reflecting the spiritual life of the church. This is not to say that heaping up words and speaking for the sake of it is in any way to be preferred. Words as such are no more spiritual than silence, but persistent silence at every meeting is an expression of something wrong in the life of the church. Surely it is an expression of an attitude of non-involvement which dominates the lives of many Christians and is a plague afflicting many churches. Faithful and wholehearted participation in the church's prayer meeting is a vital part of a Christian's service to God.

The 'let someone else do it' syndrome is a total contradiction of true Christian discipleship. The Lord Jesus calls each Christian to take up his own cross and follow him (Mark 8:34). He does not expect us to leave it for someone else to pick up and carry. Every Christian is involved in discipleship whether he likes it or not, that includes the church's ministry of prayer in the prayer meeting. It means being there too!

Some churches, however, have another problem – only one or two people lead in prayer in the meeting and they take up so much time and pray for so long that no one else has a chance. Some people do like the sound of their own voices, and that may be the reason for it, especially when they use the same phrases week after week and lose the interest of others in the meeting. Again the reason why this happens may have a deeper cause than appears on the surface.

A church that doesn't make some efforts to involve every member in its life is likely to suffer from an unbalanced emphasis and dependence on a few 'indispensable' people. Those who wield 'power' in a church can sometimes strangle a church's spiritual life by overruling the efforts of others. This is a tragic denial of the New Testament teaching on the nature of the church as the body of Christ with each member's gifts and service contributing to the health of the whole. On the other hand the problem may not be the 'power' of the few but the lack of involvement and commitment of the many. In either case believing prayer diminishes and the work of Christ suffers.

The responsibility for a well-attended, hearty and earnest prayer meeting rests with every member and not just the leaders of the church. Prayer is a vital activity of each believer in private and with the church. Perhaps the poverty of corporate prayer is but a reflection of the poverty of private prayer. One cannot make up for the deficiency of the other and there is no substitute for either private praying or the church prayer meeting. The church prayer meeting is nevertheless the 'power centre' of the church. The effectiveness of the church depends on it.

Service in fellowship

We have already spent some time considering fellowship in chapter two and we will not simply repeat what we said there; nor are we considering that private fellowship believers have with one another, although that is fostered by church fellowship where proper biblical expressions of fellowship are evident. A church that is an integrated fellowship will discover that private fellowship enhances its spiritual life, a sectionalised church will discover that private fellowship will be divisive. What we are concerned with here, however, is service in fellowship.

True biblical fellowship has to be worked at and catered for in the programme of the church's activities if it is to be a proper expression of the believer's and the church's service to God.

Fellowship is many sided (see Hebrews 10:33; Galatians 6:10; 2 Corinthians 1:7; Philippians 1:7), but it is essentially serving one another and sharing with one another in the things of the Lord. It is much more than sitting together in the same room (you can hardly be said to be enjoying 'fellowship' with your fellow sufferers in a dentist's waiting room, although some people think of it in that way). Fellowship was basic to church life from the very earliest days (see Acts 2:42) and grew and developed as time went on (Acts 2:44-45; 4:34-35; 6:1-3; 11:27-30). It was in the practical realm of true godly fellowship that the members of a church would be able to express and exercise what God the Holy Spirit had given them for the common good. 'Members should have the same care one for another' (1 Corinthians 12:25) and Paul encourages the practical outworking of that care in Romans chapter 12 when describing what being the body of Christ means for a church.

So what should a church do today to ensure that such practical service in fellowship may be enjoyed and the various members can contribute to the common good of the church? The New Testament indicates in various places that many things are appropriate. Prayer for one another in a systematic way can be encouraged. Visitation of one another and especially of the sick should be constantly taking place. Members should be encouraged to be always on the look-out for ways to serve one another in love. Church outings and social gatherings, as well as opportunity for informal fellowship on church premises on the Lord's day can all helpfully contribute to deepening fellowship. It is very important that the members of a church should know one another, and that in a deeper way than simply being able to recognise one another in the street. Fellowship is all about sharing and working together, so every opportunity should be taken to do things together as a church (decorating and cleaning are mundane examples that readily come to mind).

The church also expresses its fellowship when it meets to discuss the work of the Lord in the church business meeting. Meeting around the Lord's Table on that occasion enhances the church's fellowship, which is based on the sacrifice of the Saviour. In the breaking of bread and the drinking of the cup the members of the church demonstrate their oneness and their willingness to live and work together. Fellowship is to do with commitment and the Lord's Table speaks of the desire of the participants (the church members) to serve both the Lord and his people. As the Apostle Paul puts it: 'Submitting to one to another in the fear of God' (Ephesians 5:21).

Service in outreach

The Great Commission of Matthew 28:18-20 is still binding on the
local church as much as it has ever been. We are still to go into the
entire world with the gospel. A church should therefore have an
evangelistic programme, for it is very easy to overlook this matter
and assume that things are being done. The agent of evangelism is
the local church, so outreach should always be before the church in
the ministry of the word, in the prayer meetings, in the church business meetings and in the meetings of the elders. It should be the
church's constant desire to reach out with the gospel with every
member playing his part to the full.

Clearly preaching is to be done by those called and gifted, and
this is especially true of preaching in the open air. However all members can give invitations to meetings, most can distribute leaflets,
many can use their homes informally for reaching their neighbours,
and those with particular abilities can engage in house to house visitation. Those with other skills have their part to play in other endeavours when needed.

New Testament evangelism was church evangelism. It was church
based and the whole church did it. It was from the local church that
the word sounded out to the surrounding region (e.g. 1 Thessalonians
1:8), and it was into the local church that new converts were brought
by baptism. Missionary work was essentially the planting of
churches. The purposes of God centre in the church, and for the
church Christ came and died (Ephesians 5:26-27). The gospel and
the church go together in their message, application and presentation.

It is vital that the elders of a church seek ways consistent with
the gospel message and biblical principles of church life to reach
out with the gospel. It is also vital that they ensure that the particular gifts and talents that God has graciously given to a church are
used to the full in reaching the lost with the gospel. It is equally vital
that individual members should be eager to serve the Lord in evangelistic endeavour that all may hear the good news of Christ the
Saviour of sinners.

Service in teaching the word of God

In the work of a church the teaching of the word of God is high on the list of priorities. Nurture, instruction, building up, growth in grace and in the knowledge of the Lord are all matters associated with it. Systematic and expository preaching of the word is the normal way for this to happen in the church. Yet account must be taken of the need to teach the truth of God's word to all ages in a way suitable to the age of the person with no one left out (Deuteronomy 31:11-13; Nehemiah 8:2-3).

Ezra needed helpers to give the sense of the word of God for his hearers (Nehemiah 8:8) and so elders of churches today will similarly need helpers to give the sense and teach all ages in a way suitable to their capacity. This is a further example of the ways the members of a church can serve one another. It is necessary, therefore, in a church for some system to be worked out whereby this need can be met in a practical way. Those who do the teaching should be mature adults whom the Lord has gifted and called to this work (2 Timothy 2:2), for it is not work for a novice (Hebrews 5:12), although the whole church bears responsibility for the work.

Service and church growth

Ephesians 4:11-16 teaches that gifts are given so that a church might grow and that in various ways. A living church will grow. It will grow in understanding, in spiritual depth, in love, and in members. As each member diligently serves the Lord in the church, in those areas of life laid upon him by the Lord, the well being of the church is enhanced and it becomes more effective in the work of the gospel. The gifts given to the members are so that all the members may serve in the church. If only a few do the work, the church as a whole lacks balance; if all work, then more is done and all benefit from the service of all. A church grows in this way, for all members recognise that they are needed – and wanted. The elders of a church should always have before them the question of how each member can be used – what abilities and gifts God has given to the church for its benefit and his glory.

However growth has its dangers. Obesity is a problem not confined to physical bodies. Churches can grow fat, and overweight! Large numbers of members who do nothing can hamper the effective life of a church. If such is the case then discipline has broken down. Discipline, together with exercise and a proper diet keeps a body fit. A large membership tends to have a higher proportion of 'passengers' than does a small membership. Ten churches of 100 members can accomplish more in their neighbourhoods than one church of 1,000 members remote from the people. We must also recognise that small numbers do not guarantee effectiveness or spirituality in a church. A small church can be as dead as a large church, but it will look far more pathetic.

So, if every member of a church is to serve God fully we need to bear in mind both the size below which and the size above which a church is unable to function as a true body and effective fellowship. God alone creates a church; Christ's life sustains it; the Holy Spirit blesses it with everything it needs to be effective; the word of God governs it so that every member may serve the Lord to his full capacity and so that God's Name is honoured in the church.

Chapter 7
Membership and responsibility

Relationship to God

Each member of a church is responsible for the life the church displays, for he is responsible to Christ the church's head for his place in the church. This responsibility for the church has a very practical dimension and is expressed in many ways and activities. In this chapter we shall consider briefly some of the most important areas of responsibility that church members bear for the church.

Relationship to God is obviously basic to our consideration. The Christian believer is first of all responsible to the Lord for his life and witness and that responsibility includes responsibility for the church. The local church depends upon him, and upon every member. For instance, the spiritual health of each member affects the spiritual health of the church. In fact, the church's greatest need as far as the members are concerned is their personal holiness and spirituality. As every member walks close to Christ the local church will be holy and Christlike.

Responsibility in prayer

One of the most obvious expressions of relationship to the Lord is prayer, which is both a responsibility and a privilege. The members of a church need to pray for the work of the church as they pray for one another. Indeed they *must* pray for one another (see Ephesians 6:18-20; Colossians 4:2-4; 1 Thessalonians 5:17). The New Testament is not silent on the matter of prayer. The Lord Jesus taught his disciples to pray (e.g. Luke 11:1-4) and exercised a most profound prayer life himself. A great deal of writing on prayer has tended to concentrate on personal prayer almost to the point of neglecting the New Testament's teaching on corporate prayer in the churches. Jesus taught his disciples to pray 'Our Father....' rather than 'My Father ...' and so emphasised the importance of corporate prayer. Christians are described in 1 Corinthians 1:2 as those 'that in every place call upon the name of Jesus Christ our Lord, both theirs and ours'. The world cannot pray since it does not know God. It will not pray since it believes it to be a pointless exercise, except in dire emergencies. The church does pray, for it believes that God hears and answers prayer for his people. For this reason church members will pray for one another and for the work of the church both in private and in the prayer meetings of the church. One should not be neglected in favour of the other.

Responsibility and finance

What a man does with his money often reveals what kind of a man he is. What a Christian does with his money marks him out clearly as belonging to the Lord. The man of the world will spend his money on himself or on other man-centred items. The Christian on the other hand will exercise his responsibility for the financial support of the church and of God's work in the world through the church, as well as the proper exercise of responsibility for his family and his own personal needs.

Money is necessary for the church to function on a practical level. The work of outreach needs to be paid for. The servants of the Lord need sufficient money to live on in order to be free of financial constraints to serve the Lord and his people without worry and stress. The upkeep of the church's property and premises costs money too. Members of a local church make a commitment to that church as the centre of their Christian service and fellowship. For this reason their financial support should be directed through the local church, rather than through some other organisation. The local church should have a much higher priority in the giving of the Lord's people than any support that is shown to any of the many para-church organisations in existence today. Works not directly approved by or under the authority of the church should never take precedence, especially if support for another body leaves the church in need and without adequate support.

Tithing

In Old Testament times men were commanded by law to give a tithe (a tenth) of their earthly goods and increase to the Lord, although the practice predates the institution of the Mosaic law – see Genesis 14:20; 28:22. In the New Testament, Christ exposed the Pharisaical abuse of tithing by rebuking their failure to concentrate on matters of righteousness. He nevertheless expected the practice of tithing to continue – 'these you ought to have done, without leaving the others undone' (Matthew 23:23). At Pentecost a new motive was spontaneously demonstrated by the members of the church in Jerusalem (Acts 2:44-46; 4:32-37). Even so from time to time believers had to be encouraged and guided in their giving (2 Corinthians 8 and 9; 1 Corinthians 16:1-2; Philippians 4:10, 14-18). Members of churches committed to Christ and his people need to see clearly that all money and possessions are Christ's and that Christians are his stewards. The underlying stimulus for Christian giving must always be the sacrifice of the Lord Jesus Christ (2 Corinthians 8:9; 9:15).

Spending the church's money

A further exercise of financial responsibility concerns the spending of the church's money. Because it is the Lord's money, raised by the direct giving of the Lord's people, the church has a particular responsibility for ensuring that it is used wisely, effectively and to his glory. This responsibility is laid upon every member as they act together as the body of Christ. It is also laid upon those in whom the church places its confidence – the deacons who are responsible for practical service involving the common property of the church.

Hospitality

An important feature of a church's fellowship is the hospitality exercised by the members. In fact every member in so far as it is practicable should exercise hospitality towards fellow members and others. It is another of those marks by which a believer is distinguished from the world around. Hospitality is commended in Scripture (Romans 12:13; 1 Peter 4:9), and should be a constant feature of the life of members of a church. It is often said that an Englishman's home is his 'castle', but a Christian's home should never have a raised 'drawbridge'. It should be a place where fellow believers and those in need may find a welcome and where love and care are displayed. As the Lord blesses believers with homes, those homes should be used for his glory in a spirit of openness and fellowship. Fellowship around a meal table, a place to go in times of difficulty where burdens may be shared, provision of a bed for the night, conversation about the things of God – they all express the hospitality exercised in believers' homes.

We live in a society today where many people insulate themselves from others. Some are frightened to go out by themselves after dark. Some are friendless in densely populated inner-city areas. Others are depressed and burdened by cares and pressures of modern living. All would benefit from the ministry of hospitality exercised by members of a church. Although human society might be fragmented, a local church should not be. Hospitality can foster fellowship, friendship and unity within a church.

Acts chapter 16 contains two helpful examples of hospitality by new Christians. Lydia's heart was opened by the Lord (Acts 16:14) whereupon she opened her home to Paul and his companions (verse 15). The Philippian jailer also opened his home to Paul and Silas following his conversion to the Lord Jesus Christ (Acts 16:33-34).

Members of local churches do well to ask themselves from time to time some down-to-earth questions on this matter of hospitality, such as: 'Do the other members of the church know what the inside of my home looks like?' Some need to be invited or they will never come and they are usually the very people who need love and fellowship.

Practical care

Love and fellowship can be taken a little further as we pass on to consider the practical care that members of a church should have for one another. Once again this is one of those areas of church life that presents clear evidence of Christ's life in a church. Burdens need to be borne by others if they are ever to be made lighter. Very often those burdens are as much physical as they are spiritual, and so require the practical care of one another which is urged and commended by the Apostle Paul in such passages as Romans 12:4-18 and 1 Corinthians 12:14-27 where the picture of the church as the body of Christ provides the framework within which practical care is shown.

Baby sitting, help in a crisis, visits especially to those shut-in or bed-ridden, lifts in cars, shopping for others unable easily to visit the shops, practical help for invalids, and a host of other things when practical needs confront a church, are what come readily to mind as fulfilling the need for practical care. No one is totally self-sufficient in the end, although some like to think they are. All the members of a church need all the members of a church, whether they will admit to it or not, and we all need to remember that humility in receiving help is as important as alertness in seeing who needs it.

Faithfulness in attendance

There are a number of matters that relate to faithfulness which need to be considered in connection with a member's responsibility to the church. Attendance at the 'means of grace' (the services of worship and Bible study arranged by the church) is an essential part of Christian discipleship (see Hebrews 10:23-25). Non-attendees lose out seriously and that includes those who come only once in the week. The Holy Spirit blesses all meetings of the Lord's people, but sometimes he blesses a particular meeting in a special way. Members who are absent miss something of divine activity that is impossible to replace and also experience some sense of loss by having been apart from the body when it was specially blessed of God. (e.g. Thomas was absent from the most important occasion in John 20:19-23 and missed the blessing of fellowship with the risen Saviour. The Lord had important lessons to teach him because of that – John 20:24-29).

Persistent absence from the means of grace reflects the true state of a person's heart – it could be backsliding or even a false profession. Sympathetic pastoral enquiry is needed to determine the true state of things with a view to bringing about the restoration of the member, if possible.

Constant absence indicates a low view of the importance of God himself, because it shows that worshipping him and listening to his word are regarded as activities with low priorities. It also indicates an even lower view of the Lord's people because it is easy and even preferable to be apart from them. Yet they are the apple of the Lord's eye (Zechariah 2:8). If church members don't bother to attend services and meetings of the church, they cannot expect unbelievers to attend. Members need to be present with one another if corporate worship is to be a reality. In order to talk with one another and to support one another members need to meet with one another. The cure for loneliness is fellowship, which requires being together as well as loving one another.

The regular faithful presence of the members of the church also encourages the preacher, and all the more so if the members come in a prayerful attitude of mind and heart with a desire to give and contribute and not merely to take whatever is going.

Faithfulness in work

We can take this matter of faithfulness a little further. The faithful performance of tasks volunteered for or appointed to is always 'unto the Lord' and yet the church depends on that faithfulness too. Doing the work of the Lord in the church should not depend on personal likes or mere convenience. If someone fails to do what he has promised, he is failing the Lord, and not merely his fellow believers who have to step in and do the job for him. In the life of a church there are many things that need doing. Members should not be 'backward in coming forward'; there should be an eagerness to serve and contribute to the church's life; otherwise a very small number of diligent folk are left doing everything. That is not good for the church or for the small number of diligent people.

Each member of the church has a personal ministry to exercise which only he or she can do. The service that each member renders to the Lord and his people is vital for the proper functioning of the body of Christ. When a member volunteers for a job, he should do it, and do it well, for it is service to God. If that member fails, someone else will have to do it for him, thus increasing that member's workload, while the member who originally volunteered finds that his word and his promises are no longer taken seriously. His reputation as a Christian disciple has been damaged.

Faithfulness in discipline

Faithfulness also extends to the tricky area of discipline within the church, however distasteful it may be. It is a very important aspect of a member's responsibility to the church. There may be a time when a brother or a sister is observed to be leading a disorderly life and walking in a disobedient way. Church members may be called upon to admonish that brother or sister, seeking to restore the disorderly member to the path of consistent Christian living (see Romans 15:14; 2 Thessalonians 3:15). Sometimes, however, the discipline required is more drastic (2 Thessalonians 3:6; Romans 16:17), but the church must exercise it faithfully just the same. These things must always be done with love and humility, and never with a sense of superiority.

Discipline is not merely a negative thing, encouragement in spiritual things is equally important. Members have a particular responsibility for one another in this area of discipleship. The ministry of encouragement is important for a church's well being (see Acts 4:36-37; 9:27 – Barnabas, 'son of consolation' (or encouragement), exercised such a ministry in the church in Jerusalem). In this whole area of discipline (encouraging consistent discipleship) the avoidance of a critical spirit is vital (see Matthew 7:1-5). The member who admonishes another one day may himself need admonishing the next.

Loyalty to the church

Faithfulness leads us to consider a connected matter – loyalty, to the Lord and to his church. The true Christian will defend his church against ill-informed and prejudiced criticisms, for the glory of the Lord's name is bound up with the reputation of the church. The Christian will also defend his fellow believers against the criticisms of unbelievers. This is not to be done at the expense of the truth, but rather in a spirit of humility, so that the truth may be established. Most criticism from the world is based on misunderstanding and ignorance (it can happen among believers too). Misunderstanding and ignorance need to be cleared up. Sometimes, however, prejudice refuses to listen and defence of the truth is all but impossible.

The Christian believer will abhor gossip and will refuse to pass it on. Gossip is only gossip when it is listened to and passed on. When the child of God hears ill of a fellow member he will remain silent - a great contrast to the world, which feeds on evil and things of evil report (Philippians 4:8).

Enthusiasm

Many further things could be considered in this chapter, but one more thing will have to do. The member of the church should be known for his enthusiasm for the things of the Lord – he should be committed, to the Lord and to the Lord's people. He should be eager to worship the Lord with his fellow believers, he should be eager to hear God's word, he should be eager to do God's work. So he will be punctual, regular and reliable – he is committed to Christ and his church.

Punctuality is important. Lateness can mean many things – some of them understandable and excusable, but to be perpetually late reveals a lack of zeal, a lack of concern, and a lack of basic order to a person's life. God is a God of order and when members of churches come to the meeting place to worship him they should arrive on time.

Each and every member of a church has a responsibility to the church and for the church. The church becomes what he and his fellow members make it. The church needs every member – male and female, old and young, clever and simple, rich and poor. The Lord brings the church into being, we don't. We may be able to choose our friends, but we cannot choose our relatives. God chooses them for us. Every member of the church is related to Christ and to every other member. Christ has chosen each member and has laid down his life for each and every member. Each member is therefore vital to the life of the church; each has a place and a vital part to play. Each member is given gifts by the Holy Spirit, and each church should use to the full what the Holy Spirit gives (1 Corinthians 12:11). Nothing should be wasted.

The life of Christ in the church

The local church needs every member. It needs his prayers, his presence and his participation. Loyalty to the church is not to a merely human organisation. It is loyalty to Christ. We are not blind to the deficiencies of the church. The local church is not perfect. Christians will only be perfect in heaven, when they are presented by and to Christ without any blemish of any kind (Ephesians 5:27). While the local church remains on earth we all have a responsibility to ensure that it is always being reformed and improved – so as to be conformed to the word of God and the person of the Lord Jesus Christ. After all it is his body, the fullness of him who fills all in all (Ephesians 1:23). A true church is Christ's church, not ours, and so its life is Christ's life in our generation. Each member has a holy responsibility to ensure that what the church displays is truly the life of Christ.

Chapter 8
Membership, men and women

The creation of male and female

A local church is made up of all kinds of different people. They are different in age, different in character and personality, different in gifts and abilities, different in background and education. Its membership also contains both male and female, for those who 'have been baptised into Christ' are 'all one in Christ Jesus' (Galatians 3:27-28).

Distinctions have no place in the realm of salvation. Men are not saved because they are male but because they are sinners for whom Christ died. The same is true of women. But the differences between male and female are significant in other realms, e.g. marriage, the family, the home and in the church.

When God created man (humankind) he created both male and female (Genesis 1:26-27). However, the sacred record informs us that there was an order to that creative activity – male first and then female. It also tells us that the order is significant, for the woman was created because it was 'not good that the man should be alone'. She was created to be the suitable help to the man in the exercise of his God-given responsibilities on earth (Genesis 2:18). None of the created animals would do, only the woman would do, for she alone was 'bone of my bones, and flesh of my flesh' (Genesis 2:23).

Adam, the first man, was alone to begin with. That aloneness was incompleteness. Eve, the first woman, was from Adam and yet was not Adam, and so was the very companion to complete his life that he might fulfil his God-given purpose. This relationship is not one of superiority and inferiority but of leadership and dependence or headship and submission. This is especially true in marriage and the home; it also has a counterpart in the church.

Man and woman in the family

Although a detailed consideration of the family and of marriage is strictly outside the subject covered in this book, there are a number of areas where principles of life and conduct in the home as they arise from God's word impinge on the principles of life and conduct of the church.

The family is a basic unit of human society and the Bible shows us the true God-given order for it. Closely related is marriage. Marriage was instituted by God and involves a true and deep relationship enjoyed by husband and wife which is likened to that of Christ and his church (see Ephesians 5:22-33).

The order of creation is described for us in Genesis 2:18-25. Adam was created first and then Eve was made. In Genesis 3:16 the rule of the husband is made explicit. It needed to be so plainly stated because Eve had usurped Adam's position of headship with disastrous consequences in the Fall. In the New Testament this very order of creation is used as a basis for some plain teaching on the place of women – 1 Corinthians 11:3, 7-9; 1 Timothy 2:13-14.

Headship and submission

Relationships within marriage and the home are governed by two positions – headship and submission (Ephesians 5:22-23). The husband is the head of the family and the wife is commanded to submit to her husband. Why should this be? Biblical directions are given with good reason and so it is here. It is clear that most responsibility in the family for the children, and much else beside, will belong to the wife. So as not to overburden her with responsibility, the ultimate authority, humanly speaking, is given to the husband.

There are also more 'theological' reasons. The husband is head of the wife because that is how they were created, and because Christ is the head of the church and is its Saviour.

Underlying this marriage relationship is love. A new family unit comes into being when a man leaves his own parents and sets up home with his wife (Genesis 2:24; Ephesians 5:31); marriage involves the commitment of husband and wife to one another in love and union (Genesis 2:23-24; Ephesians 5:25; Colossians 3:19; 1 Peter 3:7). This love is to do with sacrifice and self-giving, with commitment and faithfulness, with devotion and provision of necessities, with protection and defence, with honour and respect, and with work and service. Yet the love of the husband also means leadership and headship. It means decision-making – in setting patterns of life, in setting standards, in setting an example, in uprightness, in integrity, in upholding the family name and honour. The wife shares in all this as the husband's 'help'. In partnership they both determine the character of the family. This character will be unique and will come from the joint contributions of both husband and wife and in due time, of the children.

However, the husband sets the trends and sets the pace, not ruthlessly or dictatorially, but with gentleness, with reason, with wisdom, with patience – with love. Husbands and wives are not equal – the Bible commands husbands to lead. They preside over their families – with love.

Parenthood

In many senses a family only becomes a fully complete family with the coming of children. With the coming of children husband and wife enter into another important relationship, that of parents – a father and a mother. Yet here also the order is maintained. In Ephesians 6:4 and Colossians 3:21 Paul speaks directly to fathers because they have the primary responsibility in the parental role of bringing up the children. Although most of the time when the children are in their formative years will be spent in the company of and under the authority of the mother, Paul addresses fathers. Fathers still have the primary role. They set the standards; they set the patterns and landmarks of the family. To them the mothers refer for they have the final word on matters of discipline and behaviour. Yet again the keynote is love – love for the child in desiring the best, giving the best, and advising the best.

Stability, security, justice, involvement, interest and support are all necessary, and fathers must give them. Similarly in the home the headship of the man means he will set the moral and spiritual tone of the family. He will lead in worship and the instruction of the family in the things of God. Religious matters, contrary to popular opinion, are the responsibility of men, not women, in the home. Paul's argument in 1 Timothy 2:11-15 is based on the trouble that occurred when a woman took the lead!

In our changing world where the family is constantly under threat, it is vital that the stability and security provided by homes patterned after God's word shall still be provided, otherwise the disintegration of society will be inevitable. The breakdown of the biblical patterns of authority involved in all the recent demands for equality brings with it confusion and disorder.

Men and women in society

The family is like a microcosm of human society; so much of what has been said already applies here. When we look back to Adam we note that his leadership role is emphasised. It is he who is regarded in Scripture as the one particularly responsible for the effect of the Fall on the human race (Romans 5:12-19; 1 Corinthians 15:22, 45-47) and it was as a man (the last Adam) that Christ came. Throughout the Scriptures the leadership (and responsibility) of men is displayed as a fact, unproved and without argument. From time to time women take on roles of leadership, e.g. Jezebel, Athaliah, Herodias, but seldom with good results. It is difficult to prove anything from the role of Deborah who was associated with Barak in Judges chapter 4. The weakness of Barak was emphasised by the honour for the victory over Israel's enemies going to a woman – Jael (Judges 4:9; 5:24).

Present day society is subjected to many influences, most of them antagonistic to the position presented in the Scriptures. Current patterns of behaviour often run counter to those God-honouring patterns taught in God's word. The divine order of creation is denied and therefore the divine order of the sexes. The Scriptures are by no means silent on the respective positions of men and women in society. Present society's clamour for equality will not find support in the Bible. 'Equal pay for equal work' may be a worthy principle which few right-thinking people would seriously object to, and the exploitation of women should be opposed by all legitimate means, but the passion for a 'unisex' society flies in the face of those distinctions and differences placed within the make up of both men and women by a wise creator.

Different roles

It does seem plain from the various descriptions of and references to the roles of women in human society found in God's word that their primary sphere of activity is the home. We cannot argue much from temperamental differences between men and women, although they most certainly exist. We are on much safer ground when it comes to physical differences. Men cannot bear children, women do, and so it seems that the purpose of the physical frame of women is more to do with the care of children and the home than is the case with men (see 1 Timothy 2:15; 5:14). Men are usually physically bigger and stronger. Although it is said that women can endure greater pain than men they are described in 1 Peter 3:7 as the 'weaker vessel', clearly needing support and protection – the role of men, especially husbands and fathers.

What is clear from the general thrust of the Bible's teaching is that it is given to men normally to take the leadership roles in human society. The 'bread-winner' role is usually the man's (see 1 Timothy 5:8), although Scripture does not rule out women being involved in work outside the home (see Proverbs 31:13-20). It also seems clear that moral leadership in society is to come from the men. All too often in present-day society it is the women folk who are left to make protests against moral abuse and the lowering of standards. This is work for men too, and not merely 'clergy-men'. Men should be setting the standards of honesty, reliability and trustworthiness that undergirds the strength of the nation. Men in leadership should promote righteousness in personal dealings and in national affairs. Men should be the workers and the defenders of society. Proverbs 31:3 says, 'Do not give your strength to women.' The situation is grave indeed when any society does that!

Men and women in the church

All that has been said so far about headship/leadership and submission is relevant here. We must always emphasise that 'submission' does not mean 'inferiority'. Men and women are different, were originally created differently and have different roles. Paul's teaching on the submission of the wife to her husband is prefixed by, 'Submitting to one another in the fear of God' (Ephesians 5:21) as a principle of general conduct for members of a local church. Luke records that Jesus 'went down with Joseph and Mary, and came to Nazareth, and was subject to them.' That 'subjection' or 'submission' in no way implies that he was inferior to Joseph and Mary!

What we are considering here is the different roles and positions of men and women in the local church within those basic principles of leadership for men and submission for women. There is a divine order laid down in Scripture for churches to follow. 'God is not the author of confusion' for all things are to be done 'decently and in order' (1 Corinthians 14:33, 40). The ordinances delivered to the church in Corinth, for instance, were those practices common in all the churches and they were consistent with the basic principles of headship and submission (see 1 Corinthians 11:2-3, 16). Man (and not just Christian man) is called 'the image and glory of God' (1 Corinthians 11:7) whereas 'woman is the glory of man'. The distinctions are made very clear here by the Apostle Paul and form a necessary foundation to any consideration of the relative roles of men and women in the church.

There are three particular passages that deal with the place of women in the church – 1 Corinthians 11:3-16; 14:34-36; 1 Timothy 2:9-15. It will be helpful to consider them in reverse order for we shall then move from fundamental principles to particular application. The place of men in the church is not dealt with so specifically. It may be deduced by contrast and from the general teaching given concerning officers and other responsibilities in a gospel church.

1 Timothy 2:9-15

Paul's intention in writing these words, and those which precede and follow them is 'that you may know how you ought to conduct yourself in the house of God' (1 Timothy 3:14-15). He is giving teaching about behaviour in the church - in the meetings of the church. Having given instruction on prayer for all kinds of people, even kings and others in authority – how it is to be done and by whom, he now turns his attention to the women (verses 9-10) who, 'in like manner' are to approach worship thoughtfully and modestly. The holy hands of the men lifted up in prayer are to be matched by the same spirit of holiness in the appearance of the womenfolk. Godliness of character (good works) should find expression in modest and sensible clothing. The parade of expensive and extravagant adornment is inappropriate for a woman in the church. Neatness, tidiness and good taste are appropriate. The Christian woman should never draw attention to herself either by being under or overdressed.

As outward appearance is expressive of the inward attitude of heart, so similarly a humble attitude of heart will affect a woman's attitude to teaching – receiving it and giving it. Paul goes on (verse 11) to give directions concerning the submissive attitude to be adopted by women in hearing the word of God taught. Women are not to be heard when the word is taught; they are to be silent. Further (verse 12), they are not to teach or to exercise authority over men in the church.

The reason behind these instructions is not found in the contemporary cultural setting of the ancient world. Paul indicates the permanent nature of what he is writing by giving the reason as twofold – the order of creation and the entrance of sin to the Garden of Eden (verses 13-14). To act contrary to these instructions is not only to disobey God's commands but is also to fly in the face of nature and to put men and women into positions for which they are not suited because God created man to lead and woman to follow. The entrance of sin upset that order as Eve first yielded to temptation.

Any church that fails to heed the divine instructions contained in these verses is acting disobediently and is upsetting the natural order of creation with serious consequences for the life of the church and the individuals involved. The teaching and leading roles belong to men. Women are to learn in silence when the word of God is taught; they do not have a teaching role as such and find their fulfilment within God's purposes in more domestic roles (verse 15).

1 Corinthians 14:34-36

We now take the matter a little further but still governed by the basic principles concerning the differences between and differing roles of men and women. These verses are set within the context of the worship and meetings of the church (see verses 5, 12, 19, 23 and 26) and are meant for the instruction of the churches generally (verse 34).

Paul emphasises the instruction for women to keep silent. They are not permitted to speak; they are to remain in obedience to the law of God in this matter. There are those today who wish to escape from the effects of this prohibition by claiming that Paul was referring to needless 'chatter' or 'gossip' during the meeting or was seeking to curb the influence of some argumentative women. The word translated 'speak' here is also translated 'speak' in verse 28. Paul is writing about speaking whether to God (prayer) or to man (preaching, teaching, speaking in the meeting). It is an all-inclusive word referring to ordinary as well as particular speaking, and women are not permitted to speak.

Yet others try to avoid the implications of Paul's directions by suggesting he is not writing of all women but only of married women or of unsaved women. The sense of the word 'women' used will not support this suggestion. The word translated 'women' is the ordinary and usual word for 'females' whether married or unmarried. However, there can be some misunderstanding of verse 35 until it is recognised that the word often translated 'husbands' is in fact the ordinary word for 'men' whether married or unmarried. What Paul is saying is that if women have questions or concerns they should ask their own men at home – husbands, uncles, fathers or other male Christian relatives, or if none such are available the elders of the church may be approached.

So seriously does Paul regard this abiding instruction and prohibition that he says it is shameful for a woman to speak in the church, so contrary is it to God's revealed will on the matter (verse 35). God has purposed to use men in the proclamation of his word in the church, and only men (verse 36).

1 Corinthians 11:3-16

This third passage dealing particularly with the respective roles of men and women has been a battleground of different interpretations for generations. The problems associated with the passage arise when some, for reasons best known to themselves and God, will not accept the plain and simple meaning of the words.

The headship of man is established in verse 3 with the following verse indicating how a man may dishonour Christ by entering into church worship with his head covered. Verse 5 indicates how women may bring dishonour to the men of the church by entering into church worship with heads uncovered.

The two particular areas of difficulty for some, and indeed for controversy, are: what exactly does Paul mean by 'praying or prophesying', and what exactly is the head covering required for women in the church. Let us first of all remove one fallacy before we move on. Paul is not simply expressing what was the culturally accepted custom of his day, which therefore we can ignore. His reference to the angels in verse 10 indicates that there is a timeless and abiding dimension to his instructions here. In fact, what he is teaching here is radically different from the cultural patterns of his day. He is actually creating a new and Christian culture, which means that what he writes is still binding on us now.

Praying and prophesying

The context of the instruction given in these verses is the worship activity of the local church (1 Corinthians 10:17; 11:17), and what Paul teaches in this passage is for all the churches (verse 16), not merely the church in Corinth. He is writing about church worship meetings and it is in this setting we are to understand 'praying and prophesying'. What this means therefore, is the praying or prophesying activity of the church – i.e. a corporate activity. Bearing in mind the clear directive for women to keep silent in church worship this cannot be understood here to mean that women can 'lead in prayer' in mixed meetings, nor can it mean that they may prophesy in the sense of the delivering of inspired teaching as in 1 Corinthians chapter 14. In fact, directions for the conduct of prophets and prophecy in the church (14:29-33) are followed immediately by the directive for women to keep silent (14:34-36). So what does 'praying and prophesying' mean in this context? It must be something women may do in worship.

Concerning 'praying', what Paul has in mind is corporate or congregational prayer; it is what the church does together. In Acts 4:24 we read that 'they (the church in Jerusalem) lifted up their voice to God with one accord'. In Acts 12:12, 'many were gathered together praying' (including women – Mary, the mother of John Mark, and Rhoda are mentioned). They were all praying for Peter who until that time had been in prison (12:5). If there was some form of vocal prayer of the whole company the women shared in it. If the corporate prayer was led by one individual man, the women shared in the praying silently, with perhaps a shared vocal 'Amen' at the end (cf. 1 Corinthians 14:16).

Concerning 'prophesying', again Paul is referring to a shared or corporate activity in the church. It could mean that women are to listen silently when God's word is proclaimed, but the word does suggest a more active role as with corporate and perhaps vocal prayer. What then is the prophesying which would involve the women and would not contradict the instructions concerning headship, leadership, teaching and authority being reserved to the men? Both prayer and prophecy are referred to together. Praying is a God-ward activity, surely the prophesying referred to here is also a God-ward activity. This is supported by certain references in the Old Testament to prophesying as a corporate activity in which praise is sung to God, often with musical accompaniment. 1 Chronicles 25:1-3 refers to the appointment of singers of praise who are said to 'prophesy with harp, with psalteries and with cymbals'. This ministry is also described as giving thanks and praising the Lord. Exodus 15 records the Song of Moses and the Children of Israel following the parting of the Red Sea. The women (with Miriam 'the prophetess') respond with praise to the Lord accompanied by timbrels. In Numbers 11:25-29 the seventy elders appointed to assist Moses are said to prophesy for an extended period. The Holy Spirit came upon these men to equip them for their new role. It is not surprising that this should be accompanied by joy of heart and exuberant praise of God. 1 Samuel 10:5 refers to a company of prophets who 'prophesy' accompanied by various instruments. They were together singing the praises of God.

What all this means for us in the context of 1 Corinthians 11 is that women participating in the worship of the church – corporate prayer and praise – are to conduct themselves with respect to the headship of men.

Head covering

The mark of the headship of the man is to have an uncovered head and the mark of the submission of the woman is the head covering (having 'power' or 'authority' on her head [verse 10], the head covering being the symbol of the authority under which women have been placed by God). Why is all this necessary? Paul tells us that there are very serious and theological reasons for it.

The covering of men's heads and uncovering of women's heads brings dishonour to their respective heads (verses 4 and 5). In the case of the women the exposing of their uncovered hair would be as bad as if their heads were completely shaved of all hair, which is a shameful thing for them (verse 6). Women should therefore have long hair to cover their bare heads (verse 15) and that hair is their glory and should itself be covered in worship. The woman's glory is her hair, the man's glory is the woman (verse 7) and the glory of God is to be seen in the man. It is not man's glory that should be prominent in worship, it must be God's, therefore man's glory should be covered and God's glory uncovered.

So in worship, a woman should wear a hat or some other appropriate covering for her head. However some have suggested that her own hair is given to her as a sufficient covering (verse 15). It is certainly a covering in that it hides baldness that would be a shame for a woman. Hair (long hair) is her glory, but is it an appropriate or sufficient covering in worship? Surely, the context as we have examined it gives the answer with a negative. Suppose the apostle does mean 'hair' when he speaks of 'covering', how do verses 4 to 7 read with the one substituted for the other?

> v.4. 'Every man praying or prophesying, having *hair on his head,* dishonours his head'.
>
> v.5. 'But every woman who prays or prophesies with *no hair on her head* dishonours her head, for that is one and the same as if her head were shaved [i.e. having had the hair taken off her head]'.
>
> v.6. 'For if a woman *has no hair on her head,* let her also be shorn [i.e. have the hair taken off her head)]. But if it is shameful for a woman to be shorn or shaved, let her *have hair on her head'.*
>
> v.7. 'For a man indeed ought not to *have hair on his head,* since he is the image and glory of God: but woman is the glory of man'.

Any reasonable person must see that what we have in these verses is nonsense if the long hair of the woman is the only covering required by the word of God.

What is required in worship in the church is that men's heads shall be uncovered, for their head is Christ and the glory of God is to be visible in them. Their hair is to be short – their glory is the women not their hair. The heads of women are to be covered for they are the glory of the men and only God's glory is to be seen. Their long hair is their glory and that is to be covered so that only God's glory is seen.

Harmony and balance

Uncovered and covered heads in worship are symbolic of headship and submission that are related to a whole spectrum of activities and positions within the life of the church. When both men and women understand and accept their respective positions within God's purposes in the church there can be harmony of activity and life within the church. It is when men fail to lead and women usurp the leadership of a church that the God ordained balance of a church is upset. In the experience of many churches it has also meant a dilution of spiritual life and commitment to God's word.

Men are to lead in devotion and obedience to God's word, but that is not their exclusive preserve. In the New Testament there are many examples of women being devoted to the Saviour, and in churches today we see similarly how many faithful women there are who are devoted to him. However churches must not rely on devoted women alone. They need devoted men too, to lead the people of God in the truth and in obedience to that truth. Godly balance should be aimed at.

Although the officers of a church (elders and deacons) are to be men, there is provision in the New Testament for help to be given by certain women – see 1 Timothy 3:11 (the word translated 'wives' is the ordinary word for 'women') and 5:4-10. The qualifications for officers are found in 1 Timothy 3:1-13 and Titus 1:6-9. The qualifications for the women who would assist the officers are given in

1 Timothy 5:9-10. Appointing such officers and helpers in a church, as the Lord has provided them, can only contribute to the harmonious life of the church.

A variety of tasks

As we have already noted in earlier chapters (two and six especially) there is a considerable variety about the tasks to be done in the church. There is plenty for both men and women to do. The particular leadership roles reserved to men should not prevent men from doing what some might be tempted to regard as menial tasks. Christ's service in washing the disciples' feet should give us a clear example as to what is expected of present-day disciples. The submissive position of the women folk should not create the impression that they have little to do. The New Testament indicates a considerable variety of appropriate and needful activities. A glance at 1 Timothy chapter 5 will reveal an interesting list. Many things will have to do with family life, the care of children, help for the needy and those various things which need a sympathetic and gentle touch such as a woman is able to give. Indeed in the life of a church there are many things requiring the sensitive contribution of the women folk and a church is all the better for it.

Although there are distinctive roles and positions to be occupied by men and women, whatever they do to the glory of God can contribute to the harmonious and balanced life of the body of Christ; proving to an unbelieving and watching world that Christ's love and life is a victorious and potent force for good in human lives.

PART THREE

THE LOCAL CHURCH AND ITS LEADERSHIP

Chapter 9
Leadership and service

Characteristics of the church bearing upon leadership and service

Having spent some time in the previous chapter establishing from God's word that leadership roles in the church are reserved for men, we must now consider what that leadership is and what it involves. However, we must never separate leadership from service, and we touched on their relationship at the end of the previous chapter; nor must we separate leadership and service from the nature of the church. We are considering here that leadership which is to be exercised in the local church, and the nature of the church bears considerably upon that leadership. Although we are not dealing with the nature of the church as such, it is well for us to consider those characteristics of the church that have a bearing on leadership and service within it.

Fundamentally the church is God's church (Acts 20:28; 1 Peter 2:9-10), therefore the spiritual dimension is paramount. The church is made up of those who are 'spiritual', who have been reconciled to God by the saving work of the Lord Jesus Christ, who have been born again of the Holy Spirit. Since only born again people belong to the church, only born again people can lead it and serve in it. It is not to be led by any who are outside its membership.

The church is also the body of Christ (Ephesians 2:22-23; 4:12; Colossians 1:24; 1 Corinthians 12:12ff; Romans 12:3ff). Christ is the head of the body and any service performed or leadership exercised is to be in humble submission to Christ. The bride of Christ is another description used (Ephesians 5:23-32; 2 Corinthians 11:2;

Revelation 21:2). The church is separate from all else; it is holy. That holiness is not only its status in relation to Christ but also its character as the members live holy lives. Those who lead and serve are to be holy people for spiritual qualifications are uppermost (Acts 6:3; 1 Timothy 3:1-15; Titus 1:6-9).

As the temple of the Holy Spirit the church is built upon a foundation of truth – Jesus Christ, the cornerstone of the teaching ministry of the apostles and prophets (1 Corinthians 3:16-17; Ephesians 2:19-22; 1 Peter 2:4-5). Leadership in the church is essentially to do with teaching and preaching that truth, the word of God. The temple of the Spirit is designed to 'show forth the praises' of God in the declaration of his gospel. He who is called to lead the church must first of all be a teacher and a preacher.

'But to each one of us grace was given according to the measure of the Christ's gift' (Ephesians 4:7). The work of grace brings churches into being as God saves hell-deserving sinners. His grace is constantly 'in operation' in the continuing life of the churches. He gives gifts and equips his people for service (Ephesians 4:8, 11-16). Leaders are not self-appointed; they are gifted and called by God, and subsequently recognised by the church. Leadership in a church does not depend essentially on 'natural' gifts and worldly standards (education, being a 'nice' man, being a 'strong' man etc.); it depends on spiritual gifts and godly standards.

The people of God are described as the 'flock of God' and the Lord Jesus Christ as the 'Chief Shepherd' (1 Peter 5:1-4). Leadership in a church is like shepherding a flock (Acts 20:28) and the leader of a church is its shepherd. The Chief Shepherd sets the standard for shepherding and has given us a perfect example: 'The good shepherd gives His life for the sheep' (John 10:11). He who leads in the style of the 'Good Shepherd' will love his sheep and will care for them as he expends his life in their service. Leadership after Christ's pattern inevitably involves service (Matthew 20:26-28). A 'minister' is a servant.

Leadership is not designed to be an isolated position. In the New Testament, fellowship was enjoyed within the body of apostles and within the group of elders in a local church. Each local church is itself a 'fellowship'. Evidently, fellowship is very important in God's order of things and this is hardly surprising as a most glorious fellowship exists within the Godhead itself, between Father, Son and Holy Spirit. Although God did not create man because he lacked fellowship, he has brought his church into being to have fellowship with him and to be the environment of fellowship for believers (cf. 1 John 1:3). Leadership in such an environment also enjoys fellowship within itself and with the church within which it is set.

The nature of God-appointed leadership

In the Old Testament, different purposes governed different leadership roles. Adam was head of a family and so, of course, were many others. Abraham and the other patriarchs were leaders of larger extended families or clans who were the covenant people. Moses, Joshua, the judges, Samuel, the kings, the prophets and the priests all had leadership roles which varied according to the working out of God's purposes with his people Israel and the need of the times.

Leadership of the people often had a corporate dimension (e.g. the elders of the people), but invariably overall leadership was singular. Although both Moses (Exodus 18:13-26) and Ezra (Nehemiah 8:4-8) found it helpful to have assistance in their work of declaring God's word to the people, both men remained in overall leadership. God was exercising his government of the people through godly leadership – a man appointed by him to teach his truth, helped and supported by others.

In the New Testament the Lord Jesus Christ was the great leader, but he appointed other leaders too (the apostles). He had close fellowship with these men, his companions in public ministry. Peter was appointed by the Lord to some measure of leadership among these apostles and that continued in the Jerusalem church following Christ's ascension (see Matthew 16:17-19, verse 19 is singular, but cf. 18:18; see also John 21:15-19; Acts 1:15; 2:14 etc). The apostles acted as the elders and leaders of the church in Jerusalem (Acts 4:35,37; 6:6; 9:27) until it became necessary for others to share this responsibility with them (Acts 15:2, 6, 22). Eventually, apostles faded from the scene (Acts 21:18), and James became recognised as a leader among the elders (Acts 15:13; 21:17,18). Barnabas had a similar position in Antioch (Acts 11:22-26; 13:1-2) although Paul became the leader when they both went on missionary work (Acts 13:9, 13).

All of this emphasises that when God appoints a leader he places a very high personal responsibility upon that man. It also emphasises that with his careful and loving concern he ensures that leaders will not be isolated and solitary figures. Leadership is a God-given responsibility, which is exercised first and foremost before him (Hebrews 13:17), but always within the fellowship of the church. Respect is due to those who lead (Hebrews 13:7, 17; 1 Thessalonians 5:12-13; 1 Timothy 5:17), but it must be earned. Leaders must be Christ-centred in their obedience and church-centred in their work, responsible to the Chief Shepherd and responsible for the sheep in their care. What the leader teaches he must himself fulfil, for his leadership is as much by example as by teaching with his mouth. Holy, Christ-like living from the leader is the church's great need, before ever it hears him expound God's word. Leadership of sheep means 'going before', not merely pointing from behind.

God gives leaders to the church, and we need always to recognise what God does and does not give to a church. Plurality is not essential, leadership is. The leader's work is both weighty in itself and vital to the church, for the leader carries a God-given responsibility for the church. In this connection it is significant that the Lord's letters to the seven churches in Revelation chapters 2 and 3 are addressed to the 'angels' of those churches. Who is the 'angel' of the church? 'Angel' means messenger or representative and in this highly symbolic book the title refers to the leader of the church – its pastor. He is addressed on behalf of the church and is responsible for it. He must give an account to the Lord for it (Hebrews 13:17), a heavy responsibility indeed.

Elders

The leaders of New Testament churches are called 'elders'. The word translated 'elder' originally designated an older man who by reason of age was accorded dignity and respect. However, the word became used of one who was senior by virtue of office rather than age. An elder in a church would be a leader and would be accorded seniority, dignity and respect due to his office. Elders are not necessarily therefore old men, but they must be mature men.

Elders are a proper 'carry-over' from the Old Testament into the New Testament – from synagogue to church – and that is to be expected as all the earliest churches were Jewish and would have conducted much of their life according to synagogue practices. In this case – eldership – it evidently carried the approval of the Lord. There is no equivalent of Acts chapter 6 – the appointment of deacons – in the case of elders in the Jerusalem church. In the first instance the apostles were the elders, and were more than elders; but not all elders were apostles. When other elders were appointed the apostles did not cease to function as elders initially, but eventually they appear to have left Jerusalem to engage in a more widespread ministry.

Two words are used to describe elders: 'presbyter' and 'bishop' ('presbuteros' and 'episkopos'). 'Presbyter' means 'senior' (originally 'old man') and has to do with dignity, maturity and responsibility. It can even bear the meaning of 'ambassador'. It relates to what an elder is. 'Bishop' means 'overseer' (or 'manager') and has to do with ruling, judging, overseeing, leading, feeding, teaching, shepherding (pastoring), and caring for the flock. It relates to what an elder does. The word 'shepherd' (pastor) is also used (Ephesians 4:11).

The qualifications for eldership are found in 1 Timothy 3:2-7; Titus 1:5-9 and 1 Peter 5:1-4. Eldership is not so much a status or a rank as a role within the full-orbed life of a church. So the qualifications deal with spiritual qualities and with a man's ability to lead the flock and that especially by example. That ability is proved by and demonstrated in the leadership and authority a man exercises in other spheres – in business, in the home with his wife and family.

There must be an ability to teach (aptness), and to apply the word of God to the needs of people, although this need not necessarily mean a preaching gift as such. The character of an elder must be that of a stable, mature, Christian man. He must be blameless, vigilant, wise, sober, not given to wine, not greedy, no bully, and no novice and of good reputation. Such men are rare in the life of the local church and when they appear they stand out. No man should be appointed to eldership who is not already giving evidence of eldership qualities. It is not a training ground for the immature. Appointing the right men to this office is so important because the leadership of a church determines very largely the direction, activity and character of a church. Careless elders will produce a careless church. Loving, hard working and caring elders will produce a church that is loving, hard working and caring, and such all churches should be.

In the New Testament where elders are mentioned plurals are almost invariably used e.g. Acts 11:30; 14:23 (in every church); 15:2, 6, 22; 21:18; Philippians 1:1; Titus 1:5 (in every city); James 5:14. We may safely assume, therefore, that there were a number of elders in each church. This is, however, a goal to be aimed at rather than a practical possibility for many churches. Only men who fulfil the qualifications should be appointed to the holy office – men who are holy, humble and able. Churches will only create problems for themselves if they appoint unqualified men because of motives more to do with mathematical plurality than spiritual suitability. Although plurality may be desirable it is not essential. Godly leadership is essential and where a church does not have such within its own membership it is wise if it seeks help from another church else-where. A spiritual pastoral leadership is essential for any healthy church and no church should continue long without it. A diligent and prayerful search should be conducted for God's man to lead the church when the situation arises that a church is left without pastoral leadership. Brotherly consultation with other churches can be help-ful and especially with the church from which a man is to be invited to occupy the pastoral position presently vacant.

Pastoral leadership and eldership are God's gifts to his church

(Ephesians 4:11) and those who pastor (shepherd) God's flock must do so first of all by the teaching of God's word. That is why Christian leadership requires spiritual, that is, God-given qualifications.

Deacons

The situation that arose in Acts 6 changed the whole organisation of the Jerusalem church. The heavy responsibility of organising the church was becoming too much for the apostles and a dispute arose concerning the distribution made to needy widows. Greek-speaking church members complained that Hebrew-speaking members were being favoured. The solution to the problem was to appoint seven men to assume responsibility for this practical matter. The men appointed to this new office were called 'deacons' ('diakonos' – one who serves). They all had Greek names and it is likely that they could speak Greek. It seems that the Greek-speaking element in the church was satisfied with their appointment and the crisis was overcome. They were all men of outstanding spirituality – they were wise and well respected by the whole church. Their appointment fostered the unity of the church.

Churches today are wise to appoint deacons to meet the many practical needs that arise today. The qualifications for the office are found in Acts 6:3 and 1 Timothy 3:8-13. They are to be above all, spiritual men, although their role is to 'serve'. Service is the keynote, not rank – the 'diaconate' (body of deacons) is not a 'board of directors'. Deacons are spiritual men appointed for practical service relating to the common property of the church. They are appointed to organise and ensure the smooth administration of the church's life. They are appointed to relieve the elders of practical burdens so that they can get on with their proper ministry (as in Acts 6 the seven relieved the apostles).

Being a deacon is not necessarily a life-long position because deacons were brought into being originally to address a particular situation. They should have particular responsibilities and when those responsibilities cease or the situation that required their appointment has been met they should lay down their office. We have no record in the New Testament of deacons meeting as a board, although we have many instances of the elders in a church meeting. Nevertheless it would be helpful for deacons to meet with the elders of the church from time to time to discuss and pray about matters of mutual concern relating to the practical life of the church. As overseers, elders have responsibility for all aspects of the church's life.

In 1 Timothy 3:11 the word sometimes translated 'wives' actually means 'women'. (It is strange that wives of deacons are mentioned and not wives of elders too – if the word is to be understood as 'wives'). In Romans 16:1, Phoebe is called 'a servant' ('diakonos') of the church which is at Cenchrea. Do these references suggest the existence of women deacons? 'Deacon' is a very wide word. For instance Romans 13:4 uses the word 'diakonos' to describe the civil power as 'the minister of God'! We therefore cannot automatically assume that the earlier references mean women deacons. What is clear is that certain women were associated with the deacons in some way. Many people would serve in the life of the church but would not necessarily occupy the office of deacon.

1 Timothy 5:9 suggests ('into the number') that a group of older widowed ladies performed acts of service which brought enormous benefit to the church. This service would be associated with the deacons. The 'number' of widows would be those who received support from the church in some form or another. Such service need not be limited to widows of course, but church recognition of the close association with the diaconate should perhaps be limited to older women, especially widows, who are not under a husband's authority at home.

Chapter 10
Leadership and plurality

Plurality and parity

The plurality of elders is a well established principle in the New Testament (Hebrews 13:17; 1 Thessalonians 5:12; Acts 11:30; 14:23; etc). It is evident from the many references to elders in the New Testament that they collectively exercised a caring, leading, feeding and ruling role in the local church. However plurality does not, of itself, automatically mean equality or parity. To have ' more than one' (or 'many'), which is what plurality means, does not mean that the many are equal. The cry of equality that arises from contemporary society totally overlooks God-given distinctions, both in order and function. In contemporary society this is especially true of sexual equality where the fact that God made male and female differences seems to have escaped the notice of many exerting pressure today. This failure to notice God-given differences is also true in the sphere of eldership. If we are not careful we can easily overlook God-given distinctives that are vital for the healthy life and good order of the churches.

There are those who recognise that there are distinctives and yet maintain that elders are all equal in a local church. Presbyterianism, for instance, recognises a distinction between ruling elders and teaching elders while maintaining a theoretical parity between them. The New Testament basis for this view is usually reckoned to be 1 Timothy 5:17, but even a superficial examination of this verse will reveal that the distinction is not in fact between separate functions as between ruling and teaching. Those functions are the responsibility of the same men. The distinction is on a different level altogether and we shall return to this shortly. In 1 Timothy 5:17 the Apostle Paul refers to elders who rule in word and doctrine. It is those who labour in this work who are considered worthy of double honour. What this text actually demonstrates is that ruling elders are teaching elders.

Now, if elders are equal they are all the same. To maintain both distinction and equality appears to be contradictory. You can't have it both ways – if elders are equal they can't be different. Even if 'parity' is preferred to 'equality' the contradiction is not overcome. 'Parity' means 'on the same level'. The distinction within the eldership referred to in 1 Timothy 5:17 contradicts such a notion, for Paul indicates that someone is to be treated on a different level from others. If parity (or equality) is maintained distinctions must be excluded or at least minimised, but that means God-given distinctives cannot operate properly. In fact leadership itself is all but impossible to exercise.

Singular and plural

There is little, if any, apparent difference to be found between the roles behind the various titles used in the New Testament, namely elder (presbyter) overseer (bishop) and pastor (shepherd). However it is vital that where plurality exists it should contain within it the concept of a single overall leadership too. A flock of sheep does not have a multiplicity of shepherds; it has one. Thus the flock of God, the local church, under the headship of the Chief Shepherd, the Lord Jesus Christ, will relate best to one shepherd rather than to a 'committee of shepherds'. Even where plural elders exist, single leadership is necessary. This principle – single leadership even where there is plurality – is borne out by Scripture in a number of ways.

In both Old Testament and New Testament the leadership of God's people is invariably a singular matter with the one leader often assisted and supported by others. Nowhere in the Scriptures do we find leadership exercised by a committee with one man merely acting as a kind of chairman. That unfortunately is what often happens in some churches with plural elders today. Although it is true that corporate decisions were taken, as with the apostles in Jerusalem, it is also true that singularity of leadership can be observed even in such situations. It would be helpful at this stage if we considered some of the biblical evidence for singularity of leadership.

Revelation 1 - 3

The fascinating reference to the 'angels' of the churches in Revelation chapters 1 - 3 gives us a useful starting point for a consideration of biblical evidence. In Revelation 1 verses 16 and 20 the seven stars in the right hand (the place of honour) of the exalted Saviour are identified as the angels of the churches, one for each of the seven churches. Each angel is identified with a church and yet is addressed individually and in some senses apart from it (chapter 2 and 3). Although the letters are written to the seven churches (1:11) they are addressed to the angels of those churches. The language of the letters is usually phrased in the singular for it is written to the church as an entity, an identifiable body.

Who are the angels of the churches? Clearly they are not literal angels who are being addressed here. The Lord would have no reason to write a letter to his angels, for they do his bidding and obey his word in an instant. Although they are ministering spirits serving the saints (Hebrews 1:14) and have a special interest in the activities of the churches (1 Corinthians 11:10) the Lord would not address them when he desired to speak to particular churches. Nor is the angel of the church the impersonal 'spirit' or 'character' of the church, for that could hardly be addressed in a letter.

The word 'angel' means 'messenger' and in this highly symbolic book it is to be understood here as a description of the representative of the church concerned. He is addressed on behalf of the church and is evidently responsible for it. He is one who expresses in his own person to some degree the life of the church. Here is a reference to the individual who is the leader of the church – its shepherd or pastor. The personal identification of a man with a church need not surprise us. It has a modern counterpart in the way a church is often described using its pastor's name – 'so and so's church'. He doesn't own the church, but is identified with it, and is reckoned to be responsible for it.

1 Timothy 5:17-18

Given the fact of plurality as a New Testament principle, the distinction dealt with in 1 Timothy 5:17 is all the more important. The distinction here is not between ruling and teaching, for both roles are the responsibility of the same office. The distinction taught here is within the role of ruling – some do it well (καλως), rightly, suitably (from καλος – good, profitable).

A further emphasis is given to this distinction in terms of 'labouring' in it (κοπιωντες) – those who spend themselves exhaustingly in the work; and 'especially' (μαλιστα – chiefly, most of all). So, within plural eldership there is a distinction that relates to suitability and total commitment to the work beyond anything else. These characteristics are godly and God-given. They relate to the very call of God to a man to enter into a totality of service. They relate to the leadership exercised by those who are God-appointed, whose position of leadership and commitment is recognised and acknowledged within the plural eldership.

Does the plural word 'elders' and the phrase 'they who labour' exclude the principle of singularity of leadership discovered elsewhere? The plurals used here can simply refer to the 'class' or 'category' of elder being considered. The distinction within the eldership is clear nevertheless. Perhaps there could be more than one elder who rules well or who labours in the word and doctrine. It is surely significant however that the singular is used in verse 18 when plurals could have served equally well. Although the quotation from Deuteronomy 25:4 is singular and Paul does not hesitate to interpret it of oxen as a 'class' of animal in 1 Corinthians 9:9, here in 1 Timothy 5:18 he does not do that, but concentrates attention on the single ox and the single labourer, no doubt standing for the single elder who labours especially at the word and doctrine.

The Apostle Peter

A similar singularity of leadership with the corporate function is to be noticed in other places in the Scriptures. Consider, for instance, the appointment of the apostles by the Lord Jesus Christ. Clearly with the appointment of 12 there was a plurality. Yet within that plurality there was a smaller group (Peter, James and John) and even an individual leader – Peter.

Although what the Lord said to Peter in Matthew 16:19 was also said to all the apostles in Matthew 18:18 we cannot escape the personal and individual words spoken to Peter first of all. The rock upon which the church is built is Christ; but Peter was nevertheless singled out for particular attention here, as he was in John 21:15-17. Peter is the only apostle who is specifically commissioned to feed and care for the flock.

In the Gospels, Peter was undoubtedly the spokesman for the apostolic band. He was their leader when the Lord Jesus Christ was taken from them. His leadership function within the apostolate was quite naturally carried over into the early days of the church in Jerusalem, and in the Acts of the Apostles Peter features prominently in this role (Acts 1:15; 2:14; 5:3). The apostles were the first elders of the church in Jerusalem and it would be no mistake to call Peter its pastor.

Development of the principle

In due time other elders had to be appointed as the apostles had a wider responsibility than one local church, albeit the first and most important one up to that time. Yet even among these other elders who took over the leadership of the church in Jerusalem from the apostles the same single leadership principle operated (see Acts 12:17 – James was the elder who took over individual leadership from Peter; Acts 15:7,13; 21:18; cf. Galatians 1:19; 2:9).

Evidence that the operation of this principle was not limited to the church in Jerusalem is given by the position of Barnabas in the new church in Antioch. He was the man who was undoubtedly the leader of the church there, although others assisted him (see Acts 11:22-26,30; 12:25; 13:1-2), Barnabas is named first in connection with the church's leadership in Antioch, but when he went with Saul/ Paul on the first missionary journey their roles were reversed and Paul became the leader and is thereafter named as the leader (see Acts 13:7,9 and 13).

There is no record in the New Testament of the institution of the office of elder as there is with apostle and deacon. It was an office taken over by the church without question, from the organisation of the Jewish synagogue. No doubt some adjustments took place but the role in the one was virtually identical with the role in the other. In New Testament times a group of elders or 'rulers of the synagogue' led each Jewish synagogue, and yet, even within that plurality there existed 'the ruler of the synagogue' or 'chief ruler' (see Acts 18:8). Sometimes this individual would be engaged in his duties in a full-time capacity. Because of the Jewish make up of the early New Testament churches it was inevitable that the eldership pattern of the synagogue should be followed. It would therefore need no specific comment in the New Testament as to its institution. However the synagogue pattern of a single leader within a plural eldership would undoubtedly have been followed when that pattern was transferred to New Testament churches.

Old Testament anticipations

It is usually reckoned that the synagogue concept itself dates back to the time of Ezra. Upon his return from the exile in Babylon certain men assisted Ezra in a supportive role in expounding the law of the Lord to the people (Nehemiah 8:4-8). However this need for supportive elders did not originate with Ezra. The idea goes back to Moses who needed the help of others in his work of leading and teaching the people of God (see Exodus 18:13-26). Although leadership was to a large degree shared, both Moses and Ezra occupied distinct single leadership positions with the plural elders. Scripture continually bears out the fact that leadership is essentially a singular matter.

Abraham as an individual leader, who also acted as and is understood to be a representative figure, emphasises the singularity of leadership. Even Adam, the first representative man, confirms it. Having said that, we should not put too much weight on the representative character of Adam and Abraham when discussing the representative character of the single leader of a local church – the man who is usually called the 'pastor' (shepherd).

A couple of other matters can be mentioned in passing at this point. Again, we must not make too much out of them, but they are not without their significance. In 1 Timothy 3:1, 2 the Apostle Paul refers to the office of 'bishop' ('episkopos' – overseer) in the singular, whereas a few verses later (3:8, 12) he refers to deacons in the plural. In Titus 1:5 his mention of elders is in the plural, but the word 'bishop' is singular in verse 7.

People relate to one man

It should not surprise us that the New Testament teaches a singularity of leadership within a plurality of elders, for people relate better to one man than to a corporate body or committee, and the Lord knows that perfectly well.

One or two present day examples may be helpful at this point. Among Presbyterians there has been a traditional distinguishing of ruling and teaching elders largely on the basis of 1 Timothy 5:17, which, as we have seen above will not support such a division. They regard all elders as 'ruling' and limit the role of 'teaching' usually to one man in each congregation. In their ruling capacity all elders are supposed to be equal. It is a fact, however, that over the years the teaching elder (often called the 'minister') has become more than equal in practice, certainly in the eyes of the people. Theorists among the Presbyterians may deplore this trend but it is an inevitable and natural development because people find it impossible to relate to a committee and have found it right to relate to one man whom they regard as their pastor or shepherd.

As we have been considering so far, this singleness of leadership within plurality is the institution of Christ. While all trends among professing Christians cannot be regarded as worthy, this one, detected within the ranks of Presbyterianism itself, a group which takes its name from the eldership concept, is most significant and only confirms what Scripture actually teaches concerning eldership and leadership among God's people.

Experience also teaches us that among the Christian Brethren, who traditionally have also stood for equality among elders and have opposed strongly any ideas of a 'one man ministry' as it is called, individual leadership inevitably arises within a local church. When that leadership is godly and gifted it is to be welcomed, and some enlightened assemblies have actually officially recognised such leadership in the local church. All too often it happens that someone assumes the position of unofficial leader for all the wrong reasons – e.g. a strong personality or prominence in the local business community.

Dangers and problems

In committee rule the grave danger is that of the rule of veto exercised by the man who wishes to be different or awkward. No one man should ever be allowed to be a dictator, whoever he is. No elder or single leader pastor should ever have that much authority. What Scripture teaches is the leadership *role* of the single leader (pastor). It does not support any notion of greater power or authority for him. Authority is found in God's word and not in a man. The man or men who lead do so under the authority of God's word.

In some places you get the impression that elders are so important that their appointment becomes the great goal of a church's life. What the Lord has instituted is for the benefit of the church; the church doesn't exist merely to breed elders. It has often happened that some men have sought eldership as a power base from which to operate in a church. Some consider appointment to eldership as promotion or elevation instead or concentrating on the service to be rendered to the church. As a result all manner of problems arise within the eldership and within the church. Pride, glory seeking and power seeking all create serious problems for a church. No church should belittle the role of the elder, nor should it belittle the leadership role of the one usually and sensibly called 'pastor' (shepherd). A local church needs a leader, one who is called of the Lord to be an under-shepherd and who can lead the flock under the authority of God's word, which he is responsible to teach.

It is interesting to discover that in 'the Form of Presbyterian Church Government' produced by the Westminster Assembly in 1645 the role of elders is declared to be supportive. The Baptist Confession of 1689, while it allows for plurality of elders, makes no mention of equality of elders, and implies singularity in its phrasing. The history of Particular Baptists over the years has shown that churches have normally appointed a single pastor and a group of deacons. (It was the General Baptists who had a three-fold order – pastors, elders, deacons – and a more connexional relationship between their churches). The successors of the early Particular Baptists (often known as 'Grace Baptists') rediscovered plural eldership (within say the last 30 years). Although there have been blessings, there have also been problems, largely because the principle of plurality was accepted without working out carefully its implications. Many of the problems have arisen over the emphasis made on equality among plural elders. This equality has not worked, nor can it be supported from the Scriptures.

The importance of the role of pastor

While maintaining the importance of plurality of elders in the local church where the Lord has so blessed a church with suitably qualified men, we must also maintain the leadership position of the one we usually call the pastor. This is a most suitable title for him because the word means 'shepherd' and the 'sheep' (the members of the church) find it easier to relate to one shepherd than to a number of men who engage in shepherding activity together. While the corporate responsibility of the elders for teaching, ruling and caring for the flock must be maintained, equal stress must be given to the pastor's personal responsibility in these important areas. He is to lead the church, supported in his leadership by the elders. Together all the elders, the pastor included, submit themselves to the leadership of Christ and the authority of his word. With that understanding and with a spirit of humility the way forward can be a way of blessing and progress.

Chapter 11
Leadership and commitment.

Leadership of a church requires commitment

All who work in a local church must be committed and that is
especially true of those in leadership. An office holder in a church
must be a committed man – the work of the Lord in the church is no
hobby, it is service rendered to the King of Kings. By 'office holder'
we refer to elders and deacons as the two roles of leadership and
service that are instituted in the New Testament. Although much of
what will be said in this chapter in a general sense will have
relevance to all who work in the local church and indeed all
members of it, we are concerning ourselves here particularly with
these two offices. The New Testament concentrates its directives
and qualifications upon these two offices and it is appropriate that
we do the same.

As we have already seen in previous chapters an elder is a man
called of God, recognised and set apart by the church to rule, teach
and shepherd the flock of God by the word of God. A deacon, we
have noted, is a man gifted by God and appointed by the church to
assist the elders in a particular sphere of responsibility relating to
the common life and property of the church and in so doing relieve
the elders of work they would otherwise have to do themselves. The
work of both offices is time and energy consuming. It is to be done
properly and the one who occupies the position must give himself to
it. He must be committed – but what do we mean by that?

Commitment to the Lord

First of all he who occupies any position of leadership in the Lord's church must be committed to the Lord whom he serves. This is also, of course, required of every Christian (see 1 Corinthians 6:20; 10:21; 2 Corinthians 8:5), but it is particularly required of office holders for they, in leading the church, set an example which the other members will inevitably follow. Therefore that should be an example of holy living and wholehearted devotion to the Lord (1 Peter 5:3; Hebrews 13:7).

The service rendered in the church is first of all rendered to the Lord, and this colours its quality and determines its character, (see 1 Corinthians 10:31 and also cf. Ephesians 6:6-7; Colossians 3:22-23). An elder is appointed by God (Acts 20:28) and gives an account to him (Hebrews 13:17). He is God's servant before ever he is anything else. This truth should never be forgotten – he is not a mere employee of the church! This is of the utmost importance for two reasons. First of all it prevents a church treating an elder in an improper way, and secondly it will help the man himself when problems occur and people fail him – he will carry on because he is committed to the Lord (John 21:22). There will be times when it will seem to him that all he has left is that commitment to the Lord who called him into his service.

Similarly a deacon is to be a godly man before ever he is an efficient administrator, for otherwise efficiency and the smooth running of a church become of greater importance than the spiritual issues that undergird it.

Commitment to the word of God

Commitment to the Lord involves and presupposes a commitment to his word. That may appear to be stating the obvious but it must be mentioned and emphasised. It is easy enough to make claims to be under the authority of God's word and still fail to obey it and apply its teaching to church and personal life. There are many difficult, awkward, or even costly applications that many avoid and explain away. Those who lead churches, who hold office among God's people, must lead by the principles and precepts of God's word. The application of what the Bible teaches – what it implies and involves in terms of understanding of truth and the practicalities of daily living – is what has to be made. Only those who are committed to it – not grudgingly, but with delight, can be the ones to teach the word properly. They must love the word of truth and work hard at it.

The following phrases give an idea of what that means – able to teach' (having an aptitude for teaching God's truth) (1 Timothy 3:2); 'labour in the word and doctrine' (wholly given over to it) (1 Timothy 5:17); 'holding fast the faithful word' (Titus 1:9). It is to be a major part of a man's ministry in a church if he is to lead the church as Christ's under-shepherd faithfully. Indeed every part of his life and ministry is to be related in some way or another to the word of God.

Why is this so important? The answer is simple. The word of God is our final authority in all matters of faith and practice. It is not the word of mere men – it is God's word – and that never fails or alters. The Bible is unique in all human literature, for whereas the ideas, opinions and words of men change, it remains constant, sure and reliable. It is able to make a sinner 'wise for salvation' (2 Timothy 3:15) and is the food decreed by the Lord for feeding and building up the flock (Acts 20:32).

Churches should beware of a man who is full of ideas but knows little of Scripture doctrine and practice. Quoting isolated Bible texts is not necessarily proof of biblical knowledge; nor does it guarantee that a man is committed to God's word and submissive to it. However that is what is needful if a church would be led in a God-honouring and God-ordered way.

Commitment to the church

Commitment to the Lord and his word is demonstrated particularly within the fellowship of the local church. A leader of the church must be committed to the church. That is also true of every member, and in fact has already been confessed by every member in joining the church. Baptism on profession of repentance towards God and faith in our Lord Jesus Christ involves identification with him and with his people. Baptism is an act of commitment to Christ and to his people. It is plain, therefore, that he who leads the church must be committed to it. The church is Christ's body and commitment to Christ involves commitment to his church.

There are those, of course, who claim to be committed to the church in some universal and invisible sense and so their commitment is untested, unproved and unreal. We are talking here of commitment to the local church and that is real and practical. For far too long the Lord's work has been weakened by undisciplined freelancing and so-called Christian activity that has much more to do with self glorification than the glory of God. The local church is the centre of a believer's Christian life and those who lead it are to set an example to the other members in loyalty and service. The church is bigger than any individual and it is important to have a sense of serving something bigger than yourself. Commitment to the Lord and his word find practical outworking in service to the local church.

The local church is where the believer worships with his fellow Christians, there he enjoys Christian fellowship as part of a body, there he is taught and is built up in the faith, and with the local church he evangelises the neighbourhood. This is equally true of those who are in leadership in the church; attendance, loyalty, involvement and commitment is required of both leaders and members. To be constantly absent doing other things is a total denial of this.

The man who is to take care of the church of God (1 Timothy 3:5) should be found with the church as a shepherd is to be found with his sheep. He is not free to go from church to church (the parallel with the family in the context of 1 Timothy chapter 3 emphasises this). He is to take heed to the flock, to feed it and care for it because it is specially precious to God (Acts 20:28). God forbid that anyone who leads the church should think less of it than the Lord. If the unruly are to be warned (1 Thessalonians 5:14), those doing the warning should not themselves be unruly.

Commitment to the family

It may be an embarrassing question to ask but, 'Why are the children of church leaders so often unruly?' This should not be when we bear in mind what the Apostle Paul writes about the family responsibility of church officers in 1 Timothy chapter 3 – 'one who rules his own house well, having his children in submission with all reverence', (verse 4), 'ruling their children and their own houses well', (verse 12), and Titus chapter 1 – 'having faithful children not accused of dissipation or insubordination', (verse 6). What happens in the family qualifies or disqualifies a man for office in the church; yet there does seem to be a widespread ignoring of these scriptures.

While a father's responsibility for his children is obviously limited to those under his authority in the home and he cannot be held responsible for the behaviour of his grown-up children, his responsibility for his family at home is wide-ranging. He is to exercise a loving leadership of his family especially in matters of instruction and discipline.

Discipline is as necessary in the home as it is in the church. In both settings, love and discipline go hand in hand (Hebrews 12:6). Paul's teaching in 1 Timothy 3 and Titus 1 on the qualifications required of church office holders speaks of such basic qualities as love, faithfulness, discipline and loyalty. His teaching in Ephesians 5:22- 6:4 also refers to the home and the responsibility of the men as husbands and fathers for their wives and children. When considering any man for office the church must enquire into his home circumstances and ask the important question as to whether he rules his house well (1 Timothy 3:4). Failure here brings the whole gospel into disrepute, apart from disqualifying for office.

An officer in the church must therefore be committed to his family. There is a grave danger that a man involved in the Lord's work will ignore his family, thinking only of his responsibility to the

Lord. What the scriptures mentioned above indicate is that commitment to the Lord must not be separated from commitment to the family. Family commitment is an expression of a Christian's commitment to his Lord.

To be a proper father and husband will mean care and patience. It will mean spending time with the family, learning with them, teaching them (both wives and children), leading them in worship, playing with them, enjoying time in each other's company, enquiring into and being a part of every aspect of their lives. This must all start at the beginning, when the marriage begins, when the baby is born – because it is a tragedy when it is left too late. It is all a very useful training for holding office in the church (1 Timothy 3:5) and that is why it is mentioned.

Because of the importance of family relationships in a man's life, an unmarried elder has to be a very exceptional man indeed.

Commitment to hospitality

The ministry of hospitality was reckoned to be of great importance by the Apostle Paul. In 1 Timothy 3:2 an elder is to be ' hospitable', (see also Titus 1:8 and 3 John 5-8). In other words he should be committed to it, because he shares Paul's view of its importance.

Love is seen in action in the ministry of hospitality. There is demonstrated that openness which encourages those in need to approach the man of God confident of a sympathetic reception. Hospitality shows a man to have a welcoming spirit, a concern for the needs of others, a willingness to be put out and to be involved in the affairs of others. It also means that the man of God is not ashamed of what people might discover about his home and family.

Hospitality is essentially an expression of love and fellowship. It is an open home – to the church in a general sense and by invitation, and to strangers, both the Lord's people and unbelievers.

If it is absent from a man he is hardly likely to encourage it in the church where he is to be an example. Hospitality is to have a proper place in the life of the church. Members are to be 'given to hospitality'

(Romans 12:13), and are to 'be hospitable to one to another without grumbling' (1 Peter 4:9), for good is to be done to all and especially to the 'household of faith' (Galatians 6:10). There are few things worse than an inhospitable church. Its whole character is unfriendly and repelling. A warm, friendly church commends the gospel and the Saviour. That spirit depends very largely on the openness of the homes of the church and that depends in large measure on the openness of the homes of the office holders.

Commitment to consistent Christian living

It seems obvious on the face of it for someone who is committed to the Lord and his word to be committed to consistent Christian living. Yet so much of the New Testament is given over to teaching on and appeals for consistent Christian living that we cannot leave it without comment here (cf. Ephesians 4:1-3). Verses such as 1 Timothy 3:2, 3, 7, 8; 6:11; Titus 1:6,7; Hebrews 13:7 all show its importance for officers in a church.

In both 1 Timothy 3:2 and Titus 1:6 Paul uses words which are translated 'blameless'. What does it mean to be blameless? Clearly it does not mean sinless, nor does it mean that the officer of the church has reached a particularly high level of holiness in some special way. 'Blameless' means 'to be free from blame' or 'without the possibility of a wedge being driven between a man's words and his actions'. In other words it means consistency of Christian living - not being a hypocrite. Paul uses two words – in 1 Timothy 3:2 it is ανεπιλημπτοs 'anepilemptos' which means 'not laid hold on', in Titus 1:6 it is ανεγκλητοs 'anengkletos' which means 'not accused or called in'. The idea in both cases is 'not open to accusation'.

The question that must therefore be asked is: Can anyone point the finger and say with justification, 'He doesn't live up to it'? If so, that is a disqualification for office in a local church. Paul could call others to follow his example because he followed Christ's (1 Corinthians 11:1) and every officer in a church should be able to do the same.

Every action, every activity, every part of life should be scrutinised to see if it conforms to the word of God. Even if the church officer does not do it for himself he will nevertheless be under the scrutiny of an unbelieving world (1 Peter 2:15; 4:14-16).

Commitment to the calling

Those who are called of God into office in a local church must in particular be committed to that calling. If the Lord has called, it is no optional extra on top of normal Christian service, as far as the one called is concerned. The apostle Paul wrote, 'necessity is laid upon me; yes, woe is me if I do not preach the gospel!' (1 Corinthians 9:16). If the Lord has truly called, the one called will be able to do no other than submit to the Lord's call. He cannot be the same as he was before for that call affects every part of his life.

It is actually the Holy Spirit who calls and appoints men (Acts 20:28), who sends them out (Acts 13:2) and who blesses their work (Acts 6:7). However the one called of the Spirit is himself to be committed to the work. That sense of commitment is indicated by the way Paul writes in 1 Timothy chapter 3 – 'If a man desires the position ... he desires a good work' (verse 1), 'obtain for themselves a good standing' (verse 13). Commitment is seen in willingness, eagerness, and a love of the work even when it is hard, boring and brings problems. If hospitality (1 Peter 4:9) and giving (2 Corinthians 9:7) are to be without grudging, the commitment of officers to their calling is to be without grudging too. It is to be an enthusiastic commitment.

The calling – the office – overshadows the whole of the man's life. He is no longer a private individual, nor is he ever off duty. This is particularly, and observably, the case with the pastor of a church, and it is also true for the other elders and for the deacons. Gifts which a man recognises in himself will be developed in order to be more useful in the work. Reading, learning, extra training will be done with a view to increased usefulness. Seeking to be informed about all kinds of matters relating to the work, the officer will try to develop as wide a knowledge and understanding as possible. Administration, finance and legal matters on one hand with a diligent searching of the Scriptures on a whole range of subjects on the other hand will be necessary. Attempts to improve communication skills in writing and speaking will all be part of the concern of a man committed to the work.

Conferences, courses, seminars, fraternals, will all play their part in the development of an all round ministry. Improvements will be sought in personal study methods and habits. Personal devotion and prayer will need careful cultivation. For a man who is to shepherd the flock of God, experience in these areas will enable him to help many who are finding such aspects of Christian living a particular difficulty. It all means hard work – commitment.

Dignity

As under-shepherds to Christ (1 Peter 5:2, 4) those who care for the flock of God have a certain dignity attaching to their office. This is not that contrived dignity which has to do with a special kind of dress or special voice. It is rather what Paul calls being 'sober' in 1 Timothy 3:2. Churches should never forget that there is a respect due to elders (see 1 Thessalonians 5:12-13; 1 Timothy 5:1; Hebrews 13:17) and elders should never forget that that respect must be earned. It is earned by the example of godly living, by faithfulness and by submission to God's word.

The message the church bears is a serious matter. Indeed the Christian life is a serious matter. Preaching is God's ordained means of reaching the lost with the gospel and must not be treated lightly. The work of preaching and leading a church in the things of God is a very heavy responsibility. Lightness, flippancy and levity should have no place. Enjoyment of the Christian life, true fun, and even humour in the pulpit (carefully handled) all have their proper place, but the church is engaged in the greatest work in the world – it is serving the living God, preaching his gospel and preparing men and women for eternity. Those who lead and care for the church must therefore live with that dignity which befits their office.

Assessment and appointment

No novice is to be put into office in a church (1 Timothy 3:6; 5:22), but who decides if a man is a novice or not? The preacher of Romans 10:15 is sent, by whom? The deacons of Acts 6:1-7 were appointed by somebody and those called to evangelise in Acts 13:1-3 were commissioned and sent out by somebody. The answer becomes obvious. It is the local church that must make an assessment of a man. The church appoints him, approves him, authorises him, sends him, and supports him. The church knows him, observes him, tests him and proves him to be called of God.

The ministry of the officer in the church is essentially the ministry of the church itself. No one is self-appointed in the church of the living God any more than one is self-saved. God's church is his concern and he has decreed how we shall live together in it and who will lead it. He does not leave us in ignorance about either matter.

Chapter 12
Leadership and responsibility

Responsibilities of leaders to each other

Do church officers have responsibilities for and to each other? Do pastors of churches have any responsibilities for and to other pastors? Cain asked the question in Genesis 4:9, 'Am I my brother's keeper?' and the 'silent answer' thunders out, 'Yes'! The Apostle Paul believed very strongly that he had a responsibility to a fellow apostle when he withstood Peter to his face in Antioch 'because he was to be blamed' (Galatians 2:11). Paul knew the very gospel was at stake in what Peter was doing. He certainly recognised that he had a responsibility to the Lord, to his truth and to the church in Antioch (and the churches generally) to expose error and restore gospel fellowship among God's people.

Yes, church officers do have responsibilities to each other. Pastors do have responsibility to each other! Churches have responsibilities too and in previous chapters we have dealt with this matter, having looked at it from different angles. All church leaders share in the responsibilities belonging to the churches, but that is not the end of the matter for them. The general principles of Christian behaviour laid down in God's word affect them too as much as other members of the churches. Although what is required of members in the exercise of responsibility to one another is not identical to the responsibility churches have towards one another, those who lead churches bear responsibility in both directions. The general principles of Christian behaviour do affect both individual members and their churches as 'corporate' entities, but the responsibility leaders and office bearers have for one another goes beyond that.

Under-shepherds must give an account to the Chief Shepherd and bear responsibility primarily for the flock under their care, but in an important measure they also have responsibility to other under-shepherds who must also give account to the Chief Shepherd. That responsibility relates to the calling each has entered, the gospel each preaches and the Lord each serves.

Godliness

A basic responsibility is to do with the under-shepherd's own life before Almighty God. The pastor is first and foremost to be a godly man. That is also required of all elders and all deacons. Why is this so fundamental? It is because of the enormous influence one man has over another. This is especially the case with older men over younger men. In various places the Scriptures urge church leaders to be examples and to provoke others in good things.

In 1 Corinthians 11:1 Paul urged the Corinthians to follow or imitate him as he followed Christ. In Hebrews 13:7 elders in the churches are held up as those whose life and faith should be followed. Peter encourages elders to be examples to the flock in 1 Peter 5:3. All Christians are urged to excite one another, to stir up one another, to provoke one another to love and good works. Those who lead, and indeed all Christians, are observed by others. Lifestyle, pattern of behaviour, conduct – godly or otherwise – are all observed, scrutinised and reacted to. What one will do affects others – some will imitate him, for good or ill.

What a man does with his time, the things he involves himself in, those he associates with, what he approves or disapproves, his doctrines, beliefs, emphases, they all make their mark, for they make him what he is as he is observed by others. Constantly those who lead others must ask themselves as to the nature of the example they set to those they lead and those who merely observe from a distance. Does that example help or hinder another person's appreciation of

Almighty God and their love for his truth? Is the life lived before
God and others that which may be described as 'adorning the
doctrine of God our Saviour' in all things (Titus 2:10)? Does the
one who professes to be travelling in a heavenward direction point
others in that direction too?

Support

These are difficult, confusing and hostile days, when a great deal of
misinformation is circulated - even 'character assassination' takes
place concerning those who lead God's people. Ill-informed
comment, inaccurate reporting of facts, dishonourable rumour
mongering are all too common! Those who stand for the truth of
God's word and the doctrines of the Scriptures will always be under
severe attack. The support of the brethren is therefore of the utmost
importance for the servants of God. The fellowship of kindred
spirits and like minds is needed.

There is a battle going on (cf. Philippians 2:25-30) and men
involved in pastoral work need the love and support of their brethren –
even to the extent of dying for one another! Too often those who
labour in the gospel can feel alone, cut off and isolated. They need
companionship (see Colossians 4:7-14). They also need loyalty
(contrast Colossians 4:14 with 2 Timothy 4:10) and support when
under attack, especially when misrepresented. These days how rarely
does anyone bother to find out the facts! When such qualities are
present among brethren it becomes possible to share burdens, problems, concerns and needs in fellowship.

Prayer

Christians have a responsibility to pray for each other. Church
officers have such a responsibility to each other too. If a man has
any understanding of his own needs before the Lord he will surely
understand the needs of his brethren. All who lead the people of God
need prayer. The Apostle Paul wrote, 'Brethren, pray for us'

(1 Thessalonians 5:25; 2 Thessalonians 3:1). As the Lord supplies the needs of one man he can similarly supply the needs of others.

Although those who shepherd the flock of God most certainly need the prayers of the people they lead they also need the prayers of fellow pastors. There are some things which a man cannot share with his people but which can be shared with another pastor who understands the unique problems of shepherding the flock of God. Prayer requires effort – the giving of oneself to it. Paul wrote in Romans 15:30 'strive together', in Ephesians 6:18 of 'praying always with all prayer' and in Colossians 4:2 of 'continuing earnestly in prayer'. Such phrases picture earnestness, and expending effort and energy on behalf of one another.

Paul testifies in a number of places of the importance of the people's prayer for him (e.g. Philippians 1:19). Sometimes a pastor finds it very difficult to pray for himself. In such times it is a great comfort to know of those who faithfully pray for you.

Encouragement

The ministry of encouragement is a very important one indeed. To have a spirit like Barnabas (Acts 4:36) is to be a blessing to other Christians and churches. In those things we have already been considering there are elements of encouragement, but encouragement is more than cheering up other people. It is helping another along the right way – the helping hand, the shared burden, as well as the right advice.

Responsibility for one another in the truth leads to encouragement being given to walk in the right ways and to hold to the right things by words of exhortation, advice and information. Where a lack is seen there should be a readiness to provide what is lacking. Where there is imbalance a loving encouragement to adjust the emphasis is needed.

Advice is often needed in difficult situations. Blessings can be shared and perhaps a better way of doing something can be shown. He who has experience in leadership needs to pass on that experience to those who lack it. What one has learned by the bitter schooling of 'the school of hard knocks' can be invaluable to another who is about to pass through such an 'educational process'.

In order for all this to be possible it will be necessary for men to meet one another. Telephones can help but are no substitute for face-to-face fellowship. Encouragement should therefore be given for men to attend Fraternals and Conferences where brethren can benefit from the fellowship. Personal, one to one, fellowship may be needed too, and men should make themselves available to help their brethren when such needs arise.

The Apostle Paul knew the need for encouragement provided by the physical presence of brethren (2 Corinthians 7:6; 2 Timothy 4:9; Titus 3:12).

Warning

The present period through which the churches are passing has been variously described as evil, confusing or even exciting. Whatever view is adopted, and all have some claim to accuracy depending on the point of view held, it is certainly true that these are days when great pressure is being put upon churches and pastors to conform to some pattern or form which has little to do with patterns or forms derived from the Scriptures. The shallow, pop music, glitzy, charismatic and ecumenical subculture, which passes for Christianity for some people, tempts some churches to compromise biblical principles for an appearance of attractiveness, liveliness, or even, in some cases, just to keep the peace. It is sometimes necessary for men to warn their brethren of the dangers posed by compromise and the harm that compromise of principle does to the name of Christ and the purity of his gospel.

Brethren have a responsibility to admonish one another where it is needed. Admonition is a responsibility laid upon every church member, to be exercised carefully, prayerfully and humbly (2 Thessalonians 3:15) and especially laid upon leaders in the church (1 Thessalonians 5:12). The work of warning has to be done (1 Corinthians 4:14; 1 Thessalonians 5:14), and the erring brother has to be faced with the facts of the situation. He has to be shown what is involved and what his action implies. He must be shown how he is damaging fellowship with the brethren and how he is harming trust and confidence. The aim of the exercise is to gain the brother (James 5:19-20) not to denounce him.

Some believe the procedure laid down in Matthew 18:15-17 should be followed but this is for offences within the local church. Where a problem exists between two brethren in leadership in different churches a different approach has to be made as suggested above. Responsibility does not end at the limit of church membership, but a different method of exercising that responsibility operates.

Withdrawal

Discipline is essentially a local church matter, and where it is exercised other churches should normally respect the decision of the church and recognise the sanction imposed. Note that there are times when a local church can be wrong in the exercise of discipline.

How does a man in one church act when after approaching his erring brother in another church he has failed to gain his brother? He cannot discipline him because he cannot bring the matter to the church – they belong to different churches. When the erring brother persists in error, compromise or disorderly behaviour the principles of Christian behaviour apply. Fellowship has already been broken by the error, compromise or disorder, so, as Paul teaches in Romans 16:17-18 the erring brother is to be withdrawn from and is to be avoided (see also 2 Thessalonians 3:6). No fellowship can now be enjoyed. The purpose of this withdrawal and avoidance is to bring the brother to his senses so that he will change his ways so as to enable fellowship to be restored. It is also necessary to maintain the integrity of the gospel and the purity of the faith.

Church officers have responsibility to each other both within the local church and further afield. As with every aspect of Christian living those responsibilities have to be discharged humbly in the Spirit of Christ and to the honour and glory of God.

PART FOUR

THE LOCAL CHURCH AND ITS MISSION

Chapter 13
The local church and mission

The foundational character of the 'Great Commission'

The New Testament will not allow us to think of the local church apart from mission because mission rises out of the biblical doctrine of the church. By 'mission' we mean the work and responsibility of proclaiming the gospel – the good news of the salvation of sinners by the Lord Jesus Christ. When we consider this matter it is inevitable that what has come to be called 'the Great Commission' should feature prominently. We start with it here because it is the usual starting point for considerations of evangelism and mission and also because it is fundamental to the church's role in the world. It is the commission of the risen Saviour given to his people prior to his ascension – his last words concluding his earthly ministry.

'The Great Commission' is usually identified with Matthew 28 verses 19 and 20, 'Go ye therefore, and teach [or make disciples of] all nations ... '. But each of the other Gospels and the Acts of the Apostles has its equivalent, 'Go ye into all the world ... ' (Mark 16:15); 'Ye are witnesses ... ' (Luke 24:48); 'Ye also shall bear witness ... ' (John 15:27); 'Ye shall be witnesses unto me ... ' (Acts 1:8).

Our interest in the commission is not so much that it is a divine command, supremely important as that is, but more particularly in the fact that this is the great task and responsibility laid upon the church by the risen Saviour. It is the connection with the church that is significant here. It is fundamental to the church's life, for obedience to the commission has brought the church into being. An essential expression of its life in Christ is its continuing obedience to it.

The corporate character of the commission

In the quotations above, the wording has been taken from the King James Version (1611) of the Bible to draw out this important fact: the commission is addressed to Christ's servants in the plural. The word 'ye' is used in each case. Other versions with more modern renderings obscure this important fact. The commission laid upon Christ's church is a corporate matter. The church as a body is to obey it. The people of God ('ye') are to obey Christ's command collectively or corporately. This is no general obligation laid upon the church in some universalistic sense as if it were some general Christian characteristic. The commission was given to the church already in existence, gathered and built by the Lord Jesus Christ originally from former disciples of John the Baptist, which met in the upper room before the day of Pentecost. Mission is to be done here in the world of the present. The here-and-now church is the local church that has to carry out the obligations involved in the commission. The commission has never been withdrawn and is still binding on the church – the local church, Christ's body and God's people.

Without any doubt there is an individual obedience contained within the corporate, examples of which we find in the New Testament, for individual testimony and witness is a necessary expression of the fulfilment of the commission. The agent or instrument of obedience is to be the local church, because it is the church and therefore the local church that is addressed in Christ's commission.

It follows, therefore, that evangelism and mission are not to be left to the individual believer to do what he or she can or what he or she thinks is best. It is for the church to examine what it is doing in obedience to Christ's commission and to institute a programme of endeavour in which each member is involved and to which each member's personal witness can be related. The local church will seek the guidance of the Spirit of God in this and will submit its work to the authority of God's word while taking note of the particular environment or setting of the church and the personal resources available within the church.

The church is under an obligation in this area – it is not optional. This is evident in the New Testament where the church in Jerusalem was closely involved in the outreach of the brethren in the early chapters of the Acts, and the church in Antioch was similarly involved in the labours of the Apostle Paul. We shall have cause to look again at these two churches.

The intensive character of the commission

The emphasis on 'witness' in the commission highlights its 'intensive' character. Testimony is to be borne to Christ in the lives of individual Christians and in the life of the church. A witness tells what he has seen; he testifies about what he knows. In such a way the individual believer shows by his life and testifies with his mouth concerning the saving power of Christ. In such a way also the local church witnesses to Christ. A local church is a living proof of the reality of the Christian gospel and is made up of living proofs. We, therefore, need local churches, made up of local believers, to testify concerning Christ to the localities where they are set.

The aim of local evangelistic activity must always be the local church itself. Those who are converted are to be brought into the church. Local evangelism is concerned about the church's growth, its health, its life and its work. It is intensive. In the locality, what impresses people most is not so much the individual believer and his changed life, for he can be explained away and ignored. What is more impressive is the local church living as Christ's body, where the members love one another (John 13:35), relate to one another and cope together with the problems and pressures of our present evil world.

It is hard being a local church in an area where everyone knows you but local churches, witnessing to Christ in a locality, can be anchors of hope in a sea of confusion, oases of peace in a desert of brokenness, and always colonies of heaven our home.

The local church doesn't have to be large to be a faithful witness in a locality. Although it is often difficult being a small church seeking to be true to God's word in a world where so many think that big is beautiful, it is important that each church, big or small, should understand its role as the people of God in a locality. It is simply to be witnesses to Christ. We need local churches, set where people are, where the lost are living. We need churches made up of members who themselves are local and give reality to the witness of the church.

The extensive character of the commission

What of those areas where no such church exists? Christ commanded his people to 'go'. The commission is extensive. If we are truly to obey the great commission in outreach we must reach out to those areas where no church exists. The aim of the outreach must be the planting of new churches, local churches, wherever people are. The command is to 'go'.

The command to 'wait' was only until endued with power from on high (Luke 24:49). It has nothing whatever to do with waiting for people to 'come in' to be evangelised at our convenience.

That the people of God have been 'sent' into the world is as much a fact of the divine purpose as the sending of God's Son into the world (John 20:21). Being *in* the world does not mean being *of* the world (John 15:18-19; 17:14; 1 John 2:15-17), although it does mean that contact with the people of the world is inevitable (1 Corinthians 5:9-10). The church's role in the world is to live as the people of God in stark contrast to the people of the world and to proclaim the message of Christ to them. In Matthew 5:13-16 the pictures of the church as 'salt' and 'light' suggest both its separateness and its involvement, especially in proclaiming the gospel.

The commission is extensive – into the entire world! So, how is it to be put into practice? The Lord has not left us in the dark as to how we go about obeying the commission. He tells us in his word what we are to do. He has made his mind known concerning the life and work of local churches. Similarly he has made his mind known by New Testament example and precept how we are to proceed in order to reach the goal of bringing into being new churches that will be God's instruments for reaching our ungodly generation with the gospel.

Local church activity at Jerusalem

The Acts of the Apostles is not a record of uncoordinated and unrelated activity bursting on the world following Pentecost. If any precedents are set for the long-term life of the churches during the centuries between Christ's ascension and his second coming we expect to find them here. This is indeed the case, and in the light of the corporate thrust of the 'Great Commission' we find a corporate dimension to New Testament obedience.

We turn our attention first of all to the church at Jerusalem and the activity that emanated from it. The early chapters of the Acts of the Apostles describe events which took place in Jerusalem itself, although the impact of them was felt in the surrounding towns (see Acts 5:16). Everything was related to the church itself, even Stephen's individual enterprise (Acts 6 and 7) was that of a man in whom the Jerusalem church had placed its trust (Acts 6:5). When he died, the church itself felt the repercussions in the persecution which then arose (Acts 8:1). There is no sense in which Stephen's activity was regarded as being outside the environment of the church. Devout brethren from the church buried him and mourned his passing.

It would appear at first sight that the persecution that arose following Stephen's death produced an outburst of individualistic and unrelated activity. Those who were scattered went everywhere preaching the word (Acts 8:4), and with that activity the Jerusalem church had no problem as far as we can tell. Philip, however, went to Samaria (Act 8:5), and that moved the church to send Peter and John to investigate what was going on (Acts 8:14). This was a new departure. Previously only Jews had been evangelised, now Samaritans were included. Without any doubt, the visit of Peter and John, together with the visitation of the Holy Spirit in what has been called 'the Samaritan Pentecost', ensured that Jewish and Samaritan Christianity was one and the same. God was working and the Jerusalem church both recognised it and welcomed it. Philip's work is not to be regarded as merely individualistic enterprise; there is a vital local church dimension that must not be lost sight of.

This is also the case with Peter's visit to Cornelius in Acts chapter 10. Again the visitation of the Holy Spirit in what has been called 'the Gentile Pentecost' and again Peter's response ensured that Jewish and Gentile Christianity was one and the same. Peter's report to the Jerusalem church (Acts 11:1-18) cemented this. Again the Lord was at work and the Jerusalem church recognised it and welcomed it (Acts 11:18). Peter's ministry too must not be regarded as merely individualistic enterprise. The local church dimension is plain.

Local church activity at Antioch

The formation of the church in Antioch makes interesting reading and perhaps goes some way to explaining its later prominent position in promoting missionary endeavour. It was formed out of the evangelistic zeal of believers scattered during the persecution following Stephen's death (Acts 11:19-21).

It was not 'official policy' to preach the gospel directly to Gentiles, but that is exactly what these enthusiastic believers did on arriving in Antioch. Here was the spontaneous overflowing of gospel concern. God was in it and a large number came to faith. The church in Jerusalem did not condemn what happened. Instead Barnabas was sent to investigate. Evidently, whatever report he sent back met with general approval because relationships between the two churches (Jerusalem and Antioch) remained cordial (e.g. Acts 11:27-30 where material relief was sent from Antioch to the saints in Jerusalem). Once again the local church dimension is evident in the bringing into being of the church at Antioch with the approval and support of the church in Jerusalem. Barnabas remained in Antioch to lead and teach the church. It had been a wise move to send Barnabas ('Son of Encouragement' - Acts 4:36) to Antioch. Even more were added to the Lord following his arrival (Acts 11:24).

When we turn to subsequent events in Antioch with the sending out of the Apostle Paul and his companions, the local church dimension features prominently both in the sending out of the missionaries and in their return to report fully and faithfully to those who had sent them (see Acts 13:1-3; 14:26-28).

Local church centrality

The local church dimension to the activity of these early New Testament churches emphasises the important truth that the local church was central to thinking and acting. As we look at Jerusalem and Antioch again, and consider briefly the church at Thessalonica we will find this principle demonstrated clearly.

The focus of our attention in the early chapters of Acts is the local church in Jerusalem. It is central to the moving drama of events organised and co-ordinated by the Holy Spirit. Its centrality appears at various points, even before the day of Pentecost, as Acts chapter one indicates. Acts 2:41-42 lays out the foundational characteristics of the church, including the fact that other disciples were added to or were joined to the original number (see also Acts 2:47). Peter and John returned to the church to report what had transpired before the Council (Acts 4:23) and the church as a whole engaged in prayer. Fellowship in the church was real and practical. Barnabas' gift is evidence of it (Acts 4:32-37). The perversity of Ananias and Sapphira and the judgment meted out to them by God in Acts 5 caused fear to come upon the whole church. The whole church was involved in the appointment of the seven in Acts 6, and the whole church was involved in the ministries of Philip and Peter. The whole church prayed for Peter when he was in prison (Acts 12:5).

These references demonstrate the centrality of the local church to Christian life and testimony in Jerusalem. The relationship of the brethren to one another in the church was close and real. Even before the Apostle Paul described the local church as the body of Christ the church in Jerusalem was demonstrating the rightness of such a description. Given this relationship it is unthinkable that evangelism and mission should have been engaged in without the local church being informed, involved and central to the thinking of those early Christians in Jerusalem.

The evidence concerning the church in Antioch is slender and yet all references to Antioch (in Syria) in the Acts of the Apostles have the church there in the centre of attention. It is not the city's cultural or commercial importance, or its pagan excesses which are recorded. The activities and endeavours of the church are the focus of attention in Acts. For example, expressions of fellowship with the saints in Jerusalem and apostolic concerns for truth (Galatians 2:11-21) have the needs of the local church at their heart.

Turning our attention to the church in Thessalonica we note that Paul describes the church as setting an example to believers in Macedonia and Achaia (1 Thessalonians 1:7). He then gives the reason, a most significant reason too: 'For from you the word of the Lord has sounded forth, not only in Macedonia and Achaia, but also in every place' (1 Thessalonians 1:8). For all its faults the church in Thessalonica was an out-going church and an example to others in its concern for the expansion of Christ's kingdom. The gospel had come in power to them (verse 5) and now they made sure it was passed on. Notice, however, that the church itself is commended; not just a few zealous individuals. The whole church at Thessalonica is the example to others. The whole church, undoubtedly through its various members, but the whole church nevertheless, sounded forth the word. The local church was central to this work as Paul makes plain by addressing his letters to 'the church of the Thessalonians' (1 Thessalonians 1:1; 2 Thessalonians 1:1).

Local church co-operation

Often in the New Testament, enterprise and co-operation between local churches can be observed. Relations between the various local churches were close although communications were difficult. Fellowship was real and practical. Notice in this connection the collections organised for the saints in Jerusalem and other co-operative endeavours.

In dealing with the practical arrangements for gathering funds for the poor in Jerusalem, Paul collected around him a group of men who were commended by their churches (see Acts 20:4 and 2 Corinthians 8:18-19, 23). Such co-operation had the sponsorship and support of the churches.

Although Paul was sent out as a missionary by the church in Antioch he enjoyed a close relationship with a number of churches. Philippians 4:10-17 refers to the particular bond between the church in Philippi and the apostle which was expressed in practical support as opportunity arose.

Another companion of the Apostle Paul was Timothy; he was commended to Paul by the churches at Lystra and Iconium in Galatia (Acts 16:1-3) acting in co-operation.

It is hard to see that any other way of behaving would have been appropriate for New Testament churches given the local church dimension to all New Testament Christian activity and the centrality of the local church in the records we have of New Testament life. Such precedents give us no alternative but to acknowledge that the local church according to New Testament practice is the instrument that God uses for carrying out his missionary mandate.

As that divinely chosen instrument the local church is the portrayal of the life of Christ to the world around. It bears a particular responsibility as his church to carry out the terms of his commission with respect to the world. Believers who make up the local church are his ambassadors (2 Corinthians 5:20) and the church as a whole is his representative in the world. The various descriptive titles, which we have considered earlier in this book, furnish us with helpful pointers to areas of responsibility laid upon the church relating to mission, and we will turn our attention to them now.

The church as a body

The concern of the Apostle Paul for the health of the churches is reflected in his use of the title 'body of Christ' for the local church. The dominant themes are the unity of the church with Christ its head and the mutual responsibility of members within the body. These themes predominate in such passages as Romans 12, 1 Corinthians 12 and Ephesians 4.

The headship of Christ means his rule over his people. Obedience to that rule includes obedience to his commission to go into the entire world. The exercise of the mutual responsibility of members within the body is a powerful testimony to the presence of Christ's life and the power of the gospel to a world at odds with itself, fragmented and disordered by self-seeking rebellion against God.

The teaching on the 'body' also contains other themes that direct our thoughts to local church responsibility. Attitudes to those 'outside' are dealt with by Paul's instruction to live peaceably with all men if at all possible (Romans 12:18) and to do good to those who oppose the gospel (Romans 12:14, 20). The possible presence of outsiders is to affect what takes place when the church meets together (1 Corinthians 14:23-25).

A body is a living and growing organism. The local church is to be seen in the same way. It is to grow (Ephesians 4:16) and that is not to be limited to understanding the truth or increased spiritual maturity. It is to be bodily growth. The body itself is to grow; but how does that come about? Every part, every member, is to work effectively. Every part is to do its share. The giving of gifts (Ephesians 4:11) by the ascended Lord (4:8) is so that the saints may be equipped for this ministry of bodily growth (4:12). Significantly, evangelists are included in the list of gifts for the equipping of the saints.

There are enough indications that ordinary believers evangelised by personal testimony for us to regard reaching the lost with the gospel as a regular and continuing part of the ordinary life of the churches in New Testament times (e.g. Acts 8:4; 11:20). Even so, the gift of evangelist was evidently necessary for the churches in encouraging and directing evangelistic activity. What the evangelist

actually did is hard to determine. Philip is described as one in Acts
21:8 and Timothy is urged to do the work of one in 2 Timothy 4:5.
The meagreness of New Testament information warns us against
being too dogmatic about the evangelist's role. In no way do these
scanty references justify the present-day idea of an evangelist as one
who goes about conducting large missions, campaigns or crusades
in a way detached from and unrelated to the local church.

What the New Testament references to evangelist do in fact tell
us is that preaching the gospel had a very important place in the life
of the churches, so much so that the Lord actually gave certain men
a particular gift in this direction as a service to the churches. This is
quite consistent with the emphasis on growth involved in the 'body'
motif. Any church that was alive with Christ's life by his Spirit
would engage in 'growth activity' in reaching out with the gospel.
Any church which failed to do so would merit enquiry as to the
nature of its 'life' (see Revelation 3:1-2, 17).

The church as a bride

There is a close connection between the ideas contained in 'body'
and those contained in 'bride', as Ephesians 5:22-23 shows. The
purity of the church is however the major theme of the 'bride' motif
and is derived from the church's intimate relationship with Christ.
The description of the church as the bride of Christ, therefore,
suggests separation and devotion to Christ as a bride is separated
and devoted to her husband. The church similarly takes Christ's
name and his dignity as a wife takes her husband's name and
dignity. The church is thus closely identified with Christ in the world.

That identification and intimate relationship brings constraints.
The church is motivated by a desire to please Christ in all it does.
The overriding concerns of its life will be Christ-centred areas. He
will have the pre-eminence (Colossians 1:18). The Christ-likeness
of its life will be a powerful testimony to the world of the presence
of Christ in the world. Its holy life will stand in clear contrast to the
unholy environment of the world. It will undoubtedly suffer in

consequence, but will not abandon its responsibility for all that. In the Sermon on the Mount the Saviour passed immediately from his words on the blessing of persecution to the teaching on salt and light (Matthew 5:11-16).

The church as salt and light

In order that testimony may be given to the world the church must be in the world. The salt is the salt *of the earth* and the light is the light *of the world.* The salt is to exercise its preserving ministry where it is needed - where things are going bad, where the corruption, decay and deprivation are to be found. The salt has also the effect of provoking thirst, so that needy souls will seek after the water of life. The contrast of the holy character of the church with the depraved life of much of human society should cause some to enquire after the reason for the difference; but the church has to be present in the world to do it. To escape into isolation from this present evil world is not to be salt. Separation to Christ involves separation from sin and compromise, but it also implies a ministry of testimony against sin by holy living and energetic compassion for needy souls.

Similarly the city set on the hill as the light of the world that cannot be hidden must be in the world where the darkness is in order to exercise its ministry of exposing and illuminating. The light is to shine before men so that God the Father may be glorified.

The church as a temple

The essential and unique spirituality of the church may be seen in the title 'temple of the Holy Spirit'. The Holy Spirit dwells in each believer (1 Corinthians 6:19), and in each church. The emphasis of the Apostle Paul in 1 Corinthians 3:16-17 and 2 Corinthians 6:16-17, where he described the Corinthian church as the temple of God, is upon the holy and separate character of the church. His emphasis in Ephesians 2:20-22 and Peter's in 1 Peter 2:5 is upon the structure of the church as made up of members who are built into the church as stones are part of a temple.

The church is undoubtedly a uniquely spiritual structure, for its life is derived from the presence of Christ by his Spirit. It engages in God-ward activity – the offering up of spiritual sacrifices acceptable to God through Jesus Christ (1 Peter 2:5; see also Hebrews 13:15). Yet the particular aspect of the nature of the church as the temple of God that is germane to our purposes here concerns those who are built into the temple as living stones. Gentiles as well as Jews are included. Those who are 'afar off' as well as those who are 'near' (Ephesians 2:17) are accounted now as 'no more strangers and foreigners, but fellow citizens' (Ephesians 2:19). The stones of the temple came from those previously 'outside', from the many nations of the world and from the deprived and overlooked sections of society – the foolish, the weak and the base (1 Corinthians 1:27-28).

When driving out the money changers from the Jerusalem temple the Lord Jesus quoted Isaiah 56:7 describing the temple as a house of prayer *for all nations* (Mark 11:17). The church is the temple of God in which he dwells by his Spirit. To that temple the people of the world are to be brought. The church is to reach out to bring others in to form additional living stones and members of the household of God.

The church as the people of God

Peter's description of the church as God's own special people (1 Peter 2:9) includes proclamation of praises as a dominant reason for the calling out of the chosen generation, the royal priesthood and the holy nation now identified with the church.

This proclamation has an evangelistic thrust, for those who were once not a people have now become the people of God and have now obtained his mercy (1 Peter 2:10). The church as the people of God, the new nation in which previous barriers of race, language, class and culture have been abolished (1 Corinthians 12:13; Galatians 3:28; Colossians 3:11), has a God-given command to proclaim his Name to those at present not numbered among his people.

The church as an effective instrument

We have been briefly considering the nature of the church under various headings. Each heading, as a descriptive title found in Scripture, carries with it demands made upon the church in respect of its responsibility for evangelism and mission. This is what we would expect to find if the missionary commission laid upon the church is indeed axiomatic or foundational. Note, the responsibility is a church responsibility, to be met by the local church as a church, acting in accord with its calling and its nature!

That the local church bears prime responsibility for implementing the 'Great Commission' we have found to be the teaching of the New Testament. It is therefore according to the mind of God. If this is true we should expect to find that it is effective. We expect God's ways to work. In fact, as a most efficient and effective means of accomplishing what is involved in the 'Great Commission' the New Testament concept of the local church sparkles with divine brilliance.

The presence of a local church in a community is a powerful testimony to the power of the gospel. It is in a local church that men and women see the life of Christ lived out by a body of regenerated people. It is from the local church that Christian people, born again people, go out to reach the community with the gospel.

The example of Christ's earthly life

The life on earth of the Lord Jesus Christ gives us important guidelines for the reaching of people today. He lived as a member of a human family, he appreciated friendship with others, he knew sorrow and fatigue, he shared in bereavement and sorrow, he experienced joy, he knew criticism, rejection and misunderstanding, he enjoyed the hospitality of others, yet had nowhere to 'lay his head' (Matthew 8:20). He dealt with the diseased and afflicted, the immoral and the hypocritical. Lepers, the blind, the deaf, the dumb, the lame, rich men, poor men, widows, children, the overlooked, the oppressed, the religious, the mighty, the weak, in fact, all sorts and conditions of men sought him and heard his word. Only those who refused to hear or to heed went away unblessed. No one was too bad or too small to have his full attention. He was never too busy or too tired to receive a needy soul. He came to call sinners (Matthew 9:13), and they came to him for help, and for forgiveness.

Although he preached to large companies of people and attracted a great deal of public attention, the meeting of the needs of the people in their various circumstances was more often accomplished in private and personal encounters. His personal interest in people is one of the most impressive features of the Saviour's ministry. He turned no one away, however apparently inconvenient it might have seemed. He was always ready to serve the people.

The Christian in the community

So, when we come to relate these things to the people of God today, the same factors are prominent. No Christian is ever 'off duty'. He is in the locality to serve his Saviour. He is therefore willing to serve people however inconvenient it may sometimes seem. Meeting people, needy people, means some (perhaps considerable) involvement in other people's lives as friend, neighbour or colleague. No Christian should ever cut himself off from those around him or turn away from those who come to him for help. Participation in sin he will resist, compromise of his faith he will avoid, but real people have real needs and he will seek in Christ's name to help. In so doing he will reveal Christ's life in him.

It is at this point that so much 'mass evangelism' is found wanting. It is evangelism at a distance, remote, impersonal and 'professionalistic'. Big meetings with massed choirs and special music can create a highly charged atmosphere when many may be moved to 'decide'. But it is utterly divorced from the realities of life with the problems and pressures of home and work. To dash through a town with a loudspeaker van to announce a meeting may arouse some interest, but no one has actually been met. Tract distribution without a sight of the recipients might just as well be done from an airship! Although Radio and Television need not appear to be so impersonal, real personal contact is missing, and they are, therefore, of limited effectiveness in reaching people, compared with a local church and its members living in a locality.

The broken lives of this generation need something more than is often offered to them. The well meaning, 'Cheer up, remember God loves you', will seem like a mockery to those in terrible pain, conflict or despair. The real needs of people are too deep to be treated in such a way. There are moral needs, personal needs, social needs, political needs, economic needs, and a host of others. Addressing such needs requires the presence of believers living locally and gathered into a local church.

The local church should be local

In the local community the local church has a vital role to play in serving a bewildered and fragmented society. The sense of wholeness and hope that the local church can contribute to a neighbourhood through its members can be vital in today's society. It is important therefore that church members should live locally and should be identified with the society in which they live. It is next to useless to live miles away and hope to reach a neighbourhood by 'attending church' there once a week. It is the presence of Christians in a situation which can have a profound effect upon it, bringing a sense of stability, strength and goodness which otherwise would be absent. By example to others, Christians can show how failures, frustrations and fears can be overcome.

A local church can be a unifying influence in a community if it truly reflects the cultural and racial make-up of the area. Divisions in society can be broken down in the church where what is lacking in the society around can be found and enjoyed by all. Instruction, discipleship and leadership training need have none of the social constraints of the area. All, of whatever class, group or status, can achieve their potential in the service of God in fellowship with his people.

The local church under scrutiny

The reality of the gospel needs the scrutiny of the people of the world if they are ever to see its relevance for them. They can only scrutinise it in the lives of the members of the church living before them. When members live at a distance in an area where social background and interests are quite different from those of the community the church is trying to reach, such scrutiny is impossible.

As well as the individual Christian, the local church itself is under scrutiny. Its internal relationships, in one way or another, will be observed, and will reflect on the Saviour. He said as much himself: 'By this all will know that you are my disciples, if you have love for one another' (John 13:35).

Is the gospel true? Christians say it is, but the people who inhabit our cities, towns and villages will only be able to agree as they observe its effects in the lives of Christians in their communities. That is why God brings local churches into being by the labours of other local churches. It is so that his life and being will make an impact on the lives of others through his people.

People need people, and they need Christians more than any others. Friendship, neighbourliness, help and care, are all aspects of the love Christians show their neighbours. Living in a neighbourhood, the Christian is the most effective missionary of all. His local church, supporting him, encouraging him, feeding him and praying with him, will confirm to a watching world the reality of Christ's life. He is not merely interested in enlarging the church's congregation, nor is he merely interested in people as potential 'converts'. He lives for God's glory in Christ's Name, and loves his neighbour as himself. In so doing he is aware of the real needs of real people. Because he is a real person himself, he can point men and women to a real Saviour who can meet their deepest needs. He will discover that he is the natural one to whom people turn, and the church is the natural place for them to go for help in time of trouble.

The local church exercises responsibility

A local church is God's way of reaching people with the gospel. It therefore exercises a God-given responsibility for its own locality, for the world at large and for those who are engaged in missionary work in its name.

No church can be considered to have obeyed the 'Great Commission' if it neglects the souls in its own 'back yard', however much it gives to foreign missions and however many missionaries it sends to other countries. Within the neighbourhood in which a church is set are a host of needy people who must never be ignored by the church. There is a lost and needy humanity needing the presence and ministry of the church. The local church through its members is involved in the local situation whether it likes it or not. The responsibility for reaching the people of the locality belongs first and foremost to the local church. However else will they hear of the love of Christ and salvation through his death and resurrection? Because the members of the local church live in a locality they are the very people to bring the message of salvation to the people. That is why God set the local church in the locality.

However the local church must not ignore the world at large. As the population of the world increases so the need increases, for the number of souls without Christ increases too. The local church is God's appointed way of reaching the world with the gospel and it is therefore the local church that sends out missionaries to other places and supports them, often in co-operation with other local churches. Those other local churches share the same responsibility for the gospel to be proclaimed to the 'uttermost part of the earth' (Acts 1:8). Because of the New Testament teaching on the centrality of the local church in the purposes of God here on earth, that missionary endeavour will be concerned to see more local churches gathered where the need is greatest. The church will send into this work those who are called of God and are committed to the teaching of the New Testament. They will also be convinced of the importance of the local church as the Lord's agent or instrument for reaching this generation with the gospel.

The local church is the best instrument for addressing the call, gifts and abilities of the missionaries. It knows their background, their strengths and their weaknesses. It already enjoys close fellowship with them. They will already have been working in the church and will have been observed at close quarters. The local church has had a part in their training and is already involved to a marked degree in their day-to-day living. The local church is the best instrument for sending missionaries into the work.

The sending church not only sends; it continues to be involved by prayer support, financial support, advice, encouragement and care. It continues to be responsible for its missionaries and exercises that responsibility in a personal and intimate way; but it is also responsible to ensure it remains capable of this ministry. If, for instance, its spiritual life deteriorates, its missionaries will suffer. There will be a reduction in prayer support, interest and care, and even more importantly its missionary concern will be impaired. The local church is not only responsible to send, it is also responsible for maintaining a sending spirit, for God has ordained that the local church is the most effective instrument for the work of mission.

The local church will work with others

In carrying out its responsibility for missionary endeavour further afield, a local church will often work with other churches. This encourages fellowship and help between the churches to their mutual benefit. No church has everything and will sometimes need to depend on others. This builds trust and humble dependence on the Lord who supplies what is needed through others.

Such fellowship and co-operation between sending churches can help the work of bringing a new church into being and, at the same time, strengthen and ennoble the life of each church by inculcating a spirit of fellowship and trust.

The divine aim of Christ's mission

His Father sent the Lord Jesus Christ into the world. Jesus referred to this in a number of places, e.g. John 6:39, 40,44,57; 7:16,28-29; 8:16,18,26,29. In a similar fashion he sent his disciples into the world - see John 13:20; 17:18. In various places he told us why he had come into the world, e.g. ' ... to serve, and to give his life a ransom for many'. (Mark 10:45); ' ... that they may have life, and that they may have it more abundantly' (John 10:10); ' ... to call ... sinners to repentance' (Matthew 9:13).

In Luke 24:44-47 the Lord Jesus told his disciples that the necessity of his death and resurrection was matched by the necessity that 'repentance and remission of sins should be preached in his name to all nations'. It is as if the purpose of the one receives a measure of fulfilment in the other.

Paul writes of the sacrifice of Christ as to do with the church when he says, 'Christ also loved the church and gave himself for her' (Ephesians 5:25). Similarly he described the church as that which Christ 'purchased with his own blood' (Acts 20:28). The aim of Christ's mission in the world was the saving of the church – his body, his bride. He gave himself for it; he loves it and cares for it. The church lies at the heart of God's purpose in the coming of the Lord Jesus Christ. It also lies at the heart of the consummation of God's purpose in the return of the Lord Jesus Christ. That purpose is to present the church 'a glorious church, not having spot or wrinkle or any such thing; but that she should be holy and without blemish' (Ephesians 5:27). The divine aim of Christ's mission was the church. The divine aim of the church's mission is also the church.

The church's mission

As the aim of mission is the local church, the best-qualified instrument to achieve this aim is the local church itself. This being the case we can turn to the Scriptures expecting to find instruction for the achieving of the aim. Our sovereign Lord, the head of the church, has told us in his word what we are to do to plant churches which in their turn will be God's instruments for reaching our generation with the news of salvation.

Even a superficial look at the Acts of the Apostles will reveal that the Holy Spirit had a strategy. It can be stated in simple terms: where people are, where churches are not. Guided by the Holy Spirit the apostles and their colleagues went where people were – to the population centres, the cities and towns of the ancient world. They also went to those places where Christ was not named (Romans 15:20).

It is people who are important, so it makes sense to go where large numbers of people are. This is exactly what the apostles did. 'Bible believing Christians', on the other hand, in recent years have been doing the exact opposite. They have been guilty of neglecting the cities, especially the inner cities. This has often led to spiritual decay in inner city areas as they have been denuded of gospel testimony.

People matter in God's strategy, so the church is to go where people are to be found in large numbers. The apostles didn't go too far away at first, but they went to strategic places – centres of population, communication and trade. As churches were formed they set about reaching the surrounding population and the surrounding area. The strategy has not changed. We are faced with sprawling cities with large populations living and working in a closely confined area. Local churches are needed in those very areas if ever we are to reach our generation with the gospel.

Divine wisdom

This Holy Spirit directed strategy was no haphazard or careless thing. The strategy involved practical details. There was a system that reflected the corporate nature of the instrument (the local church) and the aim (the local church). In Acts 13:1-4 two men, Barnabas and Saul, were sent out as a team into the work. No single isolated individual was being sent. It was a team, small but effective. The church in Antioch knew the importance of this corporate 'system' for it had come into being itself when a company of believers arrived in the city (Acts 11:20).

There is great wisdom in this system. Members of a team are able to enjoy fellowship with one another and this avoids that sense of isolation that many present-day missionaries have felt. There may be a diversity of gifts among the members of the team, making for greater effectiveness. Younger men can be trained, and strength of numbers is added to the testimony. These things are particularly appropriate in view of the aim to plant local churches; for such benefits are part of the normal life of local churches patterned after the teaching of the New Testament.

The man who goes off on his own trying to start something as he feels like it can find no support from the New Testament. Just as the work in Antioch needed a Barnabas to be sent from Jerusalem and then a Saul to come from Tarsus, so church-planting work should command the support and interest of the churches generally. As Barnabas went to Antioch to authenticate and encourage the new work so the authenticating and supporting fellowship of other churches is vital.

Divine aid

This is not a work that happens by accident. Each church should examine carefully what it is doing locally and further afield, to ensure that it is being true to its calling as a church of God. Although we are moved first and foremost by the Lord himself (by his command and call), we should be aware of the glaring need of our generation. Our cities have thousands of streets with thousands of homes, in which live thousands and thousands of souls; yet how few churches there are to reach them.

The divine instrument in answering this need is the local church – the body of Christ in a locality. Such an instrument can count on divine aid. The Lord's commission to go is also his call to come.

He goes before us to prepare the way. He is there before we

arrive. He is at both ends at the same time working out his purposes. This is not to say there are no problems and trials, but as they occur we can be sure of the Lord's presence and help. Matthew's record of the 'Great Commission' contains that assurance: 'I am with you always, even to the end of the age' (Matthew 28:20).

That the sovereign Lord should have chosen to use as his instruments such frail, undeserving and imperfect churches as those we belong to is a mark of his amazing grace. His treasure has been placed in truly earthen vessels, and the reason for that is so the glory and praise might be his alone (2 Corinthians 4:7).

Chapter 14
The local church and outreach

Reaching those 'outside'

The New Testament has a great deal to say about the way a local church reaches those who are outside its membership. People live in a variety of environments and circumstances, so it requires a variety of approaches on the part of the church. We shall deal with this variety in this chapter, but before we do this there are a few basic matters we need to clear up first.

First of all we must be careful lest we fall into the trap of allowing the end (the saving of the lost) to justify any and all means. 1 Corinthians 9:22 should never be used as a licence to do anything so long as it gets results. Merely to go for results at whatever cost easily leads to ways of working which bring dishonour upon the Lord and his gospel, and compromise its effects upon the ungodly.

Secondly we must never define evangelism in terms of its results. What that means is defining evangelism only as that activity which produces conversions. Anything that fails to produce conversions is then reckoned not to be evangelism. It is sometimes called 'pre-evangelism' or something similar. This inevitably produces an attitude that sees results as the all-important thing. Failure to produce them means a failure to evangelise – the gospel has not been properly proclaimed, it is said. So results control the means of evangelism, and anything which produces results is legitimate, even the slick, high-powered, costly, gaudy, entertainment-centred, gigantic crusade. It is evangelism so long as it produces results. The integrity of the gospel of the grace of God is thereby relegated to a level of secondary significance.

Evangelism is simply to proclaim the gospel in conformity with God's word to sinners outside of a saving knowledge of Jesus Christ in terms that are understood by the hearers. In evangelism we are to be governed constantly by certain biblically derived principles. We shall consider them briefly because they determine our approach to reaching those 'outside'.

The gospel message

There are two particular matters that need mention here: the doctrine of God and the grace of God.

The biblical doctrine of God is the ground from which we evangelise. We are to declare who God is and what God requires; it is not a subject for debate. Men are not to pass judgment on God – he passes judgment on men. God as creator, a holy and righteous judge, whose character is revealed in his law, is what we are to declare. When we present the truth in this way we are not so likely to be involved with things that bring the majesty of God into question or even minimise it in the eyes of men. He is the almighty God, not just a friendly old man who wants to be our friend. The gospel which is the power of God unto salvation is also the righteousness of God revealed from faith to faith (Romans 1:16-17). The gospel is about God first of all.

However our message is also centred in the grace of God. It is this that teaches so very clearly that God is not callously indifferent to the needs of men. Grace means that the undeserving receive the favour of God – so no one is to be left out of the evangelistic concern of the church. This doctrine realistically exposes the plight of sinners in the sight of God. The sinner is helpless and hopeless. To such a wretch the gospel of the grace of God comes with hope and eternal life, for God saves to the uttermost those who come to him through Christ Jesus, whom he has sent to rescue helpless sinners by his sacrifice on their behalf. He is not callous or indifferent, for in the gospel the love of God is commended (Romans 5:8).

Where the message does not present God as sovereign in grace, men will be manipulated by all possible means in order to achieve what God is unable to achieve by his own power! This is a ghastly and alarming prospect, but it is precisely what passes for so much 'evangelism' today.

Gospel motives

What moves us to proclaim the gospel to the unbeliever will also govern the manner we adopt in doing it. The Scriptures indicate that for the Christian there are certain inescapable motives.

It is first and foremost the command of the Lord Jesus Christ that drives us out into the world to proclaim the gospel. In the work of the gospel there are no volunteers. All Christians are involved. Such verses as Matthew 28:19, John 15:27 and Acts 1:8 all serve to demonstrate that the motive for the proclamation of the gospel comes primarily from the Lord himself. The gospel is invested with the power and authority of Christ. Those who obey his command can be confident that his purposes are fulfilled in the proclaiming of the gospel. We can also be confident of his presence with us as we do it (Matthew 28:20).

Secondly we must certainly follow the example of the Lord Jesus Christ, who had compassion on the multitude because they were like sheep without a shepherd (Matthew 9:36-35). It was because the people were like sheep without a shepherd and the harvest was plenteous that the Lord of the harvest was to be asked to send labourers into the harvest. The disciples were also involved in the compassion of the Lord. We who ourselves have been like sheep going astray have real understanding of the needs of our fellow human beings. We are touched with the feelings of their infirmities as Christ is with ours ((Hebrews 4:15). Having ourselves been touched by the grace of God we cannot now be unmoved by the plight of others.

Compassion is Christ-like, but it is not simply a sensitivity of heart – it leads to action. The gospel must be proclaimed to the sheep who have gone astray for it is the only thing which will do helpless sinners good. Our contacts and involvement should always be with a view to bringing people out of their danger into Christ's safety. We will not be content to leave them in peril, we will urge them to repent and trust in Christ.

Thirdly we will be motivated by concern; the concern that unbelievers have for themselves when aroused by the Holy Spirit. For example in Acts 16:30 the Philippian jailer wanted to know what to do to be saved. When the Spirit of God moves in men's hearts there is created within them a concern for the things of God. Peter urges every believer to be ready to give an answer to those who ask a reason for the hope that is in Christians (1 Peter 3:15). The answer we give is the gospel; that sinners need to be saved and Jesus Christ died to save sinners. That is the greatest help we can be to concerned people. We will not want to leave them in their concerned condition.

So, armed with the gospel message and moved by these considerations, the methods of reaching out from the church will similarly be governed by the Scriptures.

The lives of Christians

Although the day-to-day Christian living of the members of a church is not a 'method' of reaching outsiders officially organised by the church, it is nevertheless a most effective means of doing so. In fact the godly living of the members has always been the most effective way of reaching unbelievers with the truth of the gospel. Much of New Testament evangelism seems to have been the unconscious expression of the individual Christian's life in Christ making its impact on the lives of others around and on society in general (Acts 2:47; 4:13; 5:13). We also read of the natural spread of the gospel by persecuted Christians (Acts 8:4; 11:19, 21). The godly living of believers is still the most effective means and needs encouragement and constant stimulation in the teaching ministry of the church and in its fellowship. No other method can be a substitute for it.

The foolishness of preaching

The God-ordained method is preaching (1 Corinthians 1:21; Romans 10:17). For it is through this apparently foolish means that men come to faith – by hearing the word of God. The foolishness of it rules out 'professionalistic' slickness, and the centrality of the cross in it (1 Corinthians 1:18; 2:2) rules out what might compromise it. This is to be the church's work in season and out of season (2 Timothy 4:2); when convenient and when inconvenient. The preaching agent is the local church, its public ministry and its members – ordinary people using ordinary words. In this way God has chosen to confound our sophisticated age. By the simplicity and directness of preaching God has chosen to ignore man's ways of getting a hearing. The foolishness of preaching is a display of his power (1 Corinthians 1:18).

Two Greek words for preaching commonly used in the New Testament are ευαγγελιζομαι ('euangelizomai') and κηρυσσω ('kerusso'). The former word ('euangelizomai') means 'to pass on or announce good news', to 'spread the gospel, ('eu' and 'angelos' means 'good news' or gospel) and often refers to evangelism engaged in by Christians through everyday contacts. We might translate the word 'gospelising'. The latter word ('kerusso') means to 'proclaim a message as a herald' and often refers to a more public occasion when a preacher would proclaim the gospel to a group of hearers. Both words are appropriate as describing, in different settings, the outreach ministry of a local church and its members.

The way of faith

Each method of spreading the gospel that is consistent with the Scriptures is a way of faith, and teaches us not to rely on our ability and ourselves but on God alone. He does his will in his own way. But of this we can be confident – he desires to save his people from their sins. This is why Christ came into the world and also why the Holy Spirit is at work in the world. The elect will be gathered in, we can be sure of that, so we can trust God to do his saving work effectively.

As the Lord's people rely upon the Lord to do the saving of people, whatever method they adopt, they will approach each 'outreach' opportunity prayerfully, seeking God's help and blessing, as well as submitting to his guidance and direction. No gospel work should ever be done carelessly, or as a mere routine. Each occasion when Christ is presented as the Saviour of sinners is full of divine potential as the possible occasion when a soul will pass from death to life in Jesus Christ.

It is now appropriate for us to consider specific methods of gospel work. We have already considered the normal and regular meetings of the church for worship, fellowship and the exposition of God's word. They can often be fruitful occasions as sinners who have been invited by members to hear the gospel come to faith in Jesus Christ. However our attention here is to activities other than these regular and vital meetings.

In any consideration of evangelistic outreach undertaken by a church every opportunity and possibility should be considered. However, the church should be bold enough to reject anything that does not conform to God's word, and it should continually seek to ensure that all it is doing is in line with what God's word teaches. It is also possible that there are things the church is not doing which it should be doing.

Explanation of the truth

It is clear from what the apostle Peter wrote in 1 Peter 2:15 and 3:15, and from what he did on the day of Pentecost (explaining what had happened), that there is a very important place in reaching outsiders with the gospel for efforts to be made to inform people what the Christian gospel is and what the Christian faith is all about. Although it is true that the natural man cannot receive the things of the Spirit of God (1 Corinthians 2:14) unless he is first dealt with by the Spirit in regenerating grace, that is no justification for leaving misunderstandings, misconceptions and errors in his mind. Today an appalling ignorance of the truth surrounds the church. Here is a good place to start.

The local church has therefore a responsibility to pass on information about the Christian faith, explaining what a true Christian is, opening up what the word of God teaches on a host of issues and presenting the Christian answer to the needs of the present age. This will obviously be taking place in the regular Sunday services, but every encouragement should be given to the members of the church to be aware of these things themselves so as to be able to explain them to the people they meet day by day. More especially the church might usefully arrange meetings to disseminate this vital Christian information to people already in contact with the church in some way and to any others who might be persuaded to come. The purpose would be to present the relevance of God's word and the Christian gospel within the framework of discussion of some subject which would command interest. A variety of subjects may be appropriate: evolution and creation; industrial relations; honesty in business; abortion and euthanasia; the family; death, pain and suffering; the Bible; other religions, and so on. The list could be quite long.

Such meetings could be publicly announced or by invitation, on church premises, in a hired building or in a home. If a subject such as is suggested above is chosen it will be found useful to invite a speaker to open up the matter before discussion takes place. Firm leadership of such discussion is essential by a good chairman since the aim is to inform people about Christ, his word and the gospel and not simply to have a stimulating discussion.

In certain circumstances discussions can be arranged on particular topics without a speaker. The need here is for firm control by the chairman and a definite sense of direction. Although all who attend may be allowed to speak, not all opinions are equally true.

Debating the truth

As we pass on from discussions to public debate we enter a very tricky area. A debate can be a most effective way of informing the minds of the ignorant. It does two things; it enables the debater to state positively what is the Christian faith, and it also enables him to refute the arguments of those who oppose it. It is vital in certain circumstances to show men and women the great weaknesses in arguments opposed to the word of God and the Christian faith. Christians have nothing to fear in the realm of truth, reason and logic. The problem however is that of vulnerability. In a debate you lay yourself open to attack publicly. So whoever is engaged in debating needs to be good at it. He must know the subject thoroughly. He must have a quick and ready mind, able to pick up the weak argument in his opponent and use it to demolish the opposing view. In this way a debate can have a value in showing that the Christian faith can stand up to attack from any quarter.

There are problems with this method of explaining the truth to the ignorant. Winning arguments is not the same as winning people. Your defeated opponent may be all the harder to reach with the gospel after having been 'shown up' in public. That is a problem with the result obtained in using this method. The other problem is with the method itself. The truth of God is not for debate. Sinful mankind is in no position to pass judgment on God and his truth, and should never be put in the position where he thinks he is. That is precisely what a debate does. For these reasons, therefore, debating should only ever be used with the greatest care.

Literature and the media

Christian literature has proved its usefulness as a means of informing the ignorant. Christian books have a long-term ministry too – they stay with a person after a conversation has finished. In order to help its members in this kind of ministry each church might well obtain and maintain a stock of useful books on a wide range of subjects that are of concern to outsiders. The Bible is not silent on the issues of life so we have no need to fear that there is nothing to say from a Christian point of view. Apart from the good such books can be to Christians they are a special set of tools in the church's equipment for bearing testimony to Jesus Christ and informing men and women of the truth.

One disturbing fact needs to be faced. There are very few books written specifically for non-Christians. Most Christian books are written for Christians because those are the kind they buy. Few Christians seemingly have been willing to spend money on books to give away. Is this not an area where churches should be encouraging their members?

When we turn to other means of communication such as films, videos, television and radio, things are not so straightforward. Films and videos can be a useful aid to the passing on of information but great care needs to be exercised. There are many so-called Christian films which are not out to impart information as such; they are more concerned with winning a decision, and sink into emotional and pseudo-psychological attempts to influence the audience. No church should ever be tempted to replace the preaching of the word by a film or video, even occasionally.

With the use of television and radio the fundamental question is 'who controls what is said?'. If the programme is in the form of an interview with an unbeliever interviewing the Christian, his motives are nothing whatever to do with imparting Christian information. On the other hand if the church is able to buy time or is placed under no restriction as to the content of the programme, both television and radio can be very useful aids to the Church's ministry of informing the minds of the ignorant. Both television and radio should be viewed as means to that end primarily.

For the sake of completeness we might perhaps include here what the church does in informing people around in a general sort of way what it is doing and why. Newspaper reports should always tell the truth! Posters, and indeed all forms of advertising (e.g. a notice in hotels giving details of services and meetings) should be restrained, informative, clear and truthful. To make boastful claims is to lie.

Explaining what the Christian faith is and involves (including what a church is and does) is a most important aspect of reaching outsiders. It must be done well if our sovereign Lord is to be honoured in it.

Reaching out

What is in mind here is not so much providing means and opportunities for the faith to be explained on the church's own terms (as it were), but a deliberate policy adopted by a church for reaching out into the surrounding community with the intention that the members speak to others of the Lord Jesus Christ on other people's ground. How the church in Thessalonica reached out we do not know (1 Thessalonians 1:8) but their ministry was certainly effective. The church in Antioch reached out too as the Holy Spirit led them (Acts 13:1-3), but there the work was done further afield. Here we are thinking of what a church does within its own locality once it has been planted. Church planting (commonly called missionary work), is a subject to be dealt with on its own in Chapter 16.

It is clear that house to house visitation fits into this category. This is where members of the church go to call on householders in the neighbourhood of the usual meeting place of the church to speak to them of the Lord Jesus Christ. Invitations are usually given to the meetings of the church, appropriate literature is left, enquiry is made concerning any situations of need that can be met by the church through its members living in the vicinity, but above all testimony is given to the truth and reality of the Christian life and faith. A question and answer approach has often been found useful in stirring conversation on spiritual matters. Those who indicate any interest should not be forgotten, but subsequent visits should be arranged to continue the matter. All questions should be answered honestly, and where the answer is unknown at the time, it should be discovered. Interest and concern should be reflected in the careful way that information gleaned is remembered (some record might be kept) and points of need are dealt with speedily. The fact that Jehovah's

Witnesses and Mormons do this work and antagonise people should not deter us, but it should make it all the more necessary to approach people politely and kindly.

Alongside this form of house-to-house visitation might go colportage work. This is the selling of Christian literature from house to house. Christmas time is often a useful time to engage in this work as children's books are popular as presents and other books may catch the householder's eye. Often such doorstep contacts can lead to profitable conversations on spiritual issues that are then followed up by the church.

As far as the general distribution of leaflets and tracts is concerned, it can go on any time. But it must always be borne in mind that there is no such thing as the truly general tract. A church may feel it necessary to use quite a variety of tracts and leaflets according to the kind of environment and social conditions obtaining in the locality that it serves. Instead of tracts a church might consider distributing recordings of a Christian message. They can be obtained or produced quite cheaply.

Open-air work

Open-air preaching is another activity in which the local church may reach out with the gospel. It has a very long history dating back to New Testament times with John the Baptist, the Lord Jesus and the apostles involved in preaching the gospel in the open air. When we refer to preaching in the open air we are not talking about services of worship held out of doors, we mean here the public proclamation of the Christian gospel in a public place to those who are to be found there. Members of the church may be involved in some numbers by their presence in the crowd to support those actually doing the preaching. Their prayers are vital and they can use the opportunity of giving personal testimony to other people standing by. This involvement of the membership can make this a most effective way of reaching outsiders.

The preaching should be biblical, relevant, simple and direct.

Questions may be answered if those preaching are competent to answer them, for this is not the work for novices. Preaching experience should be gained first in the fellowship of the Lord's people before ever a man attempts to preach in the open air. The question of singing in an open-air meeting is a matter for discussion and very careful thought. The meeting is not a service of worship and singing of Christian songs and hymns is not a form of entertainment for unbelievers. Prayer should not be a public parade – it should be done beforehand, or if during the meeting should be silent and personal. The preacher should use no notes if at all possible, or if necessary, very few indeed. This will allow him to adjust to the circumstances confronting him – they do not remain static in the open air in quite the same way as in a church service of worship in a building.

It is also possible to use literature in the open air either in conjunction with an open-air meeting or separately. A bookstall or stand in a market or in a shopping area may be possible. Useful contacts can be made in this way quite apart from the good the books which are sold will do.

Specialised activities

We pass on at this stage to a group of activities that are somewhat more specialised. Any church thinking of engaging in these forms of evangelism would need to weigh up carefully a number of considerations i.e. finance, personnel and long term commitment. Some of these things require a significant capital expenditure and a constant and continuing ministry throughout the year. Such things as a Christian book shop staffed voluntarily by church members, a cafe which gives opportunity for Christian witness in conversation and counsel, a telephone answer service for those who feel they are in urgent need, a telephone message service which allows a caller to hear a short pre-recorded message; all require careful thought and the commitment of considerable amounts of time and money.

Another matter that will require long-term commitment is writing a regular column in a local newspaper. It is often possible to place a short, simple and direct message in a newspaper paid for as an advertisement. In this way control is maintained over what is written. Some newspaper editors will even allow a 'comment' column as part of the paper's regular feature material.

Where people gather

In the New Testament the practice of the apostles in their evangelistic work in the towns and cities they visited was to go where people gathered together in order to share the gospel with them (see e.g. Acts 17:17). The same procedure is open to us today. We have already dealt briefly with open air preaching in those locations where people gather or pass by, but there are many other such opportunities. Many public gatherings lend themselves to some form of Christian evangelistic activity. Where a lot of people are to be found it may be possible to distribute tracts, but it must always be remembered what has already been said about general tract and leaflet distribution. Such distribution can easily lose impact by virtue of its general character.

Nevertheless, taking place at some time during the year in a location reasonably close to the local church may be such an event as an Agricultural Show, a Carnival, a Fair or a Fete which may provide an opportunity for a Christian stall or stand to be included. People are more ready on such occasions to stand and chat, and this provides the church with just the opportunity it can use.

People also gather in other places somewhat less public. This usually means that the permission of those in charge will be needed before it is possible to speak for Christ. Youth Clubs, Social Clubs and even Public Houses (Pubs) come into this category. The surroundings or environment can easily present difficulties so that the gospel message is compromised if it is not handled in the right way. It may also be possible, with permission, to visit Prisons, Remand Centres and Schools. Those who are involved in such ventures need to be selected very carefully. Hospital visitation is open to more people and is a most fruitful field of ministry, as many patients at such a time are open to the loving interest of Christian people sharing the gospel with them. It may be possible to provide material for hospital Radio.

'Bait' and its dangers

A great deal of a church's evangelistic enterprise is 'invitation evangelism'. By that term is meant the worthy practice of church members inviting outsiders to some occasion organised by the church as a setting for the presentation of the gospel. There is a tendency on such occasions to use some kind of 'bait' to attract the outsiders invited.

It is important that we who believe in the primacy of preaching and the honour of God's name should not indulge in deceit or underhandedness. We should be honest enough to tell people to what we are inviting them before they assume a meeting is convened for some other non-religious purpose. Music, games for young people, barbecues and even cups of tea, can fall into the category of 'bait'. What the church lays on to entertain the outsider must be regarded as very questionable. The church should not be in the entertainment business. Its business is preaching the gospel. As people are won so people are kept. If entertainment wins them so entertainment will have to be provided continually to keep them.

There are many things which are appropriate for informal social occasions within the life of a church when church members and their families can gather to enjoy each other's company which may be inappropriate when associated with evangelistic efforts. Obviously if a meeting is held in a home, the informal atmosphere, including a cup of tea, can be a natural and necessary accompaniment to the gospel message. There is little likelihood of misunderstanding in such circumstances. Whatever is done to reach outsiders should be done honestly and in an upright and direct way. People should know they are coming to a Christian meeting, the main purpose of which is to present the gospel of the grace of God. Any form of deceit should be rejected in the service of Jesus Christ.

Any method used should be subservient to the message, and of that message we are not ashamed (Romans 1:16). We do not need to hide it or apologise for it. This is not to say we simply ram the message down people's throats. We must approach each person and each situation differently, and always prayerfully. In some cases we have to earn the right to speak. This means in some cases living as a friend or neighbour for some time before being listened to. There is a time to speak and a time to be silent. Each believer needs the help of the Lord in determining which is which.

Chapter 15
The local church and children

Children and salvation

Some basic matters need to be dealt with first of all. We need to establish what the Scriptures actually teach about children themselves, and as we do that we will be able more clearly to consider how the church ministers to them.

The New Testament teaches that everyone without exception is born as a descendant of Adam the first man. Everyone shares Adam's nature, the nature he had after his fall into sin in the Garden of Eden. When he disobeyed God he became sinful in nature and was from then on subject to death. We are born in the same condition, we all died 'in Adam' (Romans 5:12) and we belong to a humanity that is sinful and subject to death. We are born into it.

The New Testament also teaches that there is a new humanity that gets its life from Jesus Christ. Just as all of us derive our natural life from Adam by birth so we receive our new humanity from Christ by a new birth. All who are 'in Christ' in that new humanity have been given new life (1 Corinthians 15:22) and sin and death have been conquered.

This means that children, from the time of their birth, are subject to death. Because they belong to the race that is descended from Adam and therefore have a sinful nature, they are subject to the same attitudes on God's part as everybody else. They are subject to God's just condemnation like the rest of humanity. There are no exceptions to this.

Some people think that children are innocent until they've reached some kind of age of discretion, but the New Testament knows nothing of such a thing. Some believe that having Christian parents makes a difference and virtually guarantees salvation. The New Testament teaches no such thing. Although there are many blessings and advantages in having Christian parents they cannot guarantee salvation for their children. Every child who is born into the world is born into the old humanity that has come from Adam. If any child is to know salvation from sin they must be born into the new humanity in Jesus Christ. They must be regenerated. Both adults and children are in exactly the same position; they need to be born again.

Children are not saved because they are innocent as some suppose. If that were the case, then the cause of salvation would be in them and not in God alone. A child is not 'safe' until some special age of accountability, as some teach. The Bible does not speak of an age of accountability, and no one has been able to say with certainty what it's supposed to be. In fact, the idea of some special age of accountability opens up terrible possibilities. For example, a child dying only one day after he had reached that special age without believing in the Lord Jesus Christ for salvation would be lost, but if he had died only two days before, he would have been saved. That idea is horrible, and must be rejected totally.

If we hold to the teaching of the Bible that children are saved by the grace of God alone, we have true hope. The basis for our hope lies in the grace and mercy of God alone, and that brings real confidence, for the God and Father of our Lord Jesus Christ is most certainly gracious and merciful.

Children and church membership

The church is one of three institutions ordained by God for the benefit and blessing of mankind. It must never be confused with the other two. God has ordained the family, which arises from the creation ordinance of marriage (Genesis 2:21-25). He has ordained the state, so that sinful men may enjoy the benefits of living in an ordered society governed by law (Genesis 9:5-6; Romans 13:1ff;

1 Peter 2:13-14). He has also ordained the church, a people for his exclusive possession (1 Peter 2:5-6,9-10).

The family is the unit of Christian upbringing and training when the parents are Christians, but having Christian parents doesn't guarantee salvation for the children. Similarly, having Christian parents is no automatic passport to church membership. Baptism is on profession of a personal faith, not on the grounds of relationship with other Christians. Natural birth secures the rights and privileges of family membership, but it cannot secure membership in the church.

Similarly, as we turn our attention to the other divinely ordained institution, the State, it is important to stress that it is not the secular side of one coin of which the church is the spiritual side. Again, natural birth might well secure the privileges of state citizenship, but it cannot secure membership in the church. The proper basis for that is regeneration by the Holy Spirit. We must therefore reject all ideas of church membership because of parentage or citizenship. We also reject all ideas of a State church.

Children are to be regarded as non-Christian. We need to teach them in such a way that any false security or hypocrisy they might have will be destroyed. They are lost and strangers to God by nature, and that must be taken seriously. They are, therefore, to be urged to repent and believe the gospel.

The Lord Jesus Christ and children

Our Lord's teaching about children is found in two particular passages: Matthew 18:1-6 and Matthew 19:13-15 (and the parallels in Mark and Luke). In Matthew 18 the disciples asked Jesus who was the most important in the kingdom of God. He placed a child in the middle of the group and told the disciples that they had to be converted and become like little children before they could even enter the kingdom. If they wanted to be the greatest, they had to humble themselves like this child.

We need to be sure, of course, what Jesus is actually approving and commending. Is it that we must imitate children because they are humble? That can hardly be the case because children are not really noted for their humility! Jesus knew that to be true, as he pointed out in his parable of the playing children in Matthew 11:16-17. Our Lord doesn't call for us to imitate the virtue of humility as much as for us to be converted. And that can happen only by divine grace. Conversion is not something we do; God does it to us. He converts us; we don't convert ourselves. We need the grace of God to be converted and to enter his kingdom. We, like little children depending on the help of others, depend for salvation on the work of God. This passage cannot be used to support the idea that children, simply because they are children, are automatically inside the kingdom of God.

In Matthew 19 verses 13-15 the phrase 'for of such is the kingdom of heaven' obviously refers to children, but it can mean either that the kingdom belongs to such as children or it consists of them. It all hinges on the word 'for' and here it means 'because'. The children, who are not to be stopped from coming to Jesus, are also to be included in the statement about the kingdom. Our Lord means that the kingdom belongs to these children and others like them.

In the parallel passage in Mark 10:13-16 the children are used as an illustration. With them in his arms Jesus stresses the importance of receiving the kingdom as they received him. When he called, the children came and threw themselves into his arms. All who come to him like that (i.e. in faith) become heirs of the kingdom. In Matthew 18 verse 6 is the phrase 'little ones who believe in me'. The phrase is not to be limited to children (disciples are called 'little ones' in Matthew 10:42 and Mark 9:42) but it certainly includes them. Yet it is not all children, for the text explicitly refers to those who 'believe in me'. Faith in Jesus Christ is the crucial matter.

On what grounds do children and others have access to God's kingdom? By coming to Jesus (Mark 10:14) and by receiving his word (Mark 10:15). Jesus taught that children (and others) belong to the kingdom only if they come to him in simple trust. He had a tender regard for children and taught that his heavenly Father has too. Children are of genuine interest to him, and that means they should be to his people. What is of interest to him should be of interest to us. However it is vital that we understand how that interest is to be expressed. Other New Testament passages can help us in this.

Children in the letters of Paul

When the Apostle Paul writes to the churches in Ephesus and Colosse he also writes to children. His teaching to husbands and wives, and to masters and servants is accompanied by teaching to parents and children. See Ephesians 6:1-4 and Colossians 3:20-21. Although Paul writes for example, to the Colossian believers as 'saints and faithful brethren in Christ' (1:2), and then goes on to write to children that they obey their parents 'in all things, for this is well pleasing to the Lord' (3:20) we do not need to assume that these children had to be members of the church. A child doesn't need to be a church member to be encouraged to do what is right.

In line with Proverbs 22:6 ('train up a child in the way he should go, and when he is old he will not depart from it') the instruction to be given to the children is with a long term view. Although the training and upbringing of children has a church dimension the actual setting is within the family (see also 1 Timothy 3:4,12; Titus 1:6; 2 Timothy 1:5; 3:15). It is interesting to observe from Paul's words in Ephesians and Colossians that the prime responsibility belongs to the father. He is responsible for a godly example, for the teaching of the things of God, for discipline and even for general education. The mother is involved too, obviously, and will actually be far more involved in a practical sense, but the prime responsibility rests with the father, the head of the home. Although specialist help is usually needed with regard to general education, no specialist help is ever a substitute for the Christian teaching, godly example and loving discipline of a Christian home.

Children in the Old Testament

Children appear in the Old Testament in various ways. We have the stories of Isaac, Joseph, Moses and Samuel, but we are more concerned here with those matters that will help our understanding of our responsibility today towards children.

There are several passages in Deuteronomy which refer to children as receiving instruction (4:7-10; 6:7; 11:18-21; 31:11-13; 32:46). Again there is a wider corporate dimension within the worshipping community of God's people but the actual setting for the instruction is within the home with the responsibility for the actual teaching laid upon the parents. The following scriptures also indicate that parents were expected to explain the various ceremonies and practices of their religion to their children: Exodus 12:26-27; 13:8, 14; Joshua 4:6; Psalm 78:4-7.

The book of Proverbs is written (especially in the early chapters) in the form of a father speaking to his children. See Proverbs 1:8, 10; 2:1; 3:1; 4:1.

The simple conclusion from the various references above in both Old and New Testaments is that the prime responsibility for teaching and training children belongs to their parents. The place for all this to be done is the home. The standards, words and example of godly parents supported by the spiritual environment of the church point children to the Lord God and his ways. It is appropriate now, therefore, for us to turn our attention to the place of the church in the life and nurture of the young. The church's essential role is that of supporting the work and responsibility of the parents. No church must ever attempt to take over the unique role of parents. Where parents, however, fail to discharge their God-given responsibility the church will need to address the needs of the parents at this point, as well as exercising concern for the children.

The life and work of the church as it relates to children

The claim that children have on the attention and interest of the church is on two levels. The first is on the level of the church's responsibility in a general sense to all kinds and groups of people, and the second is on the level of responsibility specifically for children as children.

In the life and work of the church it is necessary to be aware of the needs of particular groups or types of people. Apart from the direct care of individuals in a pastoral sense, those with problems of various kinds will be catered for in the regular week-by-week ministry of God's word. Those problems will be addressed in the systematic exposition of the Scriptures and biblical answers will be given. For example, mothers and fathers, workers, those in leadership positions in society and a host of other categories will learn how living to the glory of God is possible within their particular set of circumstances. The climate of biblical teaching in the church will affect everyone within the church's sphere of ministry.

The families of the church will be helped. Teaching will be given which encourages holiness, love and understanding in the home. Paul's letters to the churches included instruction on marriage, work and the home. The teaching ministry of the church should do the same. This means that those responsible for the church's teaching ministry should always be aware of the presence of such a variety of folk in the congregations of the church's meetings. Various groups of people can be identified in any congregation. Children are one such group, and therefore should be able to hear teaching directly related to them.

In the presentation of truth we must always be aware of the levels of understanding in the hearers. Children should be able to understand, or at least should be encouraged to grow in understanding of what is taught, but while the teaching should be interesting it is not there merely to entertain so that all the children remember is that they enjoyed it. It must also inform their young minds concerning God's truth.

Another important consideration is that the arrangements of the patterns of church life should reflect the needs of families, and especially families with small children. Even small children should be encouraged to attend the means of grace and so times of meetings should be adjusted bearing in mind the bedtimes of the children. It is important that they should appreciate the importance of the Scriptures and Christian worship. It is tragic when a church's life is so departmentalised that children never see the church as a whole meeting, learning, worshipping and growing together. The wholeness of the church's life is a major contribution to the lives of members and their children. Children of members should be included in as many of the activities of the church as possible. The family is a part of God's 'normality' for a child. The church should reflect that normality as far as it can.

The special responsibilities of the church towards children

We have already emphasised how important it is to maintain the sense of the church's oneness. The church's special responsibility for children does not contradict this. It is possible to deal with the needs of children within the oneness of the church's ministry.

If it is recognised that the church has a God-given responsibility to pass on the truths of God's word to all, that will also include children. But the teaching of God's word is also with a view to ensuring that those who hear get the sense of it (see Nehemiah 8:1-8). This means that in the systematic instruction of the people the teaching will have to be in such a way as is understandable to them – in a way suitable to their age and mental capability. What we usually call the 'Sunday School' might well be a suitable vehicle for this teaching of children within the overall oneness of the church's ministry. Classes for that instruction will no doubt be necessary reflecting their age and ability. Classes should also be arranged for adults in the same way and at the same time.

Another useful tool for systematic instruction that a church might use is a catechism – a system of learning using questions and answers in a printed form. The place of learning truths by heart (including Scripture verses) should not be overlooked. The truth learned in such a way remains for longer than that learned by other methods. Illustrative material for child participation is also advisable as we all learn more by doing than merely by hearing.

Where a class system is in operation the teachers for the classes need to be chosen carefully. They must have a firm grasp of and love for the truth together with a proven ability to pass it on to children. They must have a love for and concern for children so as to be prepared to spend themselves for them, answering their many questions and spending time with them outside the formal teaching sessions. It is in this context that weekday activities for children feature. They are further opportunities for children to be exposed to the godly influences of Christian adults who care for them. This will supplement both the formal teaching sessions and the godly influence of the Christian home.

The teaching given should be biblical – firmly based on the Scriptures. It should be systematic, which means the child should be able to see where each Bible book, each story and each doctrine fits in to the overall biblical framework and system of Christian truth. It should be interesting, for God's truth should never be boring – it is the most exciting news of all. It should be realistic and relevant to the needs of children in a godless world. We are not dealing with fairy stories or make-believe, therefore the teaching needs to be doctrinal – we are teaching God's truth. Especially, of course, the teaching must be evangelistic – we are concerned to bring them to Christ. Teachers need to be prayerful and careful people, and adequate preparation, by study and by spending time before God's throne of grace, is vital.

Children growing up

Children are social creatures as much as adults and we need to be aware of it in the arrangement of the church's programme. For instance the church can make a contribution to the life of teen-agers. They are at the stage of withdrawing from their home environment and preparing for the setting up of their own home with their new partner. They may not see it in quite those terms but that is effectively what is happening to them. The in-between age is difficult but the church can help the young person accomplish the transition from childhood to adulthood through adolescence as smoothly as possible.

It may be possible that the careful and loving use of the homes of church members, the sacrifice of time and energy, with a sympathetic and understanding willingness to listen can prevent some of the distress and shipwreck of lives that is so often seen among the young today.

In many churches, children get to an age when they are regarded as too old for learning, and they so regard themselves. If, however, they see their parents and other older folk eager to learn the things of God, the temptation to think they are 'too old' will not be so strong. Many adults give an impression to the young that because they are adults they think they have nothing more to learn. Adults do not know it all. They are still learning too and should never forget it. If the young people see that they fit in to a learning and growing community some of their growing pains may not hurt so much.

Discipline and stability

The church has a responsibility in the area of discipline too. As in dealing with children in the home, justice must be seen to be done. Those who lead, care for and teach children and young people need to be fair and firm. For instance, among children there should be no special cases, especially among the children of church members. Church members, as part of the local church, place a great deal of confidence in those who lead and teach the young and should support children's workers, even when their own children require discipline. The work is difficult enough without having it undermined by indulgent and thoughtless parents. Those who engage in work among the young need the wholehearted support of the parents, not their criticism.

Those who work with the young do not do so for their own glory. There can be a great deal of joy and satisfaction in the work but the glory belongs to the Lord alone. Children are not to be given simply what they want – they have needs to meet, and needs are not necessarily the same as wants. When a leader is appointed he or she should be allowed to lead. If the person appointed proves to be unsuitable in some way, a new leader should be appointed. Firm, loving leadership can be one of the most valuable contributions a church can make to the lives of children who often live within a framework of indecision and instability.

The church also has a special responsibility for the children who come from homes of unbelieving parents. It is often necessary for the church to provide what is deficient in those homes. Sometimes it will be a sense of stability that is lacking, or a greater level of loving discipline. Sometimes it will be simply enough for children from deprived homes to see and perhaps occasionally share in a normal loving Christian environment. All the time, the church will want to teach the word of God and preach the gospel to unbelievers. Where contact is initially with children the opportunity often comes later to speak to unbelieving parents. Such an opportunity should be taken eagerly. It may lead to souls coming to know Christ and to transformed homes and lives.

Children in special need

Children in special need have a call on the ministry of the local church too. Handicapped children need the Saviour as much as any others. A church can surely show them love and care too. Although certain skills are sometimes needed in dealing with handicap, that is not the whole story. Often a caring, concerned interest that endeavours to encourage the handicapped child to live as normal a life as possible is just what is needed. Help given to parents in times of stress is within the power and capability of every church.

The greatest contribution that individual members can make to the welfare of the children within the orbit of the church is to live holy lives before them. If they see that the Lord Jesus Christ is truly Lord and Saviour, that he is loved, served and enjoyed, they will want to know him too. Churches need to pray for all the children within their influence, for it is only the Lord Jesus Christ who can save them and bless their lives.

The present-day world

Although many of the children the church deals with are from Christian homes, the majority of children today are not from such homes. In today's society many are from broken or deprived homes, many have suffered in one way or another and many are bewildered in an increasingly selfish and materialistic world. They are vulnerable. These children need special love, special sympathy, special understanding and special prayer. They have had little or no previous instruction in the things of God so we have very little to build on. In most cases we have to start at the beginning. They are pagan, godless and in great need. Their greatest need, apart from their own salvation, is the salvation of their parents. The church must work and pray to that end.

The environment of school, home, television and society in general is often hostile to the gospel. The church needs to do some very hard thinking about its response to that hostility. Peter was dealing with a similar situation when he wrote that by doing good the Lord's people can 'put to silence the ignorance of foolish men' (1 Peter 2:15). Hostility, however expressed should not stop the Lord's people from living the Christian life faithfully and expressing love for those around them.

Some practical questions for churches

Some people see children's work merely as a means to reaching their parents. If that is the case the commitment to the children themselves will suffer as they lose personal importance and simply become a means to an end. Some would consider that children's work is unnecessary, seeing the task of the church as reaching adults first and foremost. A church, therefore, needs to ask serious questions about its attitude to children and work among them before it starts anything for them. Experience teaches that gathering children together is easier than gathering adults. Some might be tempted to engage in children's work because of that. Again, the church needs to be very clear on motives and goals before commencing work for children.

Some children may need more individual care than others. Does the church have the resources for such a ministry? It may be possible to involve other members in such work who would not initially consider themselves suitable. A church should be using all the gifts God has given to it, and should be constantly finding out what those gifts are.

Such practical questions as, the number of children the church can cope with, and whether to have a limit to numbers with a waiting list for others, need careful consideration. Members can easily spread themselves too thinly to be able to achieve anything of lasting value.

Those who work among the young will need to think about the criteria necessary for measuring a child's response. A child will often do and say things in order to please. That is not a sufficient basis for determining whether the work is worthwhile or not.

What disciplinary standards should a church uphold, in order to ensure a proper learning atmosphere? Will it be necessary to treat children from Christian (or church) homes differently or even separately from children from non-Christian homes? Often what is taught to the one group of children is not appropriate for the other group bearing in mind their background knowledge of Christian things.

Work among the young is not easy, but those who do it know of many rewards, and blessings as they see young lives changed and shaped in a more Christ-like fashion. Many believers have cause to thank God, as they look back to their younger days, for those who showed them Christ's reality in their lives. Many Christians come to faith in Christ during their childhood or youth, and in many cases, humanly speaking, because of the testimony of faithful workers. It is a ministry requiring the wholehearted support and encouragement of the church. It is a ministry of the church as a whole not just of those who work among the young.

Chapter 16
The local church and church planting

Home or away

In view of the commission laid upon the church by the Saviour involving the evangelisation of the whole world the local church should make no essential difference in its thinking between the needs of the home land and the needs of foreign lands far away. As the local church is God's ordained base for outreach and is in fact the most effective means of reaching a community, where it is known that no local church exists the need is obviously for a church to be planted there. Christians living their Christians lives in a locality are a powerful testimony to the reality of the gospel. Long reach evangelism (weekly long distance travel to evangelise) will not do, and is totally impractical in a foreign country.

We must always seek to derive our motives, principles and practices from God's word, so we will spend some time considering what a true or scriptural church is (it is such churches we need to plant) and then how we should go about bringing such a church into being. We shall deal with both principle and practice. Discussion of principles apart from practice leads to mere theorising and does little good to the cause of the gospel. There is no difference in principle and very little difference in practice between planting a church near to home and planting one further away. So we shall consider church planting in general (i.e. in both situations).

As we are considering church planting in this chapter we will not take into account what happens as a result of church splits or what results when people come together and try to combine various Christian traditions represented in a particular area.

A New Testament church

What we have been interested in throughout this book is what a New Testament church is and what it does – its life and its work. As we have discovered, the pattern for true church life is discernible in the New Testament and conformity to that pattern is what makes a church a New Testament church.

A New Testament church is a true church. It is the Lord's church, his body, the fellowship of his people. It is the temple of the Holy Spirit, a holy people, redeemed and regenerated, saved by the grace of God. As discussed earlier we are not left to guess what its basis and form is. We know its structure and its character, because the Lord has ensured that his word reveals these matters to us. From the earliest days in the New Testament the mind of the Lord concerning his church can be clearly discerned.

Although in New Testament times churches differed from one another in certain ways, just as we would expect, what they held in common was of greatest importance. An indication of the reality and importance of this common form is found in such verses as 1 Corinthians 7:17; 11:16; 14:33.

The Jerusalem church

The basis and form of the Jerusalem church was normative for the life of subsequent churches when they came into being. A glance at Acts 2:41-47 will reveal a number of essential features. These features are expounded in detail in the New Testament epistles and we have dealt with them more fully in earlier chapters. However, notice the following:

> 'Those who gladly received his [Peter's] word were baptised'. At least two important things can be seen here. Those who joined the church on the day of Pentecost joined a company where the word of God was basic, and secondly they joined by baptism.

'They continued steadfastly in the apostles' doctrine'. It was a church based on the truth and which taught the truth. That truth could be identified, defined and systematised (see Acts 20. 27; Philippians 1:27; 2 Timothy 1:13; Titus 1:9; Jude 3).

'And fellowship'. They had a life that was expressed in practical realities (see verses 44-45).

'In the breaking of bread, and in prayers'. The church was a worshipping community where the Lord's Table had a proper place within the church. It was a praying church living its life before and to the glory of Almighty God.

Churches in the New Testament

These same marks and evidences are to be also seen in the other churches of the New Testament of which we have more knowledge than merely their name (e.g. Antioch and Corinth). These churches – the ones we know something about and others – were churches that believed the truth – the apostles' doctrine, the faith once delivered to the saints. They believed certain fundamental matters about God, Jesus Christ, man, sin and salvation. Salvation was all of God's grace through faith in Jesus Christ. They held and taught doctrines of the grace of God to hell-deserving and helpless sinners – doctrines of hope and life.

Churches in the New Testament were also baptised churches, organised and governed independently of one another yet living in close fellowship with one another.

These churches, New Testament churches, are what we are interested in planting - baptised, independent churches holding and preaching the doctrines of God's grace. It is no use thinking that issues such as the doctrines of salvation and the church do not matter in a new work. Different views of church government and baptism, for instance, cannot exist happily within the same local church. To attempt to play down such differences or to ignore them will only heap up problems for later. The doctrines of salvation and the church are basic to any thoughts of church planting and formation.

A survey of the New Testament evidence for church planting

How then did such New Testament churches come into being? How did they reproduce new churches like themselves? We will need to look at the Acts of the Apostles to see what happened and to discover patterns and principles for our action today.

For the first seven chapters our attention is centred on Jerusalem. Large numbers of believers are mentioned (2:41; 4:4;5:14; 6:1,7), thousands in fact, yet the church was able to meet as one and functioned as a unity (see 2:46; 4:23,32; 5:11-12; 6:2,5). It would appear however that many disciples lived outside Jerusalem but were not as yet organised into separate churches (e.g. many of the priests mentioned in 6:7 would live outside Jerusalem cf. Luke 1:5 and 39-40). They all looked to the apostles in Jerusalem for leadership. In the case of many of these disciples the break from Judaism was not yet complete.

Acts 8:1 however, marks the beginning of a new set of circumstances. With the scattering of disciples due to persecution came the preaching of the gospel outside Jerusalem for the first time. Judaea and Samaria were affected, particularly by Philip's ministry. Peter and John were sent by the church in Jerusalem to investigate what was happening, to support Philip's work and to authenticate it. They themselves preached in many of the Samaritan villages (8:25). Philip later preached in all the cities from Azotus to Caesarea (8:40) after first ministering to the Ethiopian.

By chapter 9:2 there were disciples in Damascus, and by 9:31 churches were firmly established in Judaea, Galilee and Samaria (they had 'rest'). In 9:32 we read of Peter visiting the saints at Lydda. There were also disciples at Joppa (9:36,38).

Chapter 10 describes the 'Gentile Pentecost' when the Spirit of God visited Cornelius, his family and his friends as Peter preached the word of God to them in Caesarea. The Jerusalem church heard of it (11:1) and Peter reported the details to them. They recognised it to be a genuine work of God (11:18).

The scattering due to persecution went wider still. Phoenicea, Cyprus and Antioch all received disciples (Acts 11:19) and their preaching. At Antioch (11:20) Gentiles turned to the Lord, and again news reached the church in Jerusalem. They sent Barnabas this time (11:22) to investigate, encourage and authenticate the work. He assumed the leadership in Antioch, but needing help went to fetch Paul (11:25). They both taught the new disciples (the church 11:26) for about a year.

Another new set of circumstances

Once again a new set of circumstances came with chapter 13, where two elders of the church in Antioch were sent out in a deliberate missionary church-planting venture. The church in Jerusalem, however, had been undergoing something of a change itself during this period. As churches were being formed in other places the responsibilities of the apostles were widening. So other leaders were appointed for the Jerusalem church – elders (11:30). James was the leader of them (12:17) as Peter was among the apostles and Barnabas was in Antioch (cf. Galatians 2:9; Acts 15:13; 21:18). As churches were eventually formed due to the labours of the sent-out missionaries, elders were appointed in each of those churches (Acts 14:23). Reports of the work of the missionaries were given to the sending church (Antioch – 14:27) and other churches (15:3) notably Jerusalem (15:4). Fellowship between the churches was close and real, with a special place being given to the advice and direction of the church in Jerusalem (cf. 16:4-5).

The churches planted due to the missionary labours of the sent-out missionaries also engaged in outreach themselves: all Asia heard the word through the Ephesian church (Acts 19:10), Macedonia and Achaia heard from Thessalonica (1 Thessalonians 1:8), and Achaia heard from Corinth too (2 Corinthians 1:1).

We can derive patterns or methods of working from the above brief survey, and to those patterns we will now turn our attention.

The scattering of believers

In both Acts 8:1-5 and 11:19-20 the phrase 'preaching the word' occurs as an activity of ordinary believers. Believers move to new places for a variety of reasons. In both references here the reason is persecution. What is significant is that they used the opportunity to testify of Christ. Although Philip's ministry was much more a proclamation of Christ (the word 'preaching' in Acts 8:5 is 'kerusso' 'proclamation' whereas the same word in Acts 8:4 is 'evangelizomai' 'evangelisation'), he was no freelancer, being involved in this whole movement of believers and their spontaneous gospel work.

This was also true of the other believers and the apostles and the church in Jerusalem took a vital interest. In Philip's case Peter and John were sent (8:14), and Barnabas was sent to Antioch (11:22). They went to investigate, encourage and authenticate. The New Testament knows nothing of freelancing individuals that are so much a feature of evangelism today.

The gathering of believers

We pass on now to those situations which arise in various ways when a number of believers in a locality meet together to serve the Lord. It will often mean seeking help from elsewhere in the matter of leadership. Sometimes it is a group of believers who live at some distance from the church's meeting place who establish their own identity (e.g. Acts 9:32, 38 – the saints at Lydda and Joppa, 25 and 35 miles respectively from Jerusalem). At other times it is a group of believers who move into an area together with the fruit of their witness (e.g. Acts 11:20- 26 – Antioch). In both cases the encouragement and authentication of the church of which they are a part is vital (cf. Acts 9:32 – Peter; Acts 11:22 – Barnabas).

The sending of missionaries

Both previous methods, which overlap one another to some degree, may be described as unorganised and unofficial ways of planting churches, although both were and still are used by the Spirit of God in his sovereign strategy. What we are now considering here are the organised and official attempts on the part of a church to plant new churches in other places where groups of their members do not exist – by sending representatives to engage in evangelistic work, to gather a company of believers and to form a church. These representatives were variously designated in the New Testament as apostles or evangelists. Today they may be called missionaries or church planters. They were capable and gifted men who were fitted to lead a church as elders (Acts 13:1-3), such as Barnabas and Saul. That should still be the case today.

In teams

It would appear from the New Testament that mission and church planting work was usually done by missionaries working in teams. As far as we can tell no one worked entirely on his own. Even when Paul was left on his own from time to time he eagerly awaited the arrival of his colleagues. Members of a missionary team could be drawn from different churches (cf. Acts 20:4) in certain circumstances. Each member of the team maintained his links with his home or sending church (e.g. Paul and Antioch). The closest possible relationship was established with the newly planted churches (e.g. Paul and Philippi; Paul's close involvement with the decision of the Corinthian church – 1 Corinthians 5:3).

Teams have many advantages – the effective use of the gifts of the men in the team, more manpower resources for the work, fellowship between team members overcoming that sense of isolation which those engaged in the Lord's work can often feel, training of younger and less experienced men. The support for the missionaries came from various sources (e.g. Philippi had a special concern for Paul), even from their own hands (e.g. Paul's work as a tent-maker). The sending and supporting churches evidently trusted the missionaries enough to make their own decisions about location, church life and practice, not to interfere in their work. Reports were made, of course, and visits between churches took place. The independency of the churches from one another did not, apparently, produce the problems independency is often accused of producing. There was constant reference back to the other churches and the common practice of the churches was valued. No new church felt restricted and none appear to have isolated themselves from the others.

Practical methods used

The basic method of missionary strategy was to go to the cities. Cities are population centres, and centres of commerce and influence. If a new church was established in a city it could then reach out to the surrounding area of towns and villages (cf. Acts 19:10; 2 Corinthians 1:1; 1 Thessalonians 1:8). Today cities are often places of great need and deprivation, neglected as mission fields for many years. They deserve our concerned interest. They are still potentially strategic centres for gospel advance, and cry out for some concerted effort to be made to reach their unsaved millions.

God is interested in cities! The prophet Jonah was sent to Nineveh, 'that great city' (Jonah 1:2; 4:11). The Lord said to the exiles in Babylon through Jeremiah 'seek the peace of the city' (Jeremiah 29:7). Paul as a missionary strategist moved from city to city as the Holy Spirit guided him. Abraham was looking for a city 'whose builder and maker is God' (Hebrews 11:10). All who share his faith have a city prepared for them (Hebrews 11:16). We seek it too (Hebrews 13:14; Revelation 21:2).

Points of contact were sought in the cities – synagogues with their opportunities to speak, and market places where the people gathered (Acts 17:17). Sometimes a house would be a kind of base (e.g. the house of Justus – Acts 18:7) or semi-public premises were used (e.g. the school of Tyrannus – Acts 19:9). On other occasions it was work done as from one house to another (Acts 20:20).

The work took time. It was not accomplished in five minutes (see Acts 18:11 – one year and six months in Corinth; Acts 19:10 – two years, and 20:31 – three years in Ephesus). It culminated, however, in a church being formed which was led by its own elders – Acts 14:23; 20:17; Titus 1:5.

Stages in the formation of a church

From what we have discovered and considered so far it should now be possible to plot the progress of church planting from its beginnings to the actual formation of a new church. There are discernible stages through which such a work passes. We have been using the phrase 'church-planting' for the whole process of bringing a new church into being. The horticultural analogy encourages us to see the process as the development of a plant growing to the point of producing flowers and fruit. Obviously this is not a rigid form, but it helps us understand what is happening. Each work is different, of course, and develops in a unique way; nevertheless we can discern certain important stages.

The first stage is the work of evangelism done by the sent-out missionaries and by believers (if there are any) living in the particular vicinity. Many of the practical methods we have discussed in earlier chapters would be appropriate at this stage (e.g. door to door visiting and literature distribution). As opportunities arise, the Lord's people will speak of him, if they have a genuine concern for the lost. Perhaps this initial witness will lead to an informal gathering of interested people who come together to consider the Christian faith and study the word of God from time to time. In fact such a gathering if carefully planned and prepared for can provide a useful focus for the evangelistic activity being carried out. When people are saved they will be baptised on the authority of the sponsoring church and will technically become a part of it but with a view to belonging to the new church when it comes into being.

The next stage is for a regular meeting to be held. This leads on naturally from the evangelistic activity of the missionaries and the gospel work of believers. As with the occasional gathering mentioned above, this meeting can provide a very useful focus for the work, a kind of base from which to operate and an activity to which contacts can be invited. However it should not be an informal get-together, but have a proper basis and form. The meeting should get down to business in the preaching of the gospel and the teaching of God's word under the direction of the duly appointed leader/ teacher. As the work is under the authority of the sponsoring church which sent out the missionaries the meeting will be encouraged and authenticated by that church, and others. This will avoid isolationism or the development of a personality-centred clique.

As the meeting is held regularly it will become clear that a group of people identify themselves with it and with each other. The next stage in the church planting process is taking place. A recognisable 'Fellowship' is coming together. As the people in the group begin to think of the group as the centre of their Christian fellowship and life and adhere to the basis already agreed with the sponsoring church it will not be long before an independent church is organised. At this stage the duly appointed leader will need the help of other leaders who will share the leadership functions of the group. They should be men who fit the eldership requirements of the Pastoral Epistles for they will begin functioning as elders in the fellowship. Although the prospective members will be known a formal membership roll will not have been drawn up yet. Even so, leadership should only be undertaken by those who adhere to the basis of the proposed church and will be members of it when it is formally organised. As yet the Fellowship will not meet around the Lord's Table, as they have not yet covenanted together as a church.

The formation of the church

As soon as it is practicably possible the 'Fellowship' – the prospective members – should commit themselves to one another with a view to the formation of a church. Then on the occasion of the organising of the church as a separate and independent body they should covenant together as foundation members of the new church, recognised and accredited by the sponsoring church. The new church needs a proper doctrinal basis and pastoral oversight. It will have meetings for worship and for the teaching and preaching of God's word. It will seek faithfully to administer the ordinances of baptism and the Lord's Supper within a disciplined and loving environment as a church of Jesus Christ.

The new church should only be formed when it can function as a viable church independent of other churches. For instance it should have a separate identifiable meeting place. If it is being formed from a group of members of another church, that planting church itself must remain a viable church when the new church comes into being. Otherwise it might just as well move its place of meeting as a whole to the new location.

There is a right time for a new church to be formed, and a wrong time. Delay can produce frustration and resentment, but premature independence can produce weakness and ineffectiveness – both are dishonouring to the Lord.

Problems, dangers and weaknesses

Any aspect of practical Christian living is full of problems and the planting of a new church is no exception. On the face of it the matter seems simple enough but the path before the new church can appear to be a veritable minefield with all manner of situations and dangers that can arise to cause a new work to founder. The devil has no love of the work we are considering here and makes it his business to make it as difficult for God's people as he possibly can.

It is inevitable that our consideration of these matters will prove to be selective and we can only touch on a few things although many others could as easily be dealt with too. We shall limit ourselves here to a few remarks on independency, the size of the new church and various deficiencies that could be thought to damage a new church.

Independency

At first sight it might appear that independency would be a hindrance to church planting. The idea is that an independent church does not have the resources or the will to plant new churches. It is often suggested that independency is inefficient, because only churches that are linked connexionally have the resources and will to plant other churches.

We have discussed independency earlier in this book. It is by no means inefficient and in fact has many advantages over other relationship systems. One local church can take decisions and make commitments more quickly than a connexion of churches. There are no boards, committees, councils and all manner of petty officials to hamper missionaries sent out by a local church. Churches working together in church planting and the sending out of missionaries in a team have genuine fellowship with one another in this work as they have confidence in one another and in those they send out. Independency is the relationship between churches that is found in the New Testament, but churches did not use their independence to justify isolationism. The go-it-alone spirit of many churches in our day finds no support from the New Testament. Such a spirit has more to do with suspicion and pride than a desire for the effectiveness of God's work.

However independency does undoubtedly have its problems. They are the problems such as local churches face within their own memberships. They are the problems of people. Many questions asked about church planting can be answered in terms of the people involved. In other words the answers are to be found in the area of the exercise of human responsibility in the Lord's work. Such questions as these: 'Why do some churches when they are formed isolate themselves from others?', 'Why do some churches leave their foundations so soon, by allowing error to get in?', 'Why do some weak churches resent offers of help from other churches who are in a stronger position?'. Those who seriously doubt the wisdom and even the rightness of the independence of the local church ask these questions and others like them. Those who believe in it would like the answers too. However, when dealt with separately, the answer to each question will very often be related to the particular people involved in each situation. Often it is a failure to grasp the implications of the New Testament teaching on fellowship between local churches. (This is a matter dealt with at some length in chapter three). Sometimes it is simply pride that leads men to believe in their own self-sufficiency, or blinds them to their own need. Churches are made up of people – sinners saved by God's grace, but frail, imperfect people still.

Size

Growth is an evidence of life, but numerical growth can bring problems. A large church can easily become complacent, and often has a higher proportion of passengers in its membership than a relatively small church. This is still true even where a large church seems to have lots of so-called converts while a small church may appear to have few. Small however, does not necessarily mean beautiful. A small church can be as dead as a large church, but it certainly looks more pathetic. Small numbers do not guarantee effectiveness or spirituality in a church. Yet small companies do have many advantages where there is genuine spiritual life. Small churches can experience a greater sense of fellowship where every member knows and is known. In smaller churches pastoral work can become a reality.

Growth should be an outward-looking thing. A growing church should seek ways of planting new churches so that new areas can be evangelised – for that is what truly local churches can do most effectively. A church planting vision is one way of preventing a growing church from becoming flabby and overloaded numerically. There is a weakness in large numbers, as there is a weakness in small.

Small churches

This leads us naturally to consider the needs of small churches. Why do some churches never seem to grow? How is it possible to get such churches moving? The answer to these questions is often to be found with the people who are the church. Perhaps they are elderly, or have responsibilities which preclude them from much evangelistic activity, or it may be that they are dispirited, or even lazy or just do not know what to do. So, how can others help? Other churches can offer help, and the small churches themselves can seek help from others. It is a two-way thing, and yet some small churches do feel there is some loss of face involved in receiving help from outside. That kind of attitude can be very damaging to the cause of the gospel. It is an inverted pride and like any pride can cause great damage to the Lord's people. Even so, receiving help does not mean a loss of independence or integrity – it is a practical expression of true biblical life and fellowship between the Lord's churches. Help can be given in a variety of ways – personnel, finance, advice, and in various other forms.

The reviving of so-called dying churches comes under this category too. A church can easily sink into low water for any of a number of reasons. It is a sign of true spiritual life if such a church recognises its state and seeks help before it is too late. In some instances it will mean that a small church will cease to be an independent work and will become part of another church that will then be able to treat the work as a church-planting venture and will be able to act accordingly. For a church that has fallen on hard times, to resort to supplying its pulpit with itinerating preachers solves nothing and only hastens the end. A ministry of sorts may be exercised, but the pastoral care and leadership of the church is missing. This does untold damage to a church.

Deficiency in leadership

There are many situations that are not ideal and many true churches exist that are deficient of some things that others consider essential. One such area is the leadership of the church. The New Testament indicates that churches should be led, cared for and ruled by a plurality of elders, and when planting a new church this scriptural ideal should be aimed at. However, we must beware of attendant dangers. It is all too possible to lay hands on a man in haste simply to satisfy adherence to this ideal and as a result ordain a man to a position for which he is not fitted.

There can be no real justification for delaying the separation and organising of a new work as an independent church just because it does not have plural elders. A church does not exist for its leaders; leadership is a God-given gift for the blessing of the church. If God does not give more than one man with pastoral gifts that is sufficient for that church at that time. Eldership is too holy an office for men to be appointed to it simply to satisfy some mathematical scruple derived apparently from Scripture. Even so it is better to delay the separation of a new work until there is a sufficiency in the leadership and an adequacy in the membership. These are judgements that have to be arrived at after thought, prayer and consultation. There is a right time and a wrong time for a church to be formed and great wisdom is needed in determining which is which.

Meeting place problems

A church can most certainly exist without owning property, and many do, as did the churches in New Testament times. There are many advantages nevertheless in having a regular and suitable meeting place. It provides a focus for the various expressions of the fellowship of the church, and a useful centre in which to arrange meetings to which outsiders can be invited. To meet in a home can also have attractions, up to a point, but there are drawbacks too. They are mostly to do with the home surroundings, the size of the room and the needs of the family living there. There can be an unhealthy dependence upon the particular family concerned in the life of the church – conflicts of interest between family and church can be difficult to resolve.

A church without a regular meeting place might consider hiring premises, or even purchasing a plot of ground on which to build a suitable meeting place.

In planting a new church it is important to have an identifiable meeting place before a church is separated, even though the church can exist without one. The new church is going to have enough problems in its early days without having to wander from pillar to post to have its meetings. Since problems concerning premises can easily take up too much of a young church's time and energy it is better to have the matter sorted out at the beginning if at all possible.

Church life deficiencies

Some may ask, 'Why does it sometimes not work?' 'Ideals are all very well, principles are fine, but what about those situations where the whole business has come to nothing?'

There are obviously many reasons for failure, but in the realm of human responsibility it is the same answer as before – the people involved. However there is more to it than that; in some instances it is to do with the quality of church life involved.

It is easy for a new church that emphasises the truth, the importance of doctrine, and the centrality of scriptural preaching and practice to be dull and austere in its services of worship and in the quality of its life and fellowship. The fear of doing anything unscriptural can become repressive. If a church holds the truth and is alive with the presence of the Lord Jesus Christ in his saving power its life and activity should be vibrant and exciting. The Lord's Day should be the most enjoyable day of the week for the Lord's people. Families should feel involved and everything the Spirit of God gives to the members of the church should have a proper place.

There is nothing wrong with having a proper, carefully planned and prayerfully organised church programme. It will ensure that everything necessary has its right place and proportion, including evangelism, which incredibly enough is overlooked in some churches.

The quality of life of a new church is often good – it is a small close-knit fellowship of people who have shared the birth pangs of the young church. Such a church must beware of being inward looking. The warm fellowship can only be saved from ossifying by encouraging others to join it –   and they bring their own living contribution to it. A church is a living body, and that life is to be expressed, not least in growth.

A church planting vision

If a church is really concerned for the saving of the lost, if it is really convinced that the local church is God's ordained way of reaching the lost, it will want to plant other churches where none at present exist. It will have a church planting vision and will adopt a church planting policy. This may be developed as follows:

First of all, if a church has a number of members living in a particular area in which it might be possible to start a work, it should consider it seriously and prayerfully, for these very members might well be God's people to form the basis of a new church. Obviously small churches would not find this easy, but should keep the possibility in mind, for, as the Lord blesses, small churches grow into large ones. It might be helpful to analyse the membership from time to time to see how the members are distributed. There may be identifiable areas of need where it may be possible to commence a work as the Lord opens up the way.

Secondly, a growing church should consider seriously how large it is prepared to grow. If a church separates off a company of members to form a new church it can often lead to more effective evangelism of the area in which the new church is planted. It also keeps the planting church alert and prevents its life from becoming flabby and complacent due to large numbers of non-working members. How big should a church be before it does such a thing – dividing to multiply? Circumstances and situations vary so there is no hard and fast rule to observe governing the size of churches. In order for the church's fellowship to be a reality and pastoral care to be a practical possibility between 100 and 150 members is likely to be the maximum size of membership.

In the third place, a church would seriously consider the many un-reached cities (especially the inner city areas), towns and villages of our land and further afield. Is it not possible for a church in fellowship with other like-minded churches to co-operate in the sending of a missionary team to a needy town near by?

Each local church can, and should, develop a church planting vision. The local church is a living body into which God has breathed his very life by the Holy Spirit. Where the Holy Spirit is present in a church it is alive – with the life of God. Where he is absent, a church is dead, and should cry earnestly to God for the Spirit to return in the fullness of his presence in revival power. The world needs to see such local living churches if it is to see Christ's life in action and if it is to hear the gospel proclaimed in God's ordained way.